CLASSICS
OF
SEA POWER

The Classics of Sea Power series makes readily available, in uniform, authoritative editions, the central concepts of the naval profession. Illustrating naval development over the centuries, these major original, book-length works relating to theory, strategy, tactics, operations, and important themes in naval warfare have been chosen for their eloquence and timelessness.

Vice Admiral S. O. Makarov's *Discussion of Questions in Naval Tactics* is the preeminent work in Russian literature of a magnetic leader expressing deeply felt—and for the Imperial Navy, badly needed—thoughts on naval tactics. Makarov also exemplifies the mode of the great naval writers at the opening of the twentieth century, which was the Golden Age of tactical thought in nations aspiring to greatness on the high seas. He blends four subjects rarely seen synthesized today:

- The tactical interrelationships of weaponry, maneuver, and search.
- The technology relationships of guns, armor, and propulsion (for in his day, tacticians regarded ship design as a tactical question).
- The central influence of the will to win.
- The strategic context.

What further distinguishes Makarov is that, until his untimely death in combat, he epitomized his own doctrines. Captain Robert Bathurst's superb Introduction portrays the character of this formidable leader in tactics, technology, energy, inspiration, and deep love of country.

SERIES EDITORS

John B. Hattendorf
Naval War College
Newport, Rhode Island

Wayne P. Hughes, Jr.
Naval Postgraduate School
Monterey, California

Discussion of Questions in
Naval Tactics

Vice Admiral S. O. Makarov, 1880

VICE ADMIRAL S. O. MAKAROV
IMPERIAL RUSSIAN NAVY

Discussion of Questions in Naval Tactics

Translated from the Russian by
Lieutenant John B. Bernadou,
U.S. Navy

With an Introduction and Notes by
Captain Robert B. Bathurst
U.S. Navy (Ret.)

NAVAL INSTITUTE PRESS   Annapolis, Maryland

Introduction and notes copyright © 1990 by the United States
Naval Institute, Annapolis, Maryland

Library of Congress Cataloging-in-Publication Data

Makarov, Stepan Osipovich, 1848–1904.
    [Rassuzhdeniia po voprosam morskoĭ taktiki. English]
    Discussion of questions in naval tactics / S.O. Makarov ;
translated from the Russian by John B. Bernadou ; with an
introduction and notes by Robert B. Bathurst.
        p.   cm.   — (Classics of sea power)
    Translation of: Razsuzhdeniia po voprosam morskoĭ taktiki.
    "This translation was originally published in 1898 by the Office
of Naval Intelligence as part of its General Information Series"—
Verso of t.p.
    Includes bibliographical references and index.
    ISBN 0-87021-779-8
    1. Naval tactics.   2. Russia.   Voennyĭ flot—History—19th
century.   3. Soviet Union—History, Naval.   I. Title.   II. Series.
V167.M2713   1990
359.4′2—dc20
                                                              90-6279
                                                                  CIP

Series design by Moira M. Megargee

Printed in the United States of America on acid-free paper ∞

            9   8   7   6   5   4   3   2

                        First printing

CONTENTS

INTRODUCTION

The Lessons of a Russian Naval Genius

Only he who does nothing never errs.—Makarov

Vice Admiral Stepan Osipovich Makarov[1] believed in the great man theory of history (that important change is more the work of innovative leaders than of historical cycles) not only because he was one but also because he understood that only through strong leadership could the Russian national character be made to produce. He also understood that the new technology and science had raced far beyond the fleet's experience in praxis. That separated him from Mahan, who believed in eternal principles uninfluenced by practical and technical considerations.

Reading Makarov's *Discussion of Questions in Naval Tactics* (hereafter referred to as *Tactics*) is an instructive, and intriguing, exercise in contemplating how a supremely energetic, scientific, Russian mind struggled to turn the weak-

---

1. The *ov* ending in Makarov is the transliteration generally adopted by modernists after the Russian Revolution. *Off*—Makaroff—was the transliteration used before the Revolution and by those who did not submit to Soviet authority.

nesses of a nation "lacking organization" into systems for tactical and strategic victory.[2] And this he tried, both by example and theory, with extraordinary energy, imagination, and charismatic leadership, to the last day of his life. That his "new thinking" could not change the pattern fast enough was a shoal upon which Makarov's ship was to founder as much as upon Japanese mines.

There are very good reasons for the modern naval officer, especially an American one, to experience Admiral Makarov's wisdom. First of all, Americans, from their island position, seem, even unconsciously, to be controlled by the ideas of Mahan. They like to think that there are "eternal principles" of sea power uncontrolled by technology or geogra-

2. S. O. Makarov, *Discussion of Questions in Naval Tactics*, trans. J. B. Bernadou (Washington: Office of Naval Intelligence, 1898), p. 167 [p. 267 in this edition]. It is easy to understand why Commander Bernadou was attracted to the works of Admiral Makarov, for they were heroes cut from the same cloth. Bernadou believed in the attack which he demonstrated in a daring assault during the Spanish-American War in 1898. Although seriously wounded and under attack from the Spanish, he calmly wrote an account of the battle. Furthermore, Bernadou was something of a universal genius, like Makarov. He was the "father" of smokeless powder in the U.S. Navy (an improvement that Makarov tested and promoted). He was a chemist, and wrote on scientific subjects—"Nitrocellulose and Theory of the Cellulose Molecule" being one. His knowledge of languages was most remarkable. Bernadou's grandparents were French, which may explain his competence in that language and his interest in learning. Astonishingly, he was also proficient in Spanish, Italian, and German. His command of Russian was remarkable, especially considering the quality of dictionaries at that time. His translation is accurate and graceful, if a little dated, but considering what sources must have been available to him during an extremely active and distinguished naval career, it is nothing short of miraculous. None of the materials I have researched gives a clue as to the origin of Bernadou's interest in Russian, much less the incentive that drove him to devote the months and years it would have required to do so. It is not known how he found Makarov, but it is certain that they were kindred spirits, drawn together through space and time.

phy. As a consequence, it is easy for them to underestimate the limitations of time and space.

For Russians, particularly Makarov, war is a problem of technology, industrial production, and organization of both men and means. It requires solutions to the problems of a great continental power that must not only achieve cooperation between the forces fighting on land and those at sea but also establish a common language. Makarov did not recognize "eternal principles" unconnected with tactical problems. Nor did he think of the navy as some kind of "thing in itself," divorced from other services. Rather, he celebrated sea power as Peter the Great had understood it: namely, a necessary attribute of a great continental power with problems at sea and on land. The navy was a resource, not a theory. The problem was to develop a mind that could command the resources, the obstacles, and the objectives practically. Although contemporaries, Mahan and Makarov were like the yin and yang of sea power.

A brilliant theoretician, Makarov nevertheless did not indulge in scientific research for its own sake. Like his Soviet successors tend to do, he maintained a constant interchange between theory and practice; his were meant to be the tactics of the possible.

Typical of the "organic" thinker—one who is not imprisoned by labels—he could, as he did in the Central Asian campaign of the 1880s, transform himself in two hours from the commander of a Caspian Sea detachment into the exemplary captain of a desert "naval" artillery battalion.[3] His observations throughout the world's oceans—in the Arctic, the Pacific, and the Black Sea—were inspired by and resulted from his concern for how equipment worked at different tem-

3. F. F. Vrangel', *Vitse-admiral S. O. Makarov* (St. Petersburg: Main Naval Staff, 1911), vol. I, pp. 219–65.

peratures, how ships handled in different waters, and how mines could be laid in different currents. Makarov also introduced into the Imperial Navy an understanding of the need for long voyages as a means of training the crews, increasing morale, making scientific discoveries, and, most important, preparing for war.

In our tumultuous times it is especially important to study Admiral Makarov as the product of the Russian culture, for he is the kind of brilliant innovator and maverick who periodically, and still somehow unexpectedly, rises out of the Russian system and makes it work. To read his *Tactics* is to experience the exciting breadth of a mind that miraculously overcomes the turgid constraints of the Russian system, giving it new energy and creativity.

At the close of the nineteenth century, the worship of science began to mean that one could not be both intuitive and rigorous. But Admiral Makarov was both. He calculated the angle for ramming a ship with accomplished mathematical precision, predicted a system for "seeing" through fog, understood that observations from the air would someday change naval war, and recommended the consideration of hypnosis in tactics. He understood various national characteristics: that while great German commanders planned battles with synchronic certitude, Russian tacticians had to fashion victory out of what they could lay their hands on. He had experienced American independence and inventiveness firsthand as a fourteen-year-old cadet on a prolonged visit to San Francisco. "An American is not at all like a Russian," he observed. "He would not even consider doing something that brought him little benefit and he doesn't allow anyone to exploit him as a Russian does."[4] This constant attention to the nature of men and their capabilities was typical of Makarov's patterns

4. Ibid., p. 7.

of thought. He, like many of his Soviet successors, maintained a realistic appraisal of the human material he had to work with and studied how to create, out of its limitations, the advantages that brought victory.

A LIFE OF IRONIES

For such a great man and a naval genius, Vice Admiral Makarov experienced many paradoxes in his life. A staunch advocate of motherland, orthodoxy, and autocracy, he was born in the revolutionary year 1848, when Czar Nicholas I, so frightened by the rising expectations of the lower classes, tried to make advanced education inaccessible to people like Makarov. Fortunately, it was determined after some investigation that his father had achieved nobility in time for Stepan's birth. That felicitous calculation made it possible for Makarov to attend a naval school. (His own patent of nobility was awarded when he was nineteen.)

Although one of Makarov's major contributions to the navy was his work on "the unsinkability of ships" (damage control), he died by going down with his flagship. One of his maxims for winning battles was to take risks, yet the risks he took at Port Arthur probably ended any hope of Russia winning the war. The circumstances of his death were also ironic. One of the seven officers saved, who had been with Admiral Makarov on the bridge, was a superfluous Romanov grand duke, an heir to a sinking throne that needed Makarov alive much more than it needed a prince saved that day.

For such a staunch defender of the autocracy, Makarov's Soviet fame is similarly ironical.[5] Memorials, ships, schools,

5. There has been a half-hearted Soviet effort to make of Makarov a class hero—a victim of bureaucracy and class jealousy—but that has not worked very well. He was too obviously recognized and valued by his supe-

and statues have been dedicated to him, and he is mentioned in all lists of naval heroes, albeit not at the top.[6]

THE POLITICAL CONSEQUENCES

In the winter of 1904, the Russian government sent the eminent Admiral Makarov to command the Pacific Squadron in hopes of turning the tide of war with Japan. Instead, his death caused such a despair as to accelerate the deluge. Admiral Makarov's loss, which foreshadowed the destruction of the Imperial Navy, was, in fact, one of several major events that seemed to hasten the Romanovs' gruesome end. A military dictatorship survives, in part, because of its mystique of power and grace. Losing a war to the Japanese who, only half a century before had learned what constituted an engine, embarrassed Russia as nothing ever had.

Imperial Russia particularly needed military heroes. The power and prestige that its victory over Napoleon should have secured for it in European affairs had been eroded by its industrial and social backwardness. The humiliating defeat and degrading peace of the Crimean War in 1855 had left the country demoralized and the navy, once a force of two fleets, reduced to one in the Baltic.

The young Makarov was one of the fortunate few young officers who benefited from the naval ministry's decision to send the vessels of the Baltic Fleet off on long-range cruises, a

---

riors, including the czar. His battles for improved conditions for the sailors, and his emphasis on morale, had a serious audience in the Imperial Navy.

It is worth mentioning that, after years of Soviet distortions of pre-revolutionary history, the news of Makarov's death so overshadowed the fact that Grand Duke Kirill Vladimirovich was saved that the latter was not mentioned in the telegram to the Emperor.

6. See, for example, A. V. Barabanshchikov, ed., *Voennaya pedagogika i psikhologiya* (Moscow: Voenizdat, 1986), p. 125.

tradition which the late Admiral Gorshkov reconfirmed. Senior naval commanders—especially the disciples of Admiral Lazarev, who had commanded the Black Sea Fleet before the war—were convinced that only such voyages created independent-minded officers. Among the advocates of such voyages was Captain and later Admiral A. A. Popov, Makarov's commander during his time with the Pacific Squadron on its deployment to San Francisco in 1863. (This is the same Popov who invented the much ridiculed *Popovka*—a circular iron-clad that made its crews too dizzy to function—but also Russia's first modern battleship, the *Petr Velikii*.)

While European powers were scrambling to create empires, Russia, no match for more industrialized nations, could only move aggressively against the Ottomans, where opposition was weakest, and against sheikdoms and emirates in Central Asia on its way to the Pacific. Although Russian society, especially the aristocracy, was largely militarized and led by an imperial family whose male members nearly all had regimental educations and careers—Nicholas I even slept on a camp bed in his palace—it coped badly with military innovations succeeding the Napoleonic wars.

A nation's military image is one of the elements of its self-recognition and a primary measure of its self-esteem. This was especially true in the nineteenth and early twentieth centuries, when strategists and engineers had to cope with the monstrous changes being wrought by the introduction of steel and machine, and the humanists had to think about the quantum leap in casualties and suffering such machinery introduced. Even though the princes were slow to understand it, gone were the courtly arts of war—the cavalry charge, the brave duels with cold steel.

General Dragomirov, whom Admiral Makarov admired and whom the Soviets still read, was a powerful voice in Russian military science. Although he proposed such modern tactical ideas as "open formations," he was most famous for recommending hand-to-hand combat as a means of developing courage and promoting a fighting spirit. But even then, warfare as he described it was no longer taking place.

After the Crimean War, the Navy was particularly demoralized. By the Treaty of 1856, and until 1871, Russia could not maintain warships in the Black Sea, a humiliating provision for a power that looked upon Constantinople as its spiritual home, Istanbul as its historic enemy, and Balkan liberation as its holy mission.

With no northern fleet, and in the Pacific only a squadron, the practice of naval strategic and tactical thought depended upon the Baltic Fleet and threats that would come from that direction. But by the 1870s, Imperial Russia had new needs for naval power. Around the Black Sea, the pan-Slavists were stirring up Balkan nationalism, and the Ottomans were in rapid decline. A Black Sea Fleet had to be built and trained. In addition, the need arose for maritime defenses of the new territories in the Pacific, where the first Japanese miracle of industrialization was taking place. Suddenly, as would occur a hundred years later with the declaration of the Brezhnev doctrine, Russia was in need of navies in seas where it had never operated. This, Admiral Makarov foresaw.

He recognized early both the strategic and economic significance of extending operations into Arctic waters. In a lecture he gave in 1899, he pointed out that with a large icebreaker, Russia would have the possibility "of transferring the fleet to the Pacific by the shortest and least dangerous, in wartime, route."[7] He was quite aware of the aggressive politics of Imperial Russia in the Far East, and made himself unpopular by constantly criticizing the government's failure to provide adequate military support and supplies, a failure for which he would eventually pay with his life. (Admiral

7. V. S. Shlomin, ed., *S. O. Makarov: Dokumenty* (Moscow: Voenizdat, 1960), vol. II, no. 163.

Rozhestvenskii, who heard Makarov's lecture on the subject of war preparation in the Far East at Kronstadt, must have been haunted by it as he sailed the Baltic Fleet, renamed the Second Pacific Ocean Squadron, to its destruction in the Straits of Tsushima.)

In fact, supplies in the Far East were so inadequate that the Baltic Fleet, had it survived in the Straits of Tsushima, would have had difficulty carrying on the war. The fleet, woefully unprepared, was supposed to achieve readiness while underway. Had it arrived, it would have sailed into a port without adequate resupplies.

ADMIRAL MAKAROV'S CAREER

Into this world for which the Romanovs were not ready was born the naval genius Stepan Osipovich Makarov in Nikolaev, a river town with shipyards and a port on the Black Sea. Much has been made by Soviets and Western writers of the fact that Makarov was not of noble birth, yet he became a vice admiral. Actually, after Peter the Great, the Russian nobility was a service class in which rank, which became hereditary, was achieved through merit. Many men of peasant origin achieved aristocratic titles, and there was a surprising degree of upward mobility in the Imperial Navy for men of peasant and serf origin.

Stepan Osipovich was enrolled as a cadet in the lower division of the naval school in Nikolaevsk-on-the-Amur, the Pacific side of Siberia. He was obviously a brilliant and probably likable student, for he attracted the attention of the port commander, who secured for him a position in the Pacific Squadron of the Imperial Navy. Makarov's first voyage was in the *Strelok,* a ship smaller than a corvette, with a screw, a clipper's bow, and rigging.

From the beginning of his career, he studied, wrote, and invented, deservedly attracting the attention of his seniors. His first article was about problems of figuring deviation at sea, and soon after, he was transferred to the Baltic and the iron-clad *Rusalka* ("Mermaid"), a monitor with a low freeboard and poor seakeeping abilities. There he began the work on damage control that made him famous and occupied him for the rest of his life. His interest was excited by the fact that after the *Rusalka* suffered minor damage, and was taking on very little water, she could only be saved from sinking by being run aground. That led to his invention of a collision mat, a damage-control device universally adopted.

Although his study was much praised, little was done to implement his ideas. The only immediate positive result of his work was that Makarov was promoted to lieutenant. It took the sinking of the ironclad *Admiral Lazarev* for his proposed ideas on damage control to be tried.

But his interest never waned. Even in the year of his death, he gave a series of lectures on damage control. He explained the lack of interest in the subject as due to the fact that "crawling around between the cofferdams was not only difficult, it was also unhealthy."[8]

Although Makarov first achieved recognition for his scientific and technological studies, one of his enduring strengths was his understanding of morale and leadership. This was manifested in one of his articles on damage control: "Man is so created that he will go to certain death when he is familiar with the danger. But he will be frightened even of the noise of water in the hold if he isn't used to it. Accustom people to this noise and they will fight penetrations of the hull up to the end."[9] His concern with the psychology of war and of sailors always accompanied his technical and tactical insights. That,

8. K. S. Velichko, ed., "Makarov, Stepan Osipovich," *Voennaya en-tsiklopediya* (Moscow: 1913), vol. XlI, pp. 117–21.
9. Ibid.

perhaps more than any other characteristic, marked his Russianness. He did not separate the idea of the operator from the instrument; he usually saw things whole. The material, psychological, and spiritual were for him all of a piece.

His *Tactics* was remarkable in that respect. Makarov's analysis always included an understanding of the needs, limitations, and emotions of men. For example, in discussing the handling of the gun crews, Makarov advised: "Battery commanders, while encouraging their men and inspiring them with energy, should remember that their own losses are always visible, while those of the enemy are invisible, and therefore they should, from time to time, notify their men of the visible or supposed losses of the enemy." [10]

He considered that it would be an effective device to name torpedo boats after their commanders, again showing the close link between tactics and morale. (Perhaps influenced by Napoleon, he wrote that three-fourths of the chances of success depend on morale and only one-fourth on material conditions.) [11]

Makarov's understanding of the close connection between national character and military capabilities was to make him famous in the naval engagements of the Russo-Turkish War of 1877–78 and to earn him a permanent place in naval history. While only twenty-nine years old, he created and developed both the torpedo boat and its tactics, a form of naval war which "closely resembles guerrilla warfare, and therefore well suits the disposition of the Russian seaman." [12] (His linking the Russian national character with guerrilla warfare probably had to do with its sudden bravado and freedom from organizational requirements, elaborate support, and sophisti-

10. Makarov, p. 148 [p. 235 in this edition].
11. Ibid., p. 31 [p. 45 in this edition].
12. Ibid., p. 167 [p. 267 in this edition].

cated technology and training. At the same time, Makarov implied his concept of "active defense," one which is again being elaborated by the general staff under Gorbachev.)

Already in 1876 Makarov had proposed that in the event of war, fast steam-powered ships be equipped with torpedo boats which, upon approaching anchored ships, could be lowered into the water for the attack against the unsuspecting enemy.[13] The plan attracted the attention and approval of the head of the naval ministry, the Grand Duke Constantine Nikolaevich.[14]

The first two attacks with the new equipment and the new tactics were not successful, but in the third, several Turkish ships were sunk. More important, perhaps, the attacks forced the superior Turkish Navy into a defensive position, taking protective measures against the new threat, which diminished the usefulness of their fleet and deprived them of the initiative. Thus, Makarov planned the tactics around the concept of "active defense." Using mine barriers in Russian ports and on the Danube—and exploring the currents at the mouth of the Bosporus in order to lay mines more effectively—he also elaborated on the concept of "passive defense." These techniques of mine warfare were put to good use later by the Japanese off Port Arthur.

Makarov's innovations in the naval battles of the Turkish wars showed another Russian characteristic: namely, the ability to improvise. The shipbuilding program for the Black Sea Fleet was hopelessly behind when the war began. The Imperial Navy had only a few boats and commandeered merchant ships fortified with artillery to defend the shores

13. In 1868 Robert Whitehead, a British engineer, first developed a torpedo, which underwent rapid development in all navies.

14. See Jacob W. Kipp, "Tsarist Politics and the Naval Ministry, 1876–1881: Balanced Fleet or Cruiser Navy," *Canadian-American Slavic Studies* 17 (summer 1983).

against a greatly superior fleet—fifteen ironclads, monitors, and many other large ships.[15] (From Peter the Great to World War II, the Russian Navy had always been extraordinarily innovative in adapting whatever was at hand to meet its tactical needs.)

Under those circumstances, it is somewhat astonishing that the Russians, who had long used mines for defense, would go on the offensive, but they did. With sure instinct, Makarov and his contemporaries led the inferior Russian forces in this tactical offensive. This "aggressive defense" helped an ill-equipped navy win through innovation, a passion for the offense, and an indifference to risk, illustrating Makarov's precepts.

Makarov was also a great communicator. He understood that to win acceptance for his ideas, he needed to embody them in short, memorable phrases; in aphorisms. Throughout his career, he created many. One, which encapsuled his idea of offense over defense, was: "A good gun brings victory while armor only postpones defeat."[16]

A RUSSIAN MIND

In writing "History has shown that we, Russians, are inclined to partisan warfare,"[17] Makarov was not thinking of Napoleon's retreat from Moscow but of naval battles, of Sevastopol and Chesma.[18] Thus, Makarov, who believed in the tactical offensive as a fundamental principle of naval war, created his first operational plan—turning defense into of-

15. S. N. Semanov, *Admiral Makarov* (Moscow: Prosveshchenie, 1971), p. 17. (There is a new edition published by Molodaia gvardiya, 1988.)
16. Makarov, p. 181 [p. 289 in this edition].
17. Ibid., p. 18.
18. Vrangel', vol. 1, p. 94.

fense. He made mines into an aggressive weapon to be used against greatly superior forces in hit-and-run operations.

Makarov's *Tactics* reflect the cast of mind of most great military leaders—to be on the offensive. His conclusion—"In general we may state that we should endeavor to concentrate a superior force upon some part of his [the enemy's] squadron, and after annihilating it to attack the other part" [19]— may not have been original, but it is so constantly rediscovered that in Soviet military doctrine it is a law. There was also something of the Soviet preoccupation with quantity of fire, and aggression for aggression's sake, in it for, although he had experimented with targeting and exercises, Makarov either had (or overrode it) little appreciation for the difficulty of fire control, especially against moving targets, with the ordnance of that time.

In order to concentrate firepower, he argued for relatively short intervals—two cables or 400 yards—between ships. That tight spacing led to the requirement for tight maneuvering in close formations, another characteristic of Soviet forces ashore or afloat.

Makarov's tactical success was not the result of a compartmentalized mind. He studied explosives, the instruments for delivering them, and the people who would place them with apparently equal interest and dedication. Not only did he experiment with all kinds of mines, he also concerned himself with the physics of explosives. Just as now, in the nineteenth century one aspect of the arms race was to produce plating most resistant to the penetration of shells. In the arms race in Europe at that time, Russia, as now, had pockets of superiority; the rifled, breech-loading Obukhov heavy artillery, for example. In any case, it was unusual for a naval officer to produce, as Makarov did, a penetrating shell superior to those in use at that time: "Makarov's Little Cap" it was called.

19. Makarov, p. 193.

With his contextual pattern of thought—he did not customarily examine reality in terms of either/or but both/and—Makarov always emphasized the importance of knowing the medium within which the action occurred. It is not surprising, therefore, that he became an outstanding oceanographer. In his *Tactics* he discussed the effects of cold water upon torpedoes, climate and geography upon ship camouflage, and depths upon maneuverability. All of this, plus his interest in the penetration of steel, naturally led Admiral Makarov to consider the problems of the Arctic and the penetration of ice.

He designed the first successful Russian icebreaker, thus providing, at one stroke, new approaches to the solution of an enormous number of Imperial Russia's strategic naval and maritime problems. The invention of the icebreaker was also of enormous economic significance since it could make vast areas of Siberia accessible through a longer season and created the possibility of the northern sea route that, a decade later, opened to navigation.

"REMEMBER WAR"

The range of his naval interests was unlimited. Having designed the world's first dedicated minelayer, Admiral Makarov then experimented with wireless communications for the Russian Navy. In 1899 a message was transmitted for over three miles. But although he pursued this invention vigorously, the naval ministry did not. In only five years, Russia was to suffer greatly for its failure to integrate, as the Japanese had, the latest wireless developments into the tactics in the Russo-Japanese War.

One of Admiral Makarov's favorite aphorisms was *Pomni voynu!* ("Remember war!"). This became his most characteristic motto, always displayed prominently above his desk. His point was that every decision should be made as if war were imminent. He applied the idea to his definition of tactics—

"The chief purpose of tactics is to maintain the fleet in condition for war"[20]—with particular urgency. During the years after the Turkish wars, when the naval budget was inadequate, the ships and crews exercised for three to four months of the year. The rest of the time, except during long cruises, the fleet was manned at a quarter strength.

Officers, far from "remembering war," occupied themselves with St. Petersburg's wonderful balls and the design of their uniforms. (The vanity of naval officers of that period, however, never reached the excesses of that of the Soviet marshals who, according to former Premier Khrushchev, decorated themselves to look like peacocks.)

As so easily happens in peacetime, the danger was that the officers and men would forget their purpose, and that the ships, being adapted for comfort, would become unsuitable for war. Makarov gave a thundering reproof: "Every military man and those connected with them, in order not to forget why he exists, would do well to have in front of himself a plaque: 'Remember War'!"[21] Makarov's reading of the Russian character deserves respect, for he was a leader who commanded enormous loyalty and devotion. He was popular with the crews, and his presence in the Far East was like a tonic, not only for the fleet but also for the whole town and its army garrison. Although there is some evidence that he had a sense of humor, most of his observations on human nature showed a stern demand for duty and discipline, a demand that was fulfilled.[22]

Makarov argued that "the Russian fighter does not serve

20. Ibid., p. 179 [p. 287 in this edition].
21. Semanov, p. 51.
22. Makarov did include the humorous story about Admiral Lazarev, who, when told that an incompetent officer had some value because he had been long at sea, replied, pointing to his trunk: "That trunk has made three voyages around the world, but it remains a trunk."

for money. He looks upon war as the fulfillment of his holy duty to which he is called by fate and does not expect money for his service."[23] The same argument, with different wording, is used to explain the modern Soviet recruit's virtual lack of pay. Makarov considered discussions of monetary rewards demoralizing, and, as a young commander in the Turkish wars, he ordered the ships he captured sunk rather than, as was the custom, sell them to reward the crew with booty.

THE *TACTICS*

At the beginning of the century, there was an enormous amount of new technology to be absorbed into naval tactics, and there were few strategic encounters to give their incorporation a sense of urgency. Lord Nelson's great battles still dominated naval minds. The preconceptions about naval maneuvers reflected the dominance of the sail. But with more powerful weapons, greater ranges, and the capability of maneuvering independent of the wind, the study of past naval battles was insufficient preparation for the present. Radio communications and the new capabilities for maneuver would radically transform naval battles. All of this required an innovative and imaginative thinker, free from prejudice and compartmentalized thinking. That was the role Admiral Makarov fulfilled in the Imperial Russian Navy.

He was decidedly familiar with the naval battles of the Napoleonic wars, as his *Tactics* shows. Lord Nelson was obviously one of his heroes, and he knew the works of Mahan and Colomb.[24] But he had a thoroughly modern mind, one which could incorporate new ideas with ease. And his think-

23. *Dokumenty*, vol. II, p. 8.
24. He had a Russian predecessor (Admiral G. I. Butakov, 1820–82) who wrote about naval tactics soon after the shift from sail to engine in *New Principles of Steam Tactics* (mentioned by Makarov in chapter XIV).

ing was very different from Mahan's. He thoroughly supported the concept of combined arms—that is, of the fleet against the shore and the fleet working with the ground forces to achieve victory—as he showed at Port Arthur and in his *Tactics*.[25] Makarov further believed that the services should be under a unified command and that the navy had much to learn, and to teach, the ground forces. This is called "organic" thinking, in which all aspects of a thing are taken into account, a concept more typical of Russian military solutions than American ones, wherein problems of tactics are more likely to be studied in isolation.

The fleet tactics Makarov introduced in Chapters XII and XIII of *Tactics* are as modern, concrete, practicable, and creative as can be found among any of the tactical thinkers of the turn of the century, a period distinguished by the quantity of writing on the subject.[26] But the Imperial Russian Navy needed more than one Makarov. There was too much new information on naval tactics to be absorbed. The tempo of the industrial revolution was increasing, and Russia, far from lagging behind, as the Soviets have wanted us to believe, tripled its industrial production in the last decade of the nineteenth century.

There was a great need for Makarov's *Tactics*. All of Europe, and some of Asia, was being transformed. As Engels observed, one of the greatest effects of industrial might was on a nation's military capabilities. But for indolent Russian naval staffs, and the even more lethargic naval ministry, the responses to change and the incorporation of new technological capabilities were so inadequate as to endanger the empire's security.

25. See Chapter I.
26. Captain Wayne Hughes, USN (Ret.), one of the few prolific tactical writers at the end of the century, is my authority for this appraisal.

For a navy, this was a serious deficiency. Ships, of course, are extremely sensitive to changes in technology since they are units of tightly interacting manufactured components. In that competition Japan, as would become apparent, had astonishingly gained the advantage in the arms race. It was not restrained by convention (having just emerged from feudalism), and all of the technology it acquired as it built its navy from scratch was the most advanced.

One of the Japanese Navy's greatest advantages was in communications. Although Admiral Makarov had immediately recognized the importance of the wireless and had urged the Admiralty to make use of it, by the opening of the Russo-Japanese War, little had been done. For Makarov, the problem of signaling, which had to be visual for most of the ships, was thus enormous. He gave detailed instructions to the fleet on how to protect the security of the signals at night and during other conditions. And the limited possibilities meant that he had to rely, almost exclusively, on fighting his ships in column formation.

While the navies of the world were fast settling on the column as the best battle formation (indeed, Admiral Togo used it at Tsushima with his flagship in the lead), the Russian Navy had no other choice. (For Makarov's own interpretation of the difficulty of maintaining control of a fleet by signals and the consequent advantages of a column, see section 198— "Choice of formation.")

Obviously, the rapid development of steam engines fundamentally changed the nature of war at sea—of maneuver, of tactics, of training, and even of discipline. Sailors could not be beaten into getting the steam pressure higher, as was the custom, while being fed rotten food and berthed under inhuman conditions. Engines could not be fired with inferior coal without giving betraying smoke signals. And artillery shells with inferior powder could not reach the enemy in time.

Makarov understood that these conditions were interrelated, and he addressed them all.

He had experimented with armor, with shells, with training, with ship design, with morale. When he took command of the First Pacific Ocean Squadron, he needed all of that knowledge, for hardly any aspect of the command functioned properly. For example, in emphasizing readiness—reducing the time it took the fleet to get under way from two days to two hours—he had to address the problem of increasing the efficiency of ships without modern boilers. Makarov's solution was to order the installation of additional steam pipes to increase the boilers' capacities.

Although he underscored the technology of warships, Makarov nevertheless emphasized the environment, rather than the hardware, of the naval battle. In *Tactics* he pays primary attention to theories of victory and questions of leadership and training. In arguing the perennial question of Russian and Soviet military thought—What is the difference between naval science and art?—he comes down on the side of tactics as the practice of naval art. During the period of Makarov's service, naval warfare underwent a revolution in ships and arms. How to integrate the new inventions and capabilities remained a largely theoretical subject since there were few wars in which to test tactical ideas. Makarov understood this, and his energies were devoted to invention and testing, to theory and praxis. Thus, his study is pertinent to our time.

The lesson he teaches, however, is that a technical and scientific genius cannot save a country whose leadership is unwilling to face a new or changed reality. Imperial Russia was, whether it wanted to be or not, in a technological race and an arms race not only with Europe but also with Japan, whose sun was rapidly rising. For Makarov, correct tactics were a problem of analysis, foresight, integration, and, most of all, training. In addition to presenting a course in modern naval praxis, his *Tactics* warned of the need to operate in a changed maritime world.

Anticipating the coming far eastern war, Admiral Makarov advised the government that if it wanted to achieve dominance in the Pacific, it would have to correlate its forces with at least a 20 percent advantage over the Japanese.[27] But that involved quality as well as quantity.

In Port Arthur, Admiral Makarov had to occupy himself not only with getting the ships to sea, improving the boilers, teaching sailors who had been used to sleeping ashore how to fight from their ships, and speeding the supplies of war but also with the shore batteries and garrison defenses that were constructed with crumbling cement. He even had to devise and then teach a spotting system for coordinating and correcting ground and naval fire on the Japanese ships that were behind the hills.

The speed and maneuverability which steam engines allowed had not, by 1898, fully changed naval warfare, and the problems of control, without the universal employment of wireless communications, were extremely restrictive. For example, the attack which Makarov greatly favored had to be accomplished by ships forming a column. In order to increase freedom of maneuver, he discouraged laying mines. To defend Port Arthur against shelling by the Japanese, he authorized only a very restrictive use of mines behind one of the hills.

In *Tactics* Makarov discusses the problem of hitting a target in surprising brevity (see Chapter VI), considering the difficulty of the subject. Obviously, he apprised other tactical problems to be more serious than that. But it would be wrong to conclude that he was unconcerned with the problems of aiming at targets. He had brought an officer named Miller, famous as an artillery expert, with him to Port Arthur.[28] Mil-

27. *Dokumenty,* vol. II, p. xxxii.
28. Ibid., no. 642.

ler devised a method for firing on Japanese ships that used quadrants, a compass, and corrections by telephone. But Makarov's preoccupation was not so much with the accuracy of firing as with action, with familiarizing men with naval warfare by getting them to sea and experiencing naval battles.

The major tactical problem Admiral Makarov faced at sea off Port Arthur was, however, that the Japanese Fleet was superior in speed, firepower, and readiness for battle. Their battle tactics were to send four destroyers ahead to engage in attack with the enemy. In the event the destroyers got into trouble, they were retired behind the main formation of light cruisers, whose speed and firepower the Russians could not match.

Admiral Makarov sent destroyers to attack in pairs, a tactic he had devised for torpedo boats. His forces were always outnumbered, his light cruisers too slow, and his communications too limited to win in these naval skirmishes. What he hoped to do was to win by daring, to disorient the enemy by showing that Russians did not fear death.

It was Makarov's final engagement, however, which was an inexplicable disaster. *Tactics* shows that he had the wisdom and the experience to have avoided it, but perhaps because of physical exhaustion (great tacticians should not have to worry about mixing cement for bastions on shore), or a sudden overwhelming attack of Weltschmerz (Russians have an extraordinary penchant for self-immolation, Edmund Wilson observed), we shall never know.

MAKAROV'S LAST BATTLE

A Russian naval hero mourned even by the czar, Makarov is praised by the Soviets with restraint. In their iconography—at least in the language of socialist realism—the end of the hero's journey must be victory. Makarov is a flawed hero, for not only the war but also his last battle was lost. On his final day, the gods of war who had so consistently awarded him the victor's laurel crown abandoned him.

There is something of a Greek tragedy in the drama of Admiral Makarov's last month. The naval battles he was to fight were the battles he had planned for all of his life, but his energetic example had been defeated by bureaucracy and procrastination. He had argued for readiness, but little was ready. (Even after a month of superhuman activity, Makarov could get only half of his ships to sea at once.) [29] Supplies that he had demanded months in advance were waiting for transshipment at Lake Baikal, a thousand miles from the front. The ships and crews, which should have "remembered war" and exercised for constant readiness, were lying idle in the port. (The ironclad *Retvizan,* for example, damaged by the Japanese, had been left aground for a month. Makarov's methods of damage control had not been applied until just before his arrival.)

The First Pacific Ocean Squadron and garrison must have presented a pitiful spectacle for this man who had spent his life preaching readiness. Even about shipbuilding he had written: "We must bear in mind the chief purpose of tactics— namely, to maintain a fleet in condition for war. If we regard the matter from this point of view, we shall make no mistakes, but if we assign too great attention to peace conditions we shall evidently remain unprepared for battle. War ships should be built as if war were to be declared to-morrow." [30]

But even Makarov's *Tactics,* which the fleet so desperately needed, had not been published as a book by the naval ministry in time to be of any use. Finally, his concept of war in the Far East as a combined arms operation (how modern he sounds!) was sabotaged by the military viceroy, who thought of the navy as useful only for coastal defense.

29. Ibid., no. 658.
30. Makarov, p. 179 [p. 287 in this edition].

If nations have styles, characteristics, and identifiable cultures in war,[31] then Russia's is that of operating at the extremes: extreme indolence followed by extreme (and usually ill-prepared) activity. Stepan Osipovich Makarov, who always operated at the extreme of energy, burst upon a somnolent Port Arthur that had grown accustomed to rousing itself infrequently to respond to Japanese attacks.

The admiral, who led not only by his brilliance but also by his example, threw himself into a frenzy of activity to get the town, the garrison, and the fleet back into the war. Immediately upon his arrival, without time for rest or consultation, he showed himself everywhere—visiting the ships, talking to the men, and giving orders for action to reverse the months of indolence. But there was much to do to reverse the ground forces' defensive mentality, which is the Russian naval disease.

Makarov instantly set about changing everything he could, but perhaps too soon.[32] Having arrived on 24 February 1904, already by the 26th he had engaged the enemy and sunk one Japanese ship, the first Russian victory of the war. But it proved to be a Pyrrhic one. The *Steregushchii*, one of the destroyers on patrol, was trapped by a superior Japanese force and knocked out.

Immediately, Admiral Makarov, in the light cruiser *Novik*, accompanied by another cruiser, rushed to the rescue in a maneuver which, considering the superior Japanese force, was ill considered. Fortunately, he succeeded in returning to port with the bodies of two sailors, although he had failed to save the stricken destroyer, which had been sunk by the surviving crew to prevent her capture.

31. See Barbara Tuchman's *Guns of August* and Edward Hall's *Beyond Culture* for convincing evidence.

32. The captain of the destroyer *Rastoropnyi* wrote: "At 8 o'clock in the morning, Admiral Makarov arrived. How energetically, suddenly, all of the work came alive after a long sleep." The captain was ordered to be ready to be underway that afternoon at 4:00! (*Dokumenty*, vol. II, no. 646.)

Although the exploit tempted disaster, Makarov's example—a vice admiral personally risking himself to save his men—excited not only all of Port Arthur but also all of Russia. Morale in the Far East rose to such a great height that its fall was all the more tragic. Unfortunately, Makarov had not had time to follow the practice he had recommended in *Tactics* of naming small ships, specifically torpedo boats, after their captains, but the originality and power of such a suggestion gives us an idea of the levels of morale and loyalty his leadership could have reached.[33]

To be more concerned with morale (which does not mean PXs, but control) than with equipment also characterizes the Russian style of war. Makarov fittingly exemplified this. In his orders-of-the-day to the squadron, he reminded the officers to compliment the men for good work in order to keep up their courage and self-confidence. He concluded with another aphorism: "He is victorious who dares well, paying no attention to his losses and remembering that the enemy is suffering even more."[34]

The final irony was Makarov's death. The commanding officer of one of his ships described how, when the flag was raised at his assumption of command, "It was obvious to each of us that this flag symbolized all of our hopes and promised a brighter future."[35] Its sinking, of course, meant the reverse.

The Greeks believed that all great men have a fatal flaw. Makarov's must have been his unbounded energy and brilliance. According to the documents of eyewitnesses, he was not a man who consulted others, or needed to. He commanded in the Russian style—decisive, unyielding, and uncompromising. Having assumed command of forces in such

33. Makarov, p. 167 [p. 268 in this edition].
34. *Dokumenty,* vol. II, no. 333.
35. Ibid., no. 379.

disarray, he must have felt that he could depend upon no one but himself. In the end, exhausted and alone, he probably suffered from the sin of hubris, for on the night before he drowned, he failed to listen to his subordinates.

When the commander of the First Pacific Ocean Squadron arrived, he found that the COs of his ships were accustomed to sleeping ashore. Makarov quickly changed that, and to set an example of good leadership, as he always did, he slept (or more probably, catnapped) on the different ships of his command. He spent the fateful night of 30 March 1904 on the cruiser *Diana*, which had guard duty at the mouth of the harbor. At least twice during the night he was awakened to be shown Japanese ships laying mines in the approaches to Port Arthur. Unaccountably, the admiral could see nothing amiss and issued no orders, either to fire on the ships or to activate the spotlights.[36]

The next morning at seven o'clock, having transferred to the *Petropavlovsk*, he went to the rescue of one of his destroyers, leading two ironclads and cruisers and destroyers in column. The ships engaged the Japanese, but were forced to retreat to port upon the appearance of the bulk of the enemy fleet. The flagship *Petropavlovsk* was nearly back into the harbor when, at 9:37 A.M., she crossed into the Japanese mine field and was blown up. In two minutes the *Petropavlovsk* sank, with only seven officers and fifty-two men pulled from the 5° C Pacific water.[37]

An important part of the legend of any hero is his death. Makarov's was not victorious. Still, in a land where the important national symbols are a cracked bell and an enormous unfired cannon, there is room for an exhausted admiral who

36. Ibid., no. 384, from the memoirs of the president of the commission that investigated the sinking of the *Petropavlovsk*.
37. This account comes from K. I. Velichko, ed., *Voennaya entsiklopediya* (Moscow, 1913), vol. XII, p. 545.

was understandably too prone to fight with the aggressive, daredevil tactics of his legendary youth.

The disaster ended in farce. Apparently, rumors had spread in Port Arthur about a new naval weapon, the submarine, and the crews were expecting to be attacked by this unknown device. When the *Petropavlovsk* went down, the ships accompanying her opened fire on the water and the survivors floating upon debris, assuming that submarines were attacking.[38] (The apprehension of new naval weapons must have been enormous. The Baltic Fleet, on its way to death in Tsushima Straits, nearly caused a war with England at Dogger Banks by firing randomly on each other and on fishing boats, having been made nervous by the news of new naval weapons, such as submarines, being employed in the West.) Another of Makarov's aphorisms was ignored: "Firing without aiming is the best way to lose."[39]

From the Pacific to the Baltic, Imperial Russia understood what it had lost. The terrible destruction of the rest of the fleet at Tsushima was an inevitable unfolding of the tragedy that fate seemed to have in store for a country where superstition played an important role in politics.

For American students of naval tactics, the importance of studying Makarov's thought and life is considerable. Although naval tactics have changed enormously since his time, the Russian way of thinking about them has not. Admiral Makarov is very modern in his ordering of priorities, his emphasis on morale, his attention to the psychology of battle, and his championing the symbiosis of theory and praxis—the holistic nature of battle. With respect to naval warfare, he is consummately Russian: speed, aggression, disorienting the enemy, taking risks, sacrificing equipment and life. There is

38. Ibid.
39. Makarov, p. 148 [p. 235 in this edition].

also a recognition of what Russians typically are not capable of, such as German organization and precision.

Reading *Discussion of Questions in Naval Tactics* is an exercise in learning to cross over into another, this time Soviet, naval culture. What can be more important than that? Admiral Makarov summed up the national character of Russian/Soviet leadership when he said: "He wins the victory who fights hard paying no attention to his losses, and keeping in mind that the enemy is suffering greater losses."[40]

Although that did not prove true for him, that is the precept he left for the Imperial Russian Navy, which is heartily embraced by its Soviet successors.

ROBERT B. BATHURST

40. *Dokumenty,* vol. II, no. 607.

INTRODUCTORY

A RECENT PUBLICATION entitled Discussion of Questions in Naval Tactics, by Vice-Admiral S. O. Makarov, Imperial Russian Navy, translated from the Russian by Lieut. John B. Bernadou, United States Navy, is published in this part of General Information Series, No. XVII, as commending itself to the naval service for the able and original manner in which it treats the broad subject of naval warfare. Vice-Admiral Makarov says:

> Above strategy is to be placed imperial [national] policy, which determines whether an end sought may be obtained without war or not—whether a demonstration will suffice, or whether military operations must be undertaken. When war is begun, strategy shows where it is to be carried on, and tactics how to conduct it so as to defeat the enemy with the least loss.

Under tactics are grouped the various special sciences of administration, command, evolutions, shipbuilding, ordnance, engineering, etc. The influence of morale upon success in battle is considered at length, as well as the training of the personnel ashore and afloat, and the general preparation for war. Several chapters are devoted to single actions and fleet actions, night torpedo attacks, and to various other important naval operations.

RICHARDSON CLOVER,
Chief Intelligence Officer.

NAVY DEPARTMENT,
OFFICE OF NAVAL INTELLIGENCE,
April 29, 1898.

1

CONTENTS

CONTENTS

CONTENTS

LIST OF ILLUSTRATIONS

PREFACE

1. Theory of seamanship. We believe that we do no injustice to our companions in arms when we say that naval seamen have never been specially given to the study of the *theory* of seamanship. Navigation, shipbuilding, and other special sciences have always had their theoretical investigators; as to seamanship, it has been considered from ancient times a matter not of theory but of practice, and all its details have been worked out exclusively in a practical way. Thus, the whole arrangement of sails has been developed in just this manner, every detail having been worked out tentatively from the basis of actual experiment.

Thanks to such customs, he knew the most who had longest followed the sea. The officer just sent forth from school was regarded as ignorant in matters of naval practice and was useful only for the performance of the most insignificant duties on shipboard, gaining his knowledge as he advanced in service. The lieutenant, for instance, knew much more than the midshipman, the captain more than the lieutenant, and the admiral more than all the rest.[1] This practical method of acquiring knowledge furnished the best means of promoting

1. "The practical method of acquiring knowledge" (that is, old hands teach the younger), is still used in training the enlisted ranks in the Soviet Navy. A sailor is not rotated until his replacement proves he is proficient enough to take over the job.

discipline afloat, and in fact, in this respect, was absolutely incomparable.

Many seamen yet remember the time when printed handbooks were very scarce, and various manuscript notes of experienced admirals passed from hand to hand and were copied by those young officers desirous of acquiring a knowledge of seamanship.

Captain Glascock,[2] in his Naval Officer's Manual, counsels the young midshipman who is eager in the pursuit of knowledge to treat the boatswain politely, for the latter then says, "that young man wishes to learn his profession; we will have to help him," and consequently explains that which the young officer is unable to understand by himself. The custom of developing everything tentatively is still preserved by seamen; so that officers may be met who, when ordering something made, are unwilling to prepare any preliminary sketch. Very skilled and worthy persons may yet be found among seamen who believe that questions in seamanship are not subject to theoretical investigation, and that everything depends upon the ability of him who undertakes the task. If seamanship possesses no theory, and is regarded as an art to be developed exclusively by practice, then still less willing are seamen to commit to paper the theory of the art of war at sea.

2. Hoste's tactics.[3] The Jesuit Paul Hoste, who accompanied Admiral Tourville in his naval campaigns and battles, was the

2. Although Captain Glascock is not identified, this reference (one of many to foreign writers and experts) illustrates the eclectic nature of Admiral Makarov's and Russian naval thought. As the Russian, and now Soviet, naval journal *Morskoy sbornik* showed and shows, Russian naval officers have always been keenly aware of naval thought abroad and at home. Foreign language has not been the problem for them that it has been for Americans. The Imperial Navy, as well as the Soviet Navy for a short time after the Revolution, made ample use of foreign experts, and knowledge of foreign languages was expected of their officers.

3. Admiral Tourville also served as a marshal under Louis XIV. In one of his many battles, he saved Brittany from an invasion by the British by

first to take up this subject. Hoste published his treatise on Naval Evolutions in 1697. In this work various battle formations and tactical manœuvers are studied in detail. In conclusion the author writes: "I have not considered it necessary to describe the method of procedure in arming and equipping a fleet, nor the nature of the military stores and supplies that are to be carried. This belongs to those specially intrusted with this duty, whose zeal and attention are to be relied upon."

This note shows that Hoste, as a farseeing man, considered that it would be well to embrace the whole field of military and naval equipment in his work, but did not do this because, probably, he did not desire to offend the amour propre of certain powerful individuals.

Hoste's work has been translated into all languages, and is to be read as a classic. The book has become a bibliographical rarity in the Russian tongue, and a new edition of it is extremely desirable. The fifth edition in English appeared not long since. The fate of the translation of this work into Russian is interesting. The first translation was made in the reign of Peter the Great, but he considered the translation incorrect. In 1736 it was again translated by Mordvinow, and in 1747 by Voltchkow, but the book only saw the light in 1764, from Golinishew-Kutusow's translation. This tardiness in translation shows how little attention was paid to theory.

3. Recognition of the necessity of higher naval training. As matters of naval theory stood in the time of Paul Hoste, so they continued until later days, and he who paid much attention to science was not regarded a professional seaman. Thus Lomonosow, in his conclusions (The Exactness of the Course at Sea) in 1759, proposed the establishment of a naval acad-

---

forcing the blockade of Brest in 1689. The Jesuit Paul Hoste accompanied Admiral Tourville during that sea campaign and wrote "Treatise on Naval Evolutions" in 1697, the oldest known work on the subject.

emy, which was only accomplished sixty-eight years later.[4] The army had long recognized the necessity of a higher military training, and there was no army in which part of the officers, at least, were not graduates of institutions where military history and the higher theory of war were taught; whereas for the navy no such school existed. Up to a short time ago our naval academy produced learned astronomers, naval constructors, and mechanical engineers, but gave no instruction in military and naval history, nor in other military and naval sciences. The first example of work in this direction was afforded by officers in the United States Navy, who in the year 1884 conceived the idea of establishing a higher naval and military school. The initiator of this work was Admiral Luce, whom the author met in the fall of 1896.[5] In support of his assertions of the necessity of military training for naval seamen, Luce cited the example of the English generals Montagu and Blake, who had commanded the English fleet. He said that the landsman with military training is more competent to control the military actions of the fleet than the professional sailor unacquainted with military science. He added that great exploits can be expected for that fleet in which the necessary scientific knowledge and skill in the art of conduct-

4. M. V. Lomonosov (1711–65), a Russian genius of peasant origin, was a brilliant scholar in physics, chemistry, linguistics, literature, and metallurgy, among many other accomplishments. Moscow State University, the most prestigious in the Soviet Union, is named after him.

5. Admiral Stephen B. Luce founded the Naval War College in Newport, Rhode Island. He met Makarov while the Russian admiral was making his second circumnavigation of the globe. (There was not another visit by a Russian admiral to the Naval War College until 1975.) Admiral Makarov started from St. Petersburg in 1894, sailing to the Mediterranean, where he was the commander of the Imperial Russian squadron, through the Suez Canal, across the Pacific to North America, and then across the Atlantic to Russia. He not only made oceanographic observations but also wrote much of his *Tactics* on this voyage, which he published the next year.

ing war are to be found combined with practical training from early years in all branches of the naval profession. Admiral Luce's representations were fruitful, and a naval war college was opened at Newport. Its work is described in General Mertwago's paper (Morsk. Sbor., 1895, No. 7).[6]

4. *The Americans in relation to scientific investigations.* The Americans are wonderful people. In no country are men more practical than in the United States, and it would seem to follow naturally that in the land of practical men a prejudice would exist against all kinds of theoretical and scientific work. But precisely the contrary is the case—the practical American considers science his helpmate. The Government is far from liberal in affording aid to the development of the arts, and allows everyone to attend to his own affairs. But in questions concerning well-established industrial pursuits money is not lacking for scientific investigation. The whole country, not excluding uninhabited portions, has long since been subdivided by the surveyor into surveyed tracts, whereby all uncertainties and misconceptions as to the boundaries of the land have been put an end to. The Government spends much money upon meteorology and the forecasting of the weather. Large expenditures have been made by the commission for the study of fishes, thanks to which valuable species have been introduced in many places. The study of the Mississippi has been in progress for more than ten years, and the results of this investigation have not only proved useful in themselves but have supplied science with very valuable data. The example presented by the United States is worthy of imitation.

The Americans afford the same aid to naval matters that they do to the various branches of human industry, and have found means to establish a naval war college.

6. Morsk. Sbor. is a reference to the Russian naval journal *Morskoy Sbornik,* published with few interruptions from 1848 until the present. It is roughly the equivalent of the U.S. Naval Institute *Proceedings.*

5. *Inauguration of naval and military courses at the Nikolaievsk Naval Academy.*[7] The necessity of higher naval training for officers has long been urged in our navy, and in 1895 special classes for the instruction of commanding officers and senior lieutenants in naval science were inaugurated at the Nikolaievsk Academy.

Instructions were given in this course in naval history, naval strategy, and naval tactics. The choice of instructors was an extremely fortunate one, namely, strategical instruction by Col. N. A. Orloff of the general staff, distinguished for his literary labors and by his activity as a professor. Tactics were taught by Lieut. N. L. Klado, well known as an instructor possessing a general knowledge of the vast literature of tactics, and who had collected a valuable library at the academy.[8] In expounding disputed questions he endeavored to give to his students the opinions of various persons who had studied the subject, and separated in a positive manner his own deductions and generalizations from those of others. In this manner his views could only be considered as fully rational. The task assigned to the above-mentioned professors was the difficult one of teaching subjects not yet regularly coordinated. We wish them all success in their efforts to estab-

7. "Academy" in Russian does not refer to a college, as in the Naval Academy at Annapolis, but to an institution for advanced studies, such as the Naval War College or the Leavenworth Command and Staff School. The academy referred to is the most prestigious Soviet naval school, which still occupies a palace in Leningrad along the bank of the Neva River.

8. Lieutenant Klado (1862–1919) was, in addition to being a tactician and historian, chief of the main naval staff during the Russo-Japanese War. This broad view of tactics was not uncommon at the turn of the century. Bradley A. Fiske, in his 1905 Naval Institute prize essay, "American Naval Policy," expounded on the intimate link between tactics afloat and the technical characteristics of the fleet executing them. Makarov felt so strongly about the breadth of tactics that he proposed (in chapter XIV) putting maneuvers—what so many people regarded as the entire subject of tactics—in a separate category called "evolutions."

lish the subject upon a better basis, and we believe that it would be well to supplement the course by one additional branch of study, "investigation of the fighting qualities of the ship." There would be no need of introducing mathematical proof, and it would suffice if formulas were presented in their final form. Vessels can be manœuvered with far greater efficiency when their qualities have been established in a suitable manner by systematic experiments.

It is very important to determine now, at the beginning of the course, in what naval strategy consists, and in what naval tactics; and we would be very glad if the conclusions upon naval tactics presented here could in any way aid this matter. It is our definite purpose to treat of tactics only, and we believe that a systematic treatment of this subject includes not only the control of ships, but shipbuilding, instruction in command, ordnance, torpedoes, etc.

6. *Uncertainty of views in naval development.* If we glance backward we shall observe that ordnance, engineering, and torpedo work have been regularly developed as independent or nearly independent sciences. Shipbuilding, however, which is most closely allied to naval progress, exhibits traces of uncertainty in development.

7. *Uncertainty of views upon systems of protection.* The greatest confusion exists in relation to thickness and method of distribution of armor. Ships were at first armored over their whole surfaces, except their extremities (*Warrior*, 1861, fig. 1). The armored bow and stern were next added (*Minotaur*, 1867). Subsequently the width of the armor belt was diminished at bow and stern and increased amidships for the protection of the battery (*Hercules*, 1868). Next, the armor was still further diminished at the extremities and the *Alexandra* (1877) type established; then, to permit the use of heavy armor, the plating was omitted at the extremities, and protection was limited in those parts to a protective deck below water level (*Nelson*, 1880, fig. 1*a*). It seemed necessary, how-

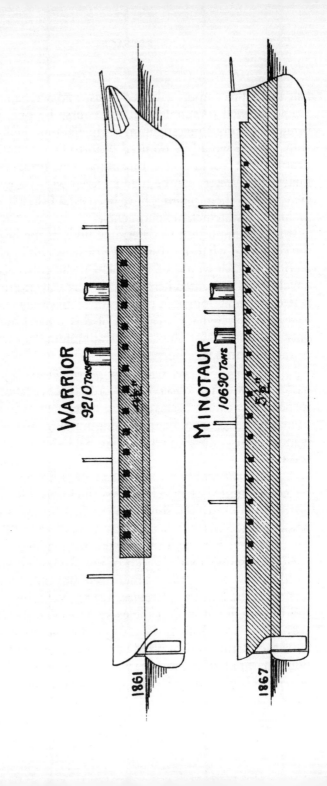

WARRIOR
9210 Tons

4½"

1861

MINOTAUR
10690 Tons

5½"

1867

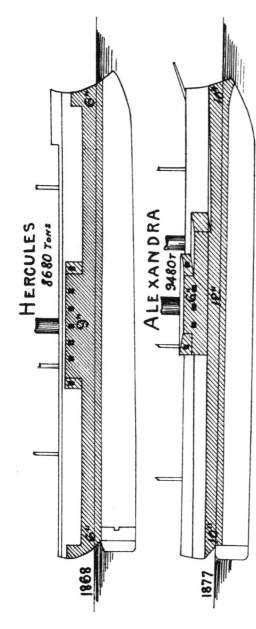

Fig. 1. Development of armor distribution afloat.

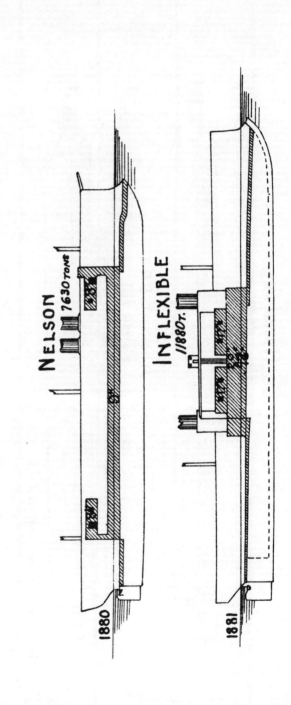

NELSON
7630 TONS

1880

INFLEXIBLE
11880 T.

1881

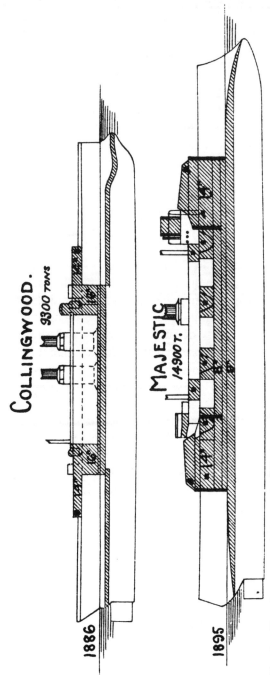

COLLINGWOOD.
9300 tons

1886

MAJESTIC
14900 T.

1895

Fig. 1a. Development of armor distribution afloat.

ever, to reduce still further the dimensions of casemates, which resulted in the *Inflexible* type (1877), in which the thickness of armor was increased to 24 inches.

When, in consequence of the above changes, the danger of the sinking of the ship from the piercing of its unarmored ends became imminent, the length of the armored casemates began to be increased again (*Collingwood*, 1886). The thickness of armor was reduced to 18 inches. Guns of moderate caliber were first placed behind armor, next were installed without armored protection, and finally were inclosed in small special casemates protected with thin plating. Finally, in ships of the present day types (*Majestic*, 1895), the main armor is reduced to 9 inches in thickness; and, as harveyized armor is now pierced by shells of special make almost as easily as unhardened armor, it may be concluded that at short range hereafter, shells of even as low caliber as 6 inches will penetrate into the vital parts of such enormous and thinly protected vessels. It is to be observed that each change in an adopted system of plating proved that previous systems were faulty. Further changes will show the faults of the present system.

8. *Uncertainty of views upon types of ships.* Still further uncertainty exists in relation to the type of vessel. Effort is made to construct each ship better than its predecessor, which has led to great confusion. Has not this arisen from the fact that naval seamen have never been able to decide what qualities they desire for their vessels? No one accuses sailors of not wishing to work; but it is impossible, also, not to state that their labors are directed to the study of details, in consequence of which the chief end in view has escaped them, which is, the battle at sea, and the question arising therefrom, what ships are needed for naval warfare?

Uncertainties of opinion concerning cruisers, and differences in views as to what their types should be, are considerable. Some say that cruisers are only intended for destroying an enemy's commerce. If so, it is inconceivable why heavy guns should be mounted upon them. Others say that in time of war an admiral would compel all his ships to fight in line of battle against the enemy, and it will be impossible then to limit the employment of cruisers to scouting duty.

An example of this uncertainty in the views of officers was presented no more than two years ago by the former English naval constructor in chief, Sir E. J. Reed. He related in Parliament an anecdote to the effect that, upon the insistence of naval officers, he increased the diameter of the captain's fighting tower; and that when a vessel was constructed with this increased tower naval captains accused him of taking a retrograde step in ship designing. This unflattering remark to naval officers remained unanswered.

9. *Uncertainty can only be obviated by consideration of data and by experiment.* Rear-Admiral Dubasow, in his torpedo-boat tactics (Morsk. Sbor., 1885, No. 5, p. 23), says:

> I openly declare myself in favor of investigations conducted in time of peace, by which I mean investigations conducted not as they now are, but as they might be. I wish to say that these investigations should possess a double character: the theoretical or, purely scientific; and the experimental, or purely practical. Both classes of research should be in close union with one another, and, moreover, no expense should be spared in conducting such investigations under circumstances most closely approximating to conditions of war.

We are in full accord with the opinion of our esteemed admiral upon the importance of deciding questions by experimental investigation.

Our companions in arms who fight upon land have never experienced such transitions. Their chief weapon, the small arm, has been gradually perfected in point of accuracy, range, and rapidity of fire. Each new type of this arm represents an improvement upon those preceding it in all three of the above-named qualities.

Notwithstanding the fact, however, that such development has advanced progressively, military tactics have undergone considerable changes, and if their tactics have changed for them, how much more have ours for us. Should we not begin by establishing the general necessary tactical conceptions, and solve in accordance therewith problems relating to special branches, and so advance up to the consideration of types of ships.

10. Some irregularities in the conception of what constitutes command of the sea. Two authorities upon strategy, Mahan and Colomb, state that the chief aim of the fleet in time of war is the command of the sea. Up to the present this has been understood to mean that the fleet commanding the sea constantly and openly plies upon it and that its beaten antagonist does not dare to leave his ports. Would this be so to-day? Instructions bearing upon the subject counsel the victor to avoid a night attack from the torpedo-boats of his antagonist, and therefore to carefully conceal his lights and to proceed at a good speed. If the victorious fleet does not observe these precautions, he will lose some units of his command upon the first night encounter, and perhaps more upon the following. Some seamen have become reconciled to this abnormality, yet if the matter were represented to a stranger he would be astounded. He probably would ask whether he properly understood that a victorious fleet should protect itself from the remnant of a vanquished enemy.

There are many of these inconsistencies, and we shall refer to them farther on. We allude here to fundamental misconceptions only. It is to be hoped that the regularly developed science of naval battle (tactics) may aid the fleet to enter upon the path of rational development.

We shall next consider the question, What are the naval tactics from which we may expect such important information?

CHAPTER ONE

THE POSITION OF NAVAL TACTICS IN THE CATEGORY OF NAVAL SCIENCES

11. Do tactics constitute a science or an art? Two high authorities upon the subject of military sciences, Jomini and Klausewitz, define the subject of tactics almost identically. Jomini calls tactics the art of war; Klausewitz defines tactics as the science of war. Both of these definitions are correct, and it might be well to unite them, for although there does not exist a positive difference between science and art, yet both are nevertheless closely allied. Thus, for example, mathematics is the science of dimensions, and no one considers mathematics as an art, yet it includes certain arts within itself, such as that of adding numbers, and of forming various other combinations from them. Astronomy is the science of heavenly bodies; it also is not regarded as an art, although it includes the art of determination of latitudes and longitudes, both of the heavenly luminaries as well as of points upon the surface of the earth. Sculpture is an art, but no one would deny that it is an art developed from scientific data. The same is true for painting, music, etc.

In sculpture and painting, art naturally possesses the primary, while in mathematics and astronomy it occupies a subordinate, position.

General Leer, in his Positive Strategy (ed. 1871, p. 4), makes the following declaration:[1]

> Every science (theory) possesses its complement (art), and conversely every art possesses its science, which is custodian of those laws underlying the foundation of the art in question. From this it is evident that the commonly employed apposition of art to science, such as the statement that "tactics is the art, strategy the science, of war" (Erzherzog Karl), is deprived of all raison d'être, since strategy and tactics each possesses in itself its own science (theory) and its own art (the application of theory to practice).[2]

The purpose of tactics is to indicate the methods of winning a battle; whence it would appear that the term "art" applies better to it than the expression "science," but as the directions for conducting a battle can only be determined as the result of the careful consideration of all elements influencing success in war, and as such investigation is a matter of theory—that is, of science—we agree with Klausewitz, and regard tactics as the science of war.

12. Comparison of the science of war on land and sea. Does there exist only one general tactical system, or is it necessary to distinguish military from naval tactics? Our companions in arms on shore reduced their profession to a science sooner than ourselves. This came about from the reason that there were more people with scientific training in their circle than in that of seamen—practical people—since war on land was conducted on a larger scale than at sea, and finally, because

1. Infantry General G. A. Leer (1829–1904) wrote about military history and theory. He recognized the unity between politics and strategy, and favored a strategy of annihilation.

2. Erzherzog Karl was a Hapsburg archduke who led the main Austrian strength against Napoleon's forces in the Austrian War of Liberation. He moved so slowly and indecisively that his forces, although nearly evenly matched, were defeated.

the method of conducting war on land was more subject to generalization than when waged upon such a capricious element as water.

Some military authorities assert that the science of war is the same for the sea as land, and they say that if naval strategy is acknowledged to be a separate science the same must be acknowledged for the strategy of the woods, the steppes, etc. (Morsk. Sbor., No. 11, 1894, p. 2.) Such a view would be just were it purposed to unite the command of armies and fleets in the hands of one commander in chief who would control the general military resources of a country. Of this there are many historical examples, beginning with Pompey and Agrippa, and ending with Orloff, the victor at Tchesma.[3] Unity of action would be secured from the fusion of fleet and army and from the centralization under one ministry of the general administration of the offensive and defensive resources of the nation. No country, however, has actually undertaken such a step, for a vast difference exists between methods of war on sea and upon land. Life itself differs greatly for the one and the other. Cases have occurred where a general who proved brave beyond question under a heavy fire on shore showed himself a coward at sea upon the first roll of the ship, when there was not the slightest danger.

Napoleon, at the time of his wars, when he ruled nearly all Europe, was unable to overcome the resistance of England. If he had felt himself able to assume command of his fleets, he would not have hesitated to do so. With such a vast military talent as Napoleon possessed it would only have required a

3. The naval battle at Chesma in the Aegean Sea (June 1770), in which the Russian Fleet destroyed a Turkish Fleet nearly twice its size, is one of the victories ritually cited by all Soviet naval authorities. The battle did change the correlation of forces and laid the groundwork for serious Russian study of naval tactics. A. G. Orlov was the brother of a lover of Catherine II and the commander of the forces that defeated the Turks at Chesma.

short time for him to grasp the essentials of our profession, and we are convinced that he would have introduced much that was fresh and healthy into our life. He himself was a native of an island, began his career at a seaport, and made a voyage with an army to Egypt. Naval conditions were therefore not altogether unfamiliar, yet he could not decide to assume command of his fleet.

The objects are the same for fleets as for armies—to defeat the enemy and compel him to yield to our demands; the methods of accomplishing the result are totally different. It is impossible not to acknowledge that the study of military history is useful to the sailor and that of naval history to the soldier. The study of history broadens the horizon of perception and determines our relations to circumstances. It is also useful to seamen to study military strategy and military tactics and to familiarize themselves with their principles; but we must proceed with caution when we apply to the sea the rules of war that have been developed from conditions that obtain on land. We should borrow from them only what corresponds to naval conditions. There are, naturally, many principles that are the same for military and naval operations— e.g., that of centralized control—but this applies to every problem of life in general. The principle of concentration of force in battle at a central point is as correct for us as for them; but another and far more important principle which stands, so to speak, at the head of every military undertaking—that of *mutual support*—must be applied with caution to the circumstances of war at sea. To the soldier it is the guiding star that must be kept in view when forming plans as well as when carrying them out upon the field of battle; general and soldier should be guided by this principle and each should be assured that aid will be afforded at the critical moment; only under such conditions will men stand firm. Villeneuve, before the battle of Trafalgar, declared that mutual support of ships was the chief end in view, but was beaten by an antagonist who always acted on the principle that it is necessary to trust the fate of some part of the fleet to chance in a sea fight.[4] If ships only busy themselves about supporting one another in battle, the enemy who is in no wise hindered will invariably win. The principle of mutual support may be remembered by seamen as far as it relates to the simultaneous attack of an adversary. The best aid to our own side is prompt attack upon our opponents.

The principle of holding a portion of an army in reserve is fundamental in military operations, and no general would ever think of so disposing his army that no part of it should be thus withheld. There are no such reserves in naval battles. A reserve is alluded to in Nelson's order before Trafalgar. He formed a third column of the fleetest ships, to unite with one of the main columns at the time of attacking the enemy. But the plan was never carried into execution, as, at the time of the engagement, he had fewer ships than he anticipated; while the assignment of the faster vessels to the third column showed that he did not contemplate holding them back for any length of time, but intended to employ them to strengthen one or the other of the main columns as speedily as possible. In fact, if any one should divide his forces in halves before battle and then enter into action first with one half and then with the other, he would enable his adversary to concentrate his entire force first upon one and then upon the other section, and would thus precipitate his own defeat. It is not intended to discuss here the question as to whether there should be a reserve or not. We can only say that it would be shortsighted to apply all military principles to conditions of naval war. The reserve is constituted in the army

4. Admiral Villeneuve led the French forces at Trafalgar on 21 October 1805, the scene of Admiral Nelson's great victory and death.

for the purpose of directing it to the turning point of the fight when the battle has developed, to crush an adversary and to compel him to retire. The enemy assumes a very unfavorable position upon retreating from a battlefield. Suvorow says, "Pursuit alone destroys a fleeing enemy."[5] For fleets the matter is entirely different. A ship retreating in the face of a head wind from an opponent is far more favorably placed for the use of her guns than the ship pursuing her. Wind and sea in nowise impede the fire of the former, while the latter is placed under many difficulties, and in the heavy sea may have to discontinue the use of his battery. It is therefore favorable for us under certain conditions to permit ourselves to be chased, while retreat with an army is only decided upon in an extremity when no other course is left open. But although retreat is disastrous on land, yet a platoon, unexpectedly meeting an enemy's regiment, should retire skillfully, and, contrariwise, if our torpedo boat should meet an enemy's ironclad unexpectedly at night or in a fog, it should immediately attack her. We only wish to show by the above that the study of miliary science is indispensable. Its application to the conditions of naval war should be made, however, with great caution and discernment. We repeat that it would be desirable to unite matters military and naval together into one compact whole, but seamanship so abounds with special conditions that the general staff officer who might desire to study them thoroughly could do so only at the cost of detriment to his ultimate purpose. This is the reason why a government should maintain one organization of matériel and personnel for naval war and another for war on land. For the purpose of avoiding unnecessary prolixity it is customary to subdivide the subject into naval strategy and

5. A. V. Suvorov (1730–1800) was one of Russia's greatest generals, noted for his attention to morale and training, rapid maneuver and bold attack. He wrote *Science of Victory*.

naval tactics. Imperial policy alone remains the same for both kinds of war.[6]

The differences between naval and military strategy and between naval and military tactics, should cause no disagreement. Sailors readily adopt weapons that the army has chosen. They imitate the movement of armies as far as they are capable in their landing expeditions, and therefore our comrades on shore would not be to blame if they hastened to adopt anything in which we were ahead of them.

13. What constitutes the subject of naval tactics? As tactics of war on land were developed first, the term "tactics" signifies military tactics. Nothing is said therein about the conditions of naval war, and we have therefore nothing left to do but to designate our tactics "naval tactics," the definition of which, in accordance with the above conclusions, is as follows:

Naval tactics is the science of naval war. While recognizing the distinction that exists between naval and military strategy, as well as between naval and military tactics, we find at the same time that they possess much in common, and we therefore deem it very useful to cite the opinions of military authorities, and to present the views of the most renowned captains, concerning them. These authorities give the following detailed explanation concerning tactics: "Tactics, according to Leer, has for its object investigation of questions concerning the relations of the military elements—armies, weapons, positions—and the most favorable conditions for utilizing them and their combinations in various cases that arise in war" (Course in Tactics, Colonel Orloff, 1896, p. 3).

The purpose of tactics, according to Dragomirow, consists in: (1) The investigation of the principles of the peace training and education of armies.[7] (2) The study of their fighting, cam-

6. "Imperial policy" is used by Makarov in a way similar to the current Soviet use of "doctrine."

7. M. I. Dragomirov (1830–1905) was a general and military scientist

paigning, and scouting capacities. (3) The study of the influence which position exerts upon the disposition, movements, and actions of armies (Text-book of Tactics, Dragomirow, 1881, pp. 1, 2). The opinions of Generals Dragomirow and Leer above presented indicate that they, like Jomini and Klausewitz, give broad scope to the field of tactics. Some naval writers consider the scope of naval tactics similarly, but there are others who confound tactics with evolutions. Occasionally, under the title of naval tactics, one will meet a book which treats only of dispositions and changes of formation of fleets. There are other books which bear the high-sounding title of naval tactics, whose contents only touch upon the advantages and disadvantages of the various types of ships.

Professor Altmeier defines tactics as follows: "Tactics, in the broadest sense of the term, teaches positions and the rules derived therefrom as to how to undertake and prosecute war under given conditions and circumstances."

This definition is extremely narrow; it limits the influence of naval tactics and throws all other naval sciences out of touch with them.

The French seamen also had narrow views upon tactics. According to their opinion, naval tactics is the art of grouping naval forces, of moving them in order with rapidity and safety, and—at the time of battle—of deriving the greatest amount of benefit from them in winning a victory.

Bainbridge-Hoff defines naval tactics in a somewhat broader way; he presents naval tactics as the most important branch of study for a naval officer, teaching him how to utilize in time

---

whose works were widely quoted and debated in the nineteenth century, and are still famous. He referred to the Russian soldiers as "grey cattle," and highly favored the psychological effects of cold steel—the bayonet attack.

of war the different weapons that constitute the fighting power of ships.[8]

14. The position of naval tactics in the list of naval sciences. If we reduce naval sciences to a system, the scope of tactics will define itself. Let us first of all agree that the *naval fleet exists for war,* and that each one of its units, personal and material, is organized with a view to successful participation in a naval battle. As naval tactics is the science of naval war, it embraces within itself everything upon shipboard. The end in view is the winning of the battle, and naval tactics should show us how to do this. To this end it should give directions in relation to all naval sciences included within its scope.

There is, however, a science higher than naval tactics—strategy. The latter investigates all the elements of war; it determines the amplitude of the resources required for war and the best mode of procedure against the enemy; it decides the type of military action best capable of accomplishing the end sought. The problem of war is how to overcome the resistance of the enemy, and the object of this science is, as above stated, to indicate the kind of military actions best calculated to defeat him and to accomplish our ends most rapidly.

Some authorities define tactics as *the science of war.* They consider strategy as the philosophy of war, or as the tactics of the theater of war, in distinction from actual tactics of the field of battle.

Above strategy is to be placed imperial policy, which determines whether an end sought may be obtained without war or not—whether a demonstration will suffice, or whether military operations must be undertaken. When war is begun, strategy shows where it is to be carried on, and tactics how to conduct it so as to defeat the enemy with the least loss.

8. Commander William Bainbridge-Hoff, U.S. Navy, published *Elementary Naval Tactics* in 1894.

Special sciences—engineering, ordnance, etc.—give detailed instruction as to how to put machinery in motion, load and point guns, etc. We present below a sketch indicating at a glance the general arrangement of naval sciences:

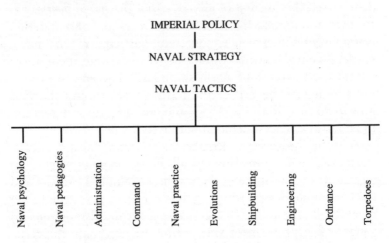

Under such a classification matters are comprehensively grouped under special subjects, and the whole science is placed upon a firm foundation. We have not yet met, in a single course in strategy or tactics, with such a coordination of subjects as is presented above, but we do not differ in our views from those of the chief contemporary authorities, Generals Dragomirow and Leer. As above stated, both of the latter regard tactics broadly. Dragomirow, for example, dwells in detail upon morale, and his text-book is filled with counsels upon matters relating to pedagogics. He not only tells us what to learn, but sometimes how to learn. Similarly, Leer does not regard tactics as a study whose theme begins and ends upon the field of battle, for fights may be won only as the results of long and careful preparation.

15. Limitations of tactics. The limitations of tactics and strategy are in accordance with the above-given definitions of these sciences. All that relates to war in general belongs to strategy; all that relates to battles of ships against ships or against fortifications, as well as the technique of all reconnaissances and scouting in general, belongs to tactics. It investigates the methods of maintaining a squadron at anchor and at sea, and considers all military elements in their general relationship to one another. The scope of tactics and of the special sciences define themselves. Every special subject, such as ordnance, engineering, etc., develops itself as fully as it may within the limits of its own sphere of extension; tactics determines the relationship existing between itself and other special sciences. If, for example, any special subject be neglected, it is the duty of tactics to adopt it to itself until it passes to the specialist's domain. This is the present status of the question of unsinkability of ships. Engineering considers it as pertaining to shipbuilding, shipbuilding to engineering. Tactics will continue to hold it in its own hands until it be definitely placed in one branch or the other.

It sometimes happens that an entirely new subject develops which does not fall within the scope of any existing branch of naval science. Artillery and ordnance can not be blamed for not giving their attention to aerial navigation. Tactics can not refuse to consider any means that may be of use to win a battle. If it should transpire that aerial navigation proves of importance in naval war, it is the duty of tactics to take the matter into its own hands, and to control it until it develops into a special branch of naval science, after which the rôle of tactics becomes limited to certain general directions relating thereto. This is why signaling, evolution, and other branches of seamanship which have not yet developed into special naval sciences, nor have been absorbed by any of the existing specialties, still remain under naval tactics.

By investigating all the elements influencing the success of naval battle, and by considering their general relationships, naval tactics points out the goal toward which each special science should strive. It is the science of the sciences of naval war, or the philosophy of naval war.

All that has been said above upon the subject of naval tactics may be summarized briefly as follows:

Naval tactics is the science of naval war. It investigates the elements constituting the fighting force of ships and the means of employing them most favorably in war under different circumstances.

16. *Relation of previous work of the author (Elements of the Fighting Qualities of Men-of-war) to naval tactics.* At the time of preparation of his treatise Elements of the Fighting Qualities of Men-of-war (Morsk. Sbor., 1894, No. 6), the author had in view the work that he is now writing, but at that time he had not yet served in command of a squadron and did not feel assured that he had collected sufficient tactical material to justify generalizations. The author now recognizes his treatise as constituting an integral part of the present work, and therefore, to avoid repetition, he will not enlarge upon investigations in relation to weapons which were therein discussed. Up to the present the opinion of the author has not changed in these respects.

17. *Relation of circumstances to tactical considerations.* There exists a difference between knowledge and understanding. There are people who know a great deal but who in fact understand very little; and, on the other hand, we meet many persons of great understanding who possess little knowledge: results are mainly obtained by the latter through the operation of their understanding. It is not enough to know rules, but understanding must be had, which will serve to indicate how to employ and utilize these rules.

Let us see what the authorities say upon this point: Jomini (Outlines of the Art of War, ed. 1840, chap. 1, p. 21) writes:

> I hope that I will not be accused of desiring to convert the art of war into a definite mechanism, or, on the contrary, of

making the assertion that anyone by reading rules may acquire the gift of command of armies. In all sciences, as in all positions in life, knowledge and the understanding of how to execute are two completely different things, and if those who prove successful are often found to possess executive ability alone, nevertheless it is the union of the two qualities that distinguishes the superior man and guarantees full success. However, to avoid being accused to pedantry I hasten to state that by the word "knowledge" I do not mean vast learning; it is not a question of knowing much, but it is necessary to know well, and to know in particular all that relates to the matter in hand.

18. General Leer's opinion. We present in detail General Leer's opinion on these matters (Positive Strategy, ed. 1871, pp. 22, 23).

Laws considered in the light in which they were viewed by the genius of Peter the Great can only be defined as to order, and not as to times and circumstances. In other words, there is no law (rule) for all cases, since the number of the latter is unlimited, and since a law can only be regarded as a general formula in which it is always necessary to introduce circumstances (time and case) in order to obtain the corresponding definite known circumstantial decision. In short, we should apply law to fact through the medium of the understanding, and not by servile obedience to the letter thereof.

19. General Dragomirow's opinion. On this point General Dragomirow states the following (Text-book of Tactics, ed. 1881, pp. 12, 13):

The verbal deduction formed from known data and under known circumstances is sometimes given to the world as absolute—that is, as true under any conditions. We must constantly be upon our guard against such one-sided propositions, especially as they are enticing, for they are always plausible. Whole epochs may be pointed out during which such opinions prevailed, and which led in the end to disaster.

It is the duty of the instructor, true to his work, to arm his hearers with salutary circumspection toward all these unquestionable deductions. He should teach them to put to themselves, in relation to any general proposition, the question, could there not be cases where an exactly opposite conclusion would be the true one?

The same writer states the following:

> The knowledge of the military relations of armies and positions is a considerable aid to obtaining success in battle, but is far from being all that is indispensable to the attainment of such success. To know is little; it is necessary to know how to apply knowledge to existing circumstances, and herein lies the whole difficulty.
>
> To acquire the former, only common sense is needed; for the latter there is required the faculty of estimating the position occupied by the enemy at a given moment, and, chiefly, of deciding upon military matters without the least hesitation, so that there may be no half measure between success and failure.

The rôle of theoretical preparation becomes still clearer when we read an extract from Dragomirow's Text-book of Tactics, where he tells us, in conclusion, how the counsels and the studies of the capabilities of armies that are presented in his work should be regarded. "The capabilities of armies—data relating thereto are available, and the more thoroughly one is acquainted with them the better. Tactical counsels we should regard as we do all other counsels; we should listen to them, but in action we should only listen to our common sense. There is no wise counsel which, under some circumstances, would not prove vain. Therefore, we should lay our hopes in no book, but trust to our own head, which can not be replaced by any book. There is no constant rule in war, since for every new case that arises a new rule has to be formed upon the spur of the moment. This is the position one has to assume in relation to the counsels herein given; and I can find no better ending to this course than the words in which Turenne used to conclude his instructions to his subordinates: 'Outre ça, messieurs, je vous recommande le bon sens' ('beyond this, gentlemen, I want you to use your common sense').[9] However good advice may be, it is never capable of comprehending and foreseeing those cases which may momentarily appear, and which may require the employment of measures exactly opposite to those originally decided upon."

We present one more extract from Dragomirow (p. 3):

> Success in war calls for very great energy, determination, and mental pliability from the military man; that energy which admits no doubt of success, even when there seems to be no hope of salvation; that determination which gives the strength never to desist from an attempted end; that pliability which in an instant upon a change of circumstance changes the means of obtaining the desired result.
>
> This is enough to show that no theoretical rule can be given for indicating how to act in any given case; that all depends upon the personality of the agent. Does it follow, therefore, that there is no theory of war? Such a theory exists, and is a most important one. The more difficult of control a weapon proves, the more thoroughly should its capabilities be studied before actually employing it. Otherwise, acquaintance with its properties can only be had through bitter experience, while such knowledge could have been had theoretically at minimum cost. The properties being known, we have in an emergency only one problem to solve—how to employ them in the case in question. If we do not know them, instead of one problem we are called upon to solve two—first to gain experience, at the cost of shedding blood, and then to utilize it. From the above it is clear that the personal fighting capabilities of a

9. Andre de la Tour d'Auvergne was a seventeenth-century general and marshal of France who, not surprisingly, considered rapid maneuver and decisive engagement the essence of winning victories.

military leader must proceed hand in hand with his theoretical knowledge, although there is no doubt that the former plays the greater rôle.

20. Napoleon's opinion. Napoleon said that all questions in higher tactics assume the form of indeterminate physico-mathematical problems, capable of solution in a number of ways. In his opinion, "a theory of military science is useful for supplying general ideas and for training the mind; but the servile application of this theory to fact is always dangerous."

In a conversation with our ambassador, Balashev, in 1812, Napoleon allowed the following remark to escape him: "All of you think that you know war because you have read Jomini; but if it could be learned from his book, would I have allowed it to be published?"

21. Conclusions upon the conceptions of naval tactics. Placing in apposition all the above extracts from the works of students of military affairs, we may make from them the following deduction: The theoretical investigation of the best means of employing the fighting power of ships—i.e., naval tactics—is indispensable. Such investigation, together with the practical exercises recommended by tactics, prove an aid in battle to the clearer comprehension of matters as they are, and to the choice of the most suitable manner of action, when we are guided by our own conceptions and by that inner voice which counsels men to bold and brave deeds. The benefit to be derived from tactics is that by constantly studying and practicing them one develops his powers of judgment, or the ability to clearly recognize existing conditions. To expect results when we are taught by practice alone means to expect the impossible, and implies great losses upon first meeting the enemy.

CHAPTER TWO

INFLUENCE OF MORALE UPON SUCCESS IN BATTLE

22. The necessity of the study of morale. It is with some hesitation that we undertake a discussion of this subject. If many military writers have overlooked it, it is not because they do not deem it of sufficient importance, but rather because the domain of military psychology remains yet practically unexplored. Here and there may be met a brief notice upon the subject, but nothing in the way of general treatment. General Dragomirow has written more than all others concerning it, but he has not considered it in its most delicate phases. The subject is a difficult one, but it is impossible to preserve silence upon it, for otherwise it would never be developed and would always remain in its original unsystematized form.

Peter the Great says "brave hearts and true are the best defenses of an empire."

Napoleon said that "in war three-fourths of the chances of success depend upon morale and only one-fourth upon material conditions." We can not but accept the opinion of such an exalted authority as Napoleon. We know that he spared no effort to instill braveness and military energy into his soldiers. The maintenance of the proper spirit on shipboard is a matter of the highest importance, in relation to which everyone in the service, from the admiral to the seaman, has his duty to perform. The employment of one or the other means of defense depends upon the administration of the navy, but cour-

45

age of the personnel is essential and all that tends to promote it is worthy of the most careful study.

Lieutenant Klado, in his lectures (p. 218) justly remarks that "at the end of a battle the only difference between the victor and the vanquished is the difference of spirit; in the vanquished they are depressed, in the victor they have reached the highest stage of exaltation, and material losses for the greater part make but little difference."

This remark is a very just one. If the victor after his victory acknowledges that he is so exhausted mentally and morally that he can fight no more, the victory has been productive of very insignificant results.

23. General Leer's opinion. We present the opinion of certain well-known authorities in relation to the effect of morale upon success in war. Leer (Positive Strategy) writes as follows:

> The moral element is one of the highest importance in war. It is not susceptible of measurement and does not lend itself readily to theoretical investigation; nevertheless, one would be hardly justified in denying the possibility of discovery in the future of laws which determine the working of the mind and heart under military conditions—the possibility of military psychology. What to-day appears as an Utopia may to-morrow be a fact. History better than all else shows how rational such a conclusion is.

In another part of the same book (p. 16) Leer says:

> The art of war is more complicated than others, because in other arts (painting, sculpture, etc.) the workman deals with lifeless elements which may be measured and weighed, and which are subject to impressions from without. In the art of war, besides other elements, man enters as the chief instrument, and with him the whole universe.

24. General Dragomirow's opinion. In speaking of moral influence in war, Dragomirow, in the preface to his Tactics (p. xvii), makes the following statement:

46

If the purpose of the theory of the art of war is the discovery of the properties of military elements, if the most important of these is the moral energy of man, how necessary it is to strive that this energy may not be destroyed, but, on the other hand, be developed and strengthened.

In another place General Dragomirow says:

If moral elasticity plays such an important rôle in the composition of the soldier, it naturally follows that every effort should be made in time of peace to develop this quality.

As regards moral training in the military sense there should be considered, first, presence of mind developed to the point where a man exhibits no hesitation when brought face to face with the unexpected; second, decision, determination; third, the ability to exercise cool judgment at the most critical moment.

The moral element possesses greater signification in naval war than war on land. In the latter, action generally begins gradually and people have time to look at one another, but in the former, with the enormous speeds that obtain at the present day, intervals of time are not to be counted by hours, but by seconds. Put the helm over five seconds earlier and you ram your antagonist; five seconds later, and he rams you. The state of spirits of the crew of a war ship depends greatly upon the mutual relations of all those persons intrusted with the performance of military duties. If we take two ships, similar in every respect, and with similar crews, we find that the morale of one has been elevated by some success, even in no wise important, and having no bearing perhaps upon military matters, while the morale of the other has been depressed by reprimands, fault findings, and dissatisfaction. The first will always succeed, but from the second it is useless to look for the initiative, or any daring, but rather we may expect timidity and lack of self-confidence. This difference may appear in time of war, with the distinction that misfortunes of peace are of little importance, while all depends upon the successes or losses of war. Advice as to how to sustain the morale and energy and to raise the spirits of the crews of war ships is frequently given, but men differ so in character and understanding that precisely the same methods will not serve for any two individuals. One must be encouraged, another restrained, and care must be taken not to discourage either one of them.

At one time the naval administration may employ severity, at another kindness, to keep up the spirits of the crews. We cite two examples to show how severity failed to develop satisfactory results, but where such results were obtained, however, through implicit trust in officers in command.

25. Measures of severity affecting chiefs of squadrons. The battle of Toulon or Isyères (in the year 1744) was remarkable for the fact that the English as well as the French commander in chief was court-martialed.[1] The English vice-admiral, Lestock, who commanded the rear guard, was charged with taking no part in the battle, but the court after hearing his explanations decided that, in accordance with the instructions received by him, Admiral Lestock was justified in not leaving his position in line as long as the signal "engage the enemy" was not made to him. Admiral Mathews, the commander in chief, was accused of destroying the line by leaving his position in it, although he did this for the purpose of engaging the enemy.

The court found Mathews incompetent to command and deprived him of his grade. The behavior of Vice-Admiral Lestock at the battle of Toulon was inexpressibly harmful and injurious; notwithstanding this, he was justified by the court, because he had not permitted himself to depart from the letter of his instructions.

1. In this famous battle off Toulon between the English and the French and Spanish fleets in the War of the Austrian Succession, the English failed to make use of their great superiority (2,144 cannons to 1,744) and lost the battle.

The French Admiral de Court was also deprived of command. Clerk says the sentence that reduced Admiral Mathews was the source of all the later disasters of the British fleet. The author of Naval Battles of Great Britain (Ekins) says—

> The fate of Admiral Mathews seems to have been peculiarly hard, and to have made a strong impression upon the mind of the unfortunate Byng, who, as will be seen, was extremely cautious, in bearing down upon the enemy, not to risk any separation from his rear; and, that a proper British spirit might again be infused into the naval service, it was found necessary to *shoot him,* as the witty Voltaire said, "pour encourager les autres!" [2]

26. *Example of confidence reposed in the chief of a squadron.* To the good fortune of the British navy the admiralty came to the conclusion that it was useless to attempt to train the fleet by measures of intimidation and that favorable results could be expected only by placing implicit trust in the officer in command.

We may cite the case of Jervis before the battle of St. Vincent. By the 1st of September, 1796, Jervis had collected in the harbor of Gibraltar fifteen ships; but three of these were driven to sea by the storm of the 6th of December, one was wrecked, while another lost all her masts. Later, upon the passage to Lisbon, Jervis lost two more ships, one wrecked at Tangier and the other at the mouth of the Tagus. Upon leaving the Tagus, he lost still another vessel; but the admiralty, instead of reproaching him for losing one third of his squadron in less than two months, immediately sent him more ships from England. Upon the 14th of February of the following

2. Admiral John Byng (1704–57) was executed, after a sensational trial, for not having taken action to relieve an English fort on Minorca, besieged by the French during the Seven Years' War. Voltaire's witticism was, "They shot him to encourage the others."

year he won a complete victory over the Spanish fleet off St. Vincent. The admiralty was liberally rewarded for its wise conclusion that the wrecking of ships is an unavoidable circumstance of war.

Much depends upon the nerve, pluck, and coolness of the commander in chief in battle. It is a notable fact that the marshals of Napoleon, hardened to war as they were, fought better and displayed more energy in those fights where Napoleon himself was present. We may cite for example a circumstance which speaks eloquently of the commendable calmness of Admiral Nakhimov at the battle of Sinope.[3] The squadron drew near to the enemy and, as noon approached, all awaited with impatience the appearance of the red flag, the signal to "open fire." Finally the long-expected flag was run up to the topmasthead, but when broken it turned out to be the midday signal; the admiral had made noon to the fleet.

My pen is incapable of expressing the full depth of meaning and the immense effect of this simple but eloquent signal.

27. *Choice of historical examples.* For the purpose of throwing light upon the influence of morale upon success in war we may cite military chiefs who knew how to arouse the enthusiasm of the armies under their command. Our choice fixes upon personages of one and the same epoch; we select Suvorow, Nelson, and Napoleon. Suvorow is nearest to us, since he understood the Russians and knew how to train armies of warriors from his full, rich personality, warriors that astounded all Europe by their deeds. We select Napoleon as the personification of genius in war on land, and Nelson in war at sea. Suvorow and Napoleon were military commanders and

3. Admiral P. S. Nakhimov (1802–55) was one of the most famous Russian admirals. He was responsible for one of the few Russian victories of the Crimean War, having sunk a Turkish squadron and captured its commander at the battle of Sinope in 1853. Later, he went ashore to take charge of the defense of Sevastopol, where he was mortally wounded.

therefore we should give more especial attention to the study of Nelson.

28. Examples from Russian history. Nelson was not alone, however, in understanding how to elevate the spirits of his ships' crews. We have our own example, still more striking, in the great founder of the Russian navy, Emperor Peter I. He it was who learned how to build ships himself and then taught his subjects; who put soul into his lifeless creations and employed them to win victories from such skilled navigators as the Swedes. A better example would be hard to find, as the case is an exceptional and unparalleled one; the Emperor himself built the fleet and put life into it by his presence and example. We may also cite the enthusiasm aroused in the Russian navy in quite recent times, in the late Crimean war, demonstrated in the battle of Sinope and the brilliant defense of Sebastopol.[4] We know that the spirit of Russian sailors at that time was worthy of the highest praise, and those who created the Black Sea fleet have won their place in history. But the manner of the elevation of the morale of the personnel has not yet been properly and sufficiently described, which compels us to seek our examples from among those foreign fleets that have experienced more naval wars than our own.

29. Suvorow and some of his views. The personality of Suvorow is too well known to render it necessary for me to describe it. A few words are insufficient; whole volumes have been written, and yet too little has been said. One of Suvorow's chief maxims was rapidity of action, or, as he expresses it, "money is dear, life is dearer, and time is dearest of all."

---

4. Here Makarov uses some hyperbole. The defense of Sevastopol was heroic, though perhaps not "brilliant." One of the actions consisted in sinking the Russian Black Sea Fleet across the entrance to the harbor. The loss of the Crimean War was a humiliation that made reform of the imperial system inevitable. Russian defeat in the Russo-Japanese War, where Admiral Makarov died, produced a similar effect.

(Fuchs, II, 118.) Actual experience in war taught him the true value of time.

We extract the following from Orloff's work (Suvorow, ed. 1892, p. 346):

> In field movements Suvorow attached the greatest significance to that rapidity which gives rise to the unexpected—the best way of preparing an attack, or, as he well expresses it in words, "bayonets, rapidity, surprise; the enemy thinks that you are one or two hundred versts away; double your pace, my fine fellows, and come upon him unexpectedly; the enemy is drinking or promenading; he seeks you in the open, and you fall upon him from the mountains and the woods like snow upon his head; strike, press hard upon him, drive him, chase him, give him no time to think; he who is frightened is half beaten; fear has large eyes; one seems ten; keep a sharp look out; keep your wits about you and your end in view."
>
> At Trebbia, Bagration went to Suvorow and asked him in a low voice to postpone the attack until the stragglers came up, as there were not 40 men to a regiment. Suvorow whispered in his ear, "But Macdonald has not 20 men; attack him immediately, in the name of God!"

When Suvorow heard the rumor that people were attributing his success in war to luck he said, "Lucky to-day, lucky to-morrow—must have skill sometimes."

30. *Extracts from Dragomirow upon Suvorow's Science of Victory.* Dragomirow in his tactics treats this subject in detail. The portion of Suvorow's rules relating particularly to methods of instruction might with propriety be presented in another chapter of this work, but as with him war and instruction were one and the same thing we consider it more suitable to present his instructional methods and rules for war together—the more so as the rules applied by Suvorow to his own men indicate to us the proper way to develop men in the ranks to-day.

Dragomirow says (p. 459) that Suvorow's "Science of Victory" was not published during the lifetime of its great author, and called forth no comment on the part of those who instructed, or who were trained under the supervision of Suvorow himself, and would have been quite forgotten at the present time if, thanks to the Italian campaign of 1799, Suvorow had not considered it advisable to communicate it to the Austrians. In these instructions, which are usually very brief, he explained the fundamental principles of his "Science." They constitute a commentary upon the work; but in them, true to his custom, Suvorow says only what it is necessary to do, very rarely entering into explanations, assuming that the circumstances of the individual case itself will justify the means employed.

"The Science of Victory," says Dragomirow, further on, "is built up from disconnected phrases, and that is the reason why, in our opinion, it was so taken to heart by the soldiers, and also why it did not arouse the slightest interest among the trained contemporaries of Suvorow or those who had pretensions to military knowledge. Suvorow's "Science" seems at the first glance a singular and eccentric production; but, thanks to its peculiarities, it made a deep impression upon simple minds, so that some of its contained aphorisms are to-day proverbial, not only among ourselves, but with others, while the "Science" itself has been thrown aside and almost forgotten.

Suvorow's contemporaries regarded him as an extremely fortunate madman, rather than one who had been endowed with the divine fire of military genius; they regarded his "Science of Victory" from this standpoint. His victories were so characterized by departures from the methods of the day, and were based upon such simple measures, that scholars who sought for deep motives in them could only regard them as pieces of great good fortune.

What were the simple measures that Suvorow employed? They were all founded upon the fact that if moral buoyancy be not only cultivated, but also developed to its possible limit of growth, the most desperate undertakings may be attempted without risk of failure; they may even be attempted under conditions that are far from favorable. Suvorow, moreover, was well aware of the simple fact that the mind of every man is capable of rapid action; but to be able to decide at a critical moment what is best to be done is a gift inherited from nature only by those endowed with military talent. He endeavored, therefore, to develop the faculty of military decision as far as it could be done in the case of ordinary men. Men fit for war have always been obtainable, and wars have occurred about every ten years. Suvorow trained his army so that it should attain its ends through the utilization of determined, if not of skilled, hands.

These conceptions of genius—this logic developed in war— his contemporaries could not appreciate, for they were adherents of Frederick's method of training armies, the waning influence of which, according to Dragomirow, was nevertheless realized by all. Under Frederick's system, says Dragomirow, everything was determined in feet and inches. Moral independence upon the part of the solider was not only not required, but was, on the other hand, considered completely superfluous, if not professionally injurious. It was a system that had been established as the result of the brilliant victories of a commander who, great himself, would have conquered under any circumstances.

It is to be noted that, notwithstanding Suvorow's great capacity for training armies for war and the real merit of his "Science of Victory," it did not occur to anyone to induce him to expound his system with a view of making it more intelligible to others—in such little confidence was he held and so little was he understood. Therefore it was only at the end of seventy years that people began to comprehend how closely his manner of training was in accordance with the principles of war and how well adapted to the instincts of the masses. The "Science of Victory" seems to be one of those productions whose form may grow old, but whose spirit remains perpetually young and as immutable as the unalterable moral nature of man.

"Arms may change, and with them tactics; but the hands that control the arms and the hearts which put the hands in motion remain forever the same."

31–33. Dubocage upon Suvorow's Science of Victory. Dragomirow cites extracts from the words of Dubocage's Précis Historique sur le Maréchal Suvorow, in which the author describes Suvorow's methods of training and his celebrated attack at close quarters. We select the following as typical: "The art of war," writes Dubocage, "whether exemplified in the soldier or the officer, consisted, in Suvorow's opinion, in rapidity of execution and in fearlessness, hesitating at no obstacles; military virtues crowned by implicit obedience.

"To develop rapidity and fearlessness, it was necessary, in his opinion, to accustom the army to the appearance of war by means of manœuvers, the conditions of which should approximate those of actual war, so that the soldier might regard an actual attack as a manœuver.

"In consequence of this, and relying upon his favorite method—not to await an attack, but to make the attack himself—all Suvorow's manœuvers concluded in an engagement. For this purpose his troops were divided into two bodies, placed at some distance from each other, and drawn up in open formation or in columns, from which they were put in motion simultaneously. Having approached within 100 paces, each leader gave commands necessary for an attack, which the infantry executed on the run and the cavalry on the gallop. Sometimes the infantry attacked the cavalry, firing as the latter galloped to meet them. Sometimes the infantry awaited the cavalry at a halt in open field, withholding fire until the latter had advanced within 20 paces.

"Such manœuvers were not without danger when cavalry attacked cavalry or infantry. I often chanced to see men thrown from the saddle, with resulting sprains and bruises that kept them upon the sick list for days and sometimes weeks.

"It is evident that in an army trained by Suvorow's method cavalry acquired the habit of attacking briskly and fearlessly, while the infantry met this attack steadily and calmly. Such soldiers used the bayonet in war as if in manœuvers. Under such training recruits were soon converted into old, tried soldiers.

"From time to time he gave his instructions upon very dark nights, always concluding with a bayonet attack. In his first campaign he had become convinced of the necessity of training armies in night manœuvers, so as to familiarize them with the circumstances of battle at night, and from that time on he never abandoned this manner of training, the maintenance of which was justified by many successes.

"Finally, to accustom the army to attack fortifications with open force, he built forts, strengthened them with chevaux-de-frise, palisades, and deep trenches, and surrounded them with abatis, etc. Having occupied these fortifications, he set his army at work to attack them during the day as well as by night. Each division was trained in turn in attack and defense.

"We must say, in conclusion, that Field Marshal Suvorow was in the habit of conversing with his armies, and concluded every exercise and every parade with discourses, in which he clearly indicated what was necessary to learn or do in order to become a good soldier or a good officer. He pointed out mistakes made by the armies on one hand and praised what they did well on the other; and, finally, he gave them general instructions upon the art of war."

Sailors could borrow much that is useful from Suvorow's system of instruction and from his system of attack at close quarters. Suvorow himself fully realized that parade-ground movements were useless for training people for war, and that peace manœuvers should assimilate as nearly as possible to war conditions. It was with this end in view that he built fortifications, devised problems, etc. Nothing can be said in favor of a commander who coolly refuses to burden his mind with any such schemes and does everything in accordance with the requirements of established routine; for routine training, while conducive to regularity, draws the attention of the men away from many things that are liable to occur in war. The less people see of war conditions in peace, the harder war will appear to them. As Suvorow said: "Easy in training, hard on the march (that is, in war); hard in training, easy on the march."

34. Nelson. Let us now consider what Nelson was and why he was successful.

We turn instinctively to Nelson, for in him we find energy combined with fearlessness in war and with unusual daring as a seaman. Nelson was a captain at the age of 25, and consequently performed responsible duties always. His whole active life in service he spent at sea. War in that day was almost continuous, and all of Nelson's views were developed at sea in war. We shall endeavor to illustrate through an analysis of Nelson's character the means he employed to inspire his crews, and, besides this, we shall endeavor to prove that he knew not only how to train a squadron and arouse the enthusiasm of his men, but that he knew also how to dispose his ships to bring about conditions favorable for the achievement of naval victory—that is, he acted in accord with the principles of naval tactics and not in opposition to them, as many have supposed.

35. Nelson's career affords a brilliant illustration of the fact that true energy is indomitable. Although there were always to be found at the head of the English naval administration admirals who had spent their whole life of active service at sea, and who were fully competent to estimate the qualities of seamen, nevertheless employment in administrative positions had the effect of throwing, as it were, a veil over their perceptions, so that they ceased to be able to distinguish talented officers from those of ordinary capacity.

In the early days of his command of ships Nelson displayed his abilities in a favorable light in a few naval engagements in the West Indies. After peace was declared, his energy and determination helped to increase the prestige of England in those seas and gained him attention. He was at that time 26 years of age, and indicated by his activity the possession of those qualities indispensable to a future naval chief. "Nevertheless," Jurien de la Gravière writes, "Nelson was one of those restless spirits, those agitators who arouse the suspicion of administrative bodies whose calm they disturb. This is the reason why they determined to give no support to his restless activity and fiery zeal." When, in 1788, worn out with what were to him the fatigues of inactivity, he urgently requested to be sent to sea again, not even the influence of Prince William was sufficient, both Herbert, secretary of the admiralty, and the Earl of Chatham, in 1790, opposing his solicitations. At last Nelson lost all hope and prepared to go into retirement, although he felt that he was worthy of employment. "Sure I am," he said, "that I have ever been a zealous and faithful servant, and have never intentionally committed any errors."

The administration was well aware that energetic men were needed for command, but at same time Nelson was regarded as an agitator—as if one can be energetic without disturbing any of those around him.

Nelson's chiefs always placed a high value upon his talents. Thus, after Jervis, who regarded him rather as a companion than as a subordinate, assumed command, another captain said to Nelson: "You did just as you pleased in Lord Hood's time, the same in Admiral Hotham's, and now again with Sir John Jervis; it makes no difference to you who is commander in chief."

Jurien de la Gravière repeats the statement several times that the administration was incapable of appreciating Nelson.

Referring to the inadequate reward received by Nelson after the battle of Aboukir, he says: "It was Nelson's lot to suffer the test of humiliating experiences throughout his whole life."

Notwithstanding Nelson's enormous services he did not even receive independent command after the battle of Aboukir, and won a victory at Copenhagen while under the command of Sir Hyde Parker, who almost ruined everything by hoisting the signal to cease action at the very time when retreat was out of the question. As is well known, Nelson placed his telescope to the eye that he had lost at the battle of Calvi and said to the captain of his own flagship, "I really do not see the signal." To his signal officer he gave special orders to keep the signal hoisted for "close action." In this affair Sir Hyde Parker compelled Nelson to commit the highest transgression of which an officer may be capable—to disobey the signal of his chief in battle. Probably this is one of the reasons why the battle of Copenhagen was not valued by Nelson's countrymen in proportion to the energy required on his part to bring it to a successful issue.

Examining into the causes which may have led to the doubtful disposition of the Admiralty toward Nelson, the question unwittingly presents itself, was he not actually a burden to the administration? We find an answer to this question in Jurien de la Gravière's book, in many parts of which are presented extracts from Nelson's letters, and in which he writes of his complete satisfaction, both with his own chiefs, whom he constantly praises, as well as with his own subordinates. Even in his relations to economical measures, upon the necessity for which the Admiralty laid such great stress, Nelson may serve as an example to others.

If all that Nelson did, who passed his whole life in war, if all the wounds received by him were insufficient, what more could he have done to gain the full confidence of the Admiralty? We shall have occasion to point out the esteem in which Napoleon held those who were useful to him in war, and how much he appreciated them. The simple appearance of Nelson in the fleet was enough to inspire energy in every ship and bind all together in the performance of one common task—the annihilation of the enemy. With Nelson in command all became convinced that the battle would be waged with full energy along the whole line, and that victory was assured. There would be no hesitation, and this in war is of vast importance. Evidently the English Admiralty was not immediately convinced that Nelson carried full success with him, even with the facts before them. Other admirals had been contented with some measure of success, unproductive of decisive results, but now complete victory was required.

Admiral Calder had limited himself to capturing two ships from the allied French and Spanish squadron under Villeneuve in the battle off Finisterre, and later, upon the following morning, did not decide to reopen the attack. In the meantime England began to be threatened by an immense army collected by Napoleon in the ports of the English channel, where 2,000 vessels had been prepared for transporting troops to the coast of England. Villeneuve was at Cadiz with a large and well-equipped fleet, and if he could succeed in appearing in the channel and in holding command there for only a few days, successful disembarkation in England would be assured. Napoleon would have given much at that time to have had a commander like Nelson in his navy; even the British Admiralty now began to realize that without Nelson nothing could be done, and they addressed him in another tone.

"The British Admiralty," writes Jurien de la Gravière (p. 105, Chap. II), "who up to this time had remained ill disposed toward Nelson, finally began to show him the consideration to which his brilliant deeds entitled him. Lord Barham gave unlimited power to his command, the sphere of action of which extended from Cadiz over the whole Mediterranean Sea."

Jurien de la Gravière, citing a few examples bearing witness to Nelson's popularity before Trafalgar, and the devotion of the sailors to him, says: "Never was such devotion more needed, for Nelson had given his word to deal the final blow." "I will lay down my life in the attempt," he said. Sometimes in the midst of his daring plans he begins to lament the insufficiency of his own strength, but, he adds, "I am not come forth to find difficulties, but to remove them."

In September, 1805, Nelson was assigned to command, and on the 21st of October he annihilated the fleet of Villeneuve at Trafalgar, paying for his victory with his life.

The question may be again asked, why was the Admiralty unable to appreciate Nelson? Such a question is easier to ask than to answer. To the good fortune of England, no injustice could quench his energy, and while the pulse beat in his body that energy did not weaken. What his pride endured he kept to himself and thereby exhibited in himself a brilliant example of discipline.

By active participation in honorable disasters Nelson taught his captains to regard the preservation of ships as a matter of secondary importance, and the primary duty to be the prompt fulfilment of orders. "I own myself one of those who do not fear the shore," he wrote the First Lord of the Admiralty, "for hardly any great things are done in a small ship by a man that is; * * * nor do I regret the loss of the *Raven* compared to the value of Captain Layman's services, which are a national loss. * * * If I had been censured every time I have run my ship, or fleets under my command, into great danger, I should long ago been *out* of the Service, and never *in* the House of Peers." "Here are the measures," said Jurien de la Gravière, "that Nelson employed to render his captains capable of supporting him in his daring enterprises. We shall see further on that Napoleon regarded the loss of ships in exactly the same manner."

36. *Views of Nelson upon expenditures.* It is often inaccurately stated that great people can not be moderate in their requirements, and that they are unaware of the cost of the things which they expend. The following extract from Jurien de la Gravière shows that one may be a great commander and yet be moderate in his expenditures. The preservation and economic expenditure of naval stores was an object of Nelson's special attention. Thanks to the rigid economy practiced by him, recollection of which is still fresh in England, Nelson never had occasion to regret, like other admirals, the meagerness of supplies that he received.

37. *Views of Nelson and Jurien de la Gravière upon the measure of power to be vested in the commander in chief of a squadron.* Nelson well understood that when a squadron is formed from a number of vessels the duty of the admiral commanding is to bind together these units of war, destined to the attainment of a common end, into one homogeneous whole. The success of the efforts of the chief of a squadron depends greatly upon his personal talents and also upon the degree of power vested in him. Nelson, in his letter to Earl St. Vincent (Jervis), expresses the following opinion: "The officers of the fleet should look up to the commander in chief for their reward: for otherwise the good or bad opinion of the commander in chief would be of no consequence."

Jurien de la Gravière says upon this point—

The most skilled administration can not change existing conditions. Creative forces are only vested in the military commanders in chief. When France shall have more confidence in her agents, when her chiefs of squadrons and ports shall have power to distribute rewards in the name of their Government, then her chiefs of fleets will be found ready to make her fleets what Jervis and Nelson made those of England. Then may we look for the birth of that devotion which the French sailors never yet had for their own chiefs in command.

It is impossible not to agree with the opinions of these two authorities, for if commanders in chief are only accorded limited powers and have not vested in themselves powers of encouragement they are left without means of obtaining positive results in their squadrons. Whatever they may attempt will appear weak and unstable. In many cases a chief so situated is afraid to attempt anything, and in this he may be justified, for creation in one direction implies destruction in another, and, having no power to build anew, he may hesitate to destroy what is old.

38. Views of Napoleon and Nelson upon executives. There exists a difference between the views of Napoleon and Nelson regarding executives and subordinates in general.

No one knew better than Napoleon how to value merit and to reward distinguished services. He took people as he found them and forgave their faults when they did not interfere with the accomplishment of the chief end in view, which was the destruction of the enemy. Nevertheless Napoleon frequently regretted the absence of talent in those whom he intrusted with the execution of his plans.

Nelson also took people as he found them, but the perusal of his correspondence suffices to convince us that even in his most emotional confidences no place is to be found where he speaks regretfully concerning his own officers, ships, or crews. All are devoted, excellent, and filled with energy. (Naval Wars, Part I, p. 41).

39. Opinions of Jervis and Nelson on discipline. In what relates to discipline Nelson was a pupil of Jervis, who knew how to raise the English fleet to a high degree of efficiency. Jervis was of the opinion that unquestioning obedience was indispensable to the maintenance of order. He required his officers and men always to observe the outward signs of respect and submission, and used to say that when discipline appears in outward forms we may rest assured that it really exists. "I dread not the seamen," he wrote Nelson; "it is the indiscreet, licentious conversation of the officers which produces all our ills, and their presumptuous discussion of the orders they receive." The words of Jervis, which were just in his day, are no less so now, and there is no officer who should not reproach himself if guilty of carelessness in this direction.

40. *Nelson's views upon the health of his crews* are also worthy of attention. In those arduous times, when fresh water was preserved in wooden casks, Nelson understood how to maintain the health of his crew during long sea cruises. "After sixteen months at sea," says Jurien de la Gravière, "throughout which Nelson had remained almost constantly between Cape San Sebastian and Sardinia, there was not a single sick man among the 6,000 men in his squadron. It is instructive to note what attention this great man gives to little things which might affect the health of the seamen." If the matter be that of forming plans of attack he outlines his views in a few vigorous words. "Signals . . . are useless," he says, "when every man is disposed to do his duty. The great object is for us to support each other, and to keep close to the enemy, and to the leeward of him." Nelson led an extremely active life. He rose at 4 or 5 in the morning and never breakfasted later than 6, generally sharing his breakfast with one or two midshipmen. He was fond of pleasant association with young officers, was not afraid to make fun with these youngsters, and often showed himself to be as much of a child as any of them.

41. *Views of Nelson and Jurien de la Gravière upon the education and training of naval officers.* We may present here with propriety Jurien de la Gravière's views upon the proper time for beginning the education of a young man who desires to become a naval officer. "Naval life," he writes, "demands an impressionable and pliable nature. Too great a store of knowledge at the beginning of a career sometimes proves rather superfluous than useful, since much has to be acquired by perception and much by experience."

Nelson, whose opinion has great weight, frequently says it is impossible to become a naval officer without uniting in one's self the practical knowledge of the seaman with the qualities of a gentleman, and when questioned upon this point counseled young men who wished to follow the sea, after the study of navigation and French, to take lessons from a dancing master.

The views of Jurien de la Gravière and of Nelson upon the education and training of young seamen are shared by many at the present day, and there is a great deal of justice in them.

42. *Nelson as a seaman.* Speaking from a purely naval standpoint, Jurien de la Gravière continues, "What naval officer is not filled with pride at the contemplation of Nelson's last cruise, when he led his ships upon journeys of almost unheard-of duration, journeys which to us of the present day such ships seem hardly capable of performing." There were no difficulties in seamanship to which the English did not become accustomed in such a school. Invaluable were those prolonged sojourns at sea that kept the French ports and coasts blockaded and in a state of alarm, even in midwinter. Experience gained at sea affords the best explanation of those rapid movements which shattered the plans of the French, those unexpected concentrations, when England seemed to cover the sea with her ships. Therefore in Nelson's case, who united in himself infinite activity with rare daring, it is even more necessary to study his energy as a seaman than his boldness in war.

43. *How Nelson regarded victory.* Nelson's merits as a seaman do not diminish his importance as a military leader, and we must consider what he understood the word "victory" to mean. In this regard his views are in accordance with those of other great commanders. Victory, in his opinion, only produced the desired results when it was complete, and under other circumstances developed but a temporary and partial advantage. Nelson was indefatigable in his efforts to inflict

the greatest possible injury upon his opponents in battle. His words, "I had rather see half my squadron burnt than risk what the French fleet may do in the Mediterranean," were significant.

Nelson was of this opinion when he commanded the *Agamemnon,* and when, at the end of an indecisive battle in the Gulf of Genoa, on the 14th of March, 1795, he went to Admiral Hotham and asked him to leave the injured ships under the protection of a few frigates and proceed with the remaining eleven ships in pursuit of the enemy. "But he," wrote Nelson to his wife, "much cooler than myself, said 'We must be contented, we have done very well.'" Two ships had been captured. Then, he adds, "Now, had we taken ten sail and allowed the eleventh to escape, when it had been possible to have got at her, I could never have called it well done." We should note that Nelson approached the admiral with his proposition after he himself had taken part with his own vessel in the battle for two days. Untiring energy and persistence made his own victories decisive.

Later, we see Nelson at the battle of St. Vincent, when, with his ship, the *Captain,* he hastened to cut off the retreat of the enemy, preventing them from uniting with the leeward division and thus avoiding a decisive engagement—a manœuver which resulted in the full and complete defeat of the Spaniards.

When admiral, Nelson prepared his squadron and framed all his military instructions upon a basis of the assumption of complete defeat of the enemy; and, actually, Aboukir, Copenhagen, and Trafalgar present examples of complete disasters, possessing enormous strategical and political signification.

An eminent military authority with whom we have conversed on this subject considers it correct to state of Nelson that he knew how to perfect his victories. Take the parallel case on shore: he is the victor who retains the field of battle. If the enemy retreat, the victory may justly be claimed, yet it may prove very insignificant if not perfected; that is, if the pursuit of the enemy, which might result in the final annihilation of his army and the seizure of his country be not undertaken. In a naval battle, to allow an antagonist to retire from the field of action does not imply victory, which can only be defined as the annihilation of the opposing force in whole or in part. If, after the annihilation of a portion of this force, the rest be not pursued, the victory is not complete; while, on the other hand, pursuit may assure the complete destruction of the enemy. By perfection of victory upon the sea we can only understand victory followed by the seizure of the enemy's transports, if he possesses them, or of his harbors, if he is protected by them. Upon this basis we assume that it is correct to employ in reference to the fleet the expression "complete victory."

44. *Causes of Nelson's victories.* Let us now examine into the causes of Nelson's victories to ascertain whether they were the results of blind chance or whether attributable to the well-laid plans of a skilled commander. Upon this point Jurien de la Gravière says: "It should be carefully borne in mind that the English owed their victories (1796–1814) not to the strength and numbers of their ships, not to their wealth in naval population, not to the influence of their admiralty, nor to the conceptions of their great seamen: they conquered because their squadrons were the better trained and disciplined." The development of this superiority was the work of Jervis and of Nelson—unassuming, long-sustained effort, which must be studied. If we wish to understand Nelson fighting with such daring, we must follow him preparing his squadron for battle. He had learned from Jervis how to preserve the health of his crews without shortening the duration of sea cruises; how to maintain his ships at sea for whole years without visiting a port; and, most important of all, how to direct attention to military and naval training of the fleet. His fortunate disposition was an aid to him in the latter work, and he

converted the personnel of his well-disciplined ships into a circle of brothers and friends. His wish was that mutual love and esteem should bind together those called to fight under the same flag. In the most critical situations he always found time to investigate the smallest difficulties, and settled dispute with a steady hand. Following this renowned man at the times when he condescended to these little efforts toward the maintenance of friendly relations, it is easy to understand what an immense influence such a beloved chieftain could exert upon his squadron.

But the chief cause of the devotion of his officers to Nelson—that which incited all to aid him in everything he undertook—was the unusual simplicity and clearness of his orders and instructions. Each of his subordinates knew what the admiral expected from him, and this was of the highest importance in avoiding confusion and preventing hesitation. "Nelson," wrote Jurien de la Gravière, "never blamed an officer because he was unlucky. In his opinion his captain was always right. If he lost a ship, he believed he should be given another."

Let us now see how Nelson observed the rules of tactics; that is, did he dispose his ships advantageously with respect to an enemy or not?

On this point the English historian James makes the following statement: "Approaching as near as possible to the enemy, so as to defeat him as quickly as possible—here, in fact, are Nelson's complete tactics. He knew that complicated evolutions frequently lead to errors and often produce results contrary to those originally intended."

In this way James does not recognize in Nelson the skilled tactician, arranging his ships in more favorable formations than those of his antagonist. The opinion of Jurien de la Gravière (Chap. II, p. 158) corroborates James' views:

> The general who would reverse Nelson's tactics and place his antagonist in the positions in which the renowned admiral

frequently placed his own ships would adopt the most certain means of insuring the defeat of the enemy's army. Such eccentric tactics are more evident in Nelson's deeds than in his orders. To adopt them as a general guide, to be followed in an engagement with an equally skilled antagonist, would be to make efforts toward one's own complete destruction. On the other hand, under the circumstances in which the fleets of both nations existed from the years of 1798–1805, these bold onslaughts produced victories more complete than ever known before in naval war, and Nelson's mistakes were turned to his own advantage, if inspirations crowned with success can be regarded as mistakes.

In the opinion of the same author (Chap. I, p. 3)—

Nelson developed his plans of action opportunely and endeavored to familiarize his officers with them, but when in the presence of the enemy he only sought to close in with him as quickly as possible, and thus acted more like a happy child of fortune than the patient suitor for her favors.

Thus Jurien de la Gravière considers Nelson's tactical evolutions as mistakes, and pardons them as the efforts of genius crowned with success. He is willing to regard him as a favored child of fortune, but not as a man who knows really what he wishes to do and what he can do. Such an opinion of Nelson may lead to the conclusion that there is no need of studying conditions of naval war, and that it is enough upon sighting an enemy to throw oneself upon him and crush him; but the conclusion would be faulty, and everyone would blame a captain who would rashly attack without taking the necessary precautions. Such actions reveal the existence of the qualities of boldness and decision in the commander in chief, but success can only be secured when to these is added a third quality, that of tactical ability. We shall endeavor to show hereafter that Nelson's tactical views were always correct, but that to insure success with him implicit confidence in him was required, and that, actuated by this opinion, he attached the greatest importance, not to tactics in the abstract, but to burning words, capable of arousing enthusiasm.

45. Did Nelson actually disregard naval tactics? Most authorities state that in time of battle naval tactics were really disregarded by Nelson. It is impossible to agree with such views. Thus, at Aboukir he threw his whole squadron upon the windward portion of the enemy's line, for the purpose of preventing the leeward division from affording aid to their companions. From a tactical standpoint this manœuvering was entirely correct.

The bombardment of Copenhagen was an extremely risky matter on account of the inequality of the forces engaged and difficulties attending its accomplishment on account of the existence of shoal water, but the manœuvers were so performed that it is impossible to accuse Nelson of disregarding any tactical laws. Nelson urged Admiral Parker to begin the bombardment, not because he was overanxious to fight, but because each day's delay made the matter more difficult, for the Danes were making extensive preparations. Such conceptions are in full accordance with tactical laws, which assert that the attainment of the unexpected is one of the surest guarantees of success. Parker postponed the commencement of the Copenhagen affair, and thus made the matter more difficult, but we can not blame Nelson in any way in this connection.

It must be acknowledged that the means employed by Nelson in his attack in the battle of Trafalgar constitute the chief motive for the accusation that he neglected tactical precautions. In this battle Nelson threw himself directly upon the line of the enemy's ships, and in Clerk's opinion the fleet attacking another in a perpendicular direction from his line will be beaten.

46. Selections from Nelson's instructions before the battle of Trafalgar. Let us see if Nelson actually disregarded laws of tactics (fig. 2).

70

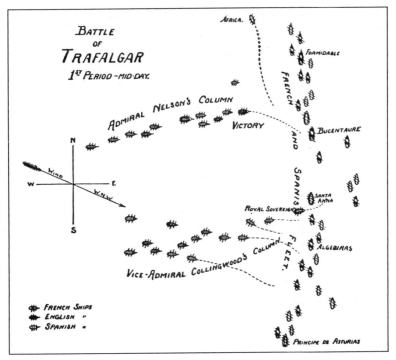

Fig. 2.

Before Trafalgar Nelson disposed his fleet of 40 ships, dividing it into two columns of 16 vessels each, and a third composed of 8 two decked ships possessing greater speed, "which will always make, if wanted," he wrote in his instructions (memorandum) before the battle, "a line of twenty-four sail, or whichever line the commander-in-chief may direct. The second in command will, after my intentions are made known to him, have the entire direction of his line to make the attack upon the enemy, and to follow up the blow until they are captured or destroyed."

Later on in the instructions it is stated that the center and rear must be attacked in such a manner that the number of

English ships shall always exceed by one-quarter the number intercepted from the enemy. Finally,

> Something must be left to chance; nothing is sure in a Sea Fight beyond all others. Shots will carry away the masts and yards of friends as well as foes; but I look with confidence to a Victory before the Van of the Enemy could succour their Rear, and then that the British Fleet would most of them be ready to receive their twenty Sail of the Line, or to pursue them, should they endeavor to make off.

> The Second in Command will in all possible things direct the movements of his Line, by keeping them as compact as the nature of the circumstances will admit. Captains are to look to their particular Line as their rallying point. But, in case Signals can neither be seen or perfectly understood, no Captain can do very wrong if he places his ship alongside that of an Enemy.

The plan of battle sketched out by Nelson is very clear. He divides his fleet of 40 ships into three squadrons, two of which are the principal, and the third, composed of the swiftest ships, an auxiliary, which is to join one of the main squadrons. The plan of battle was to throw the full force upon the enemy's center and rear guard and defeat him before the van could come to his aid. Nelson wished all of his ships to break away through the enemy's lines and take a position to the leeward. The manœuver of piercing the line is a very difficult one to accomplish successfully; but his ships never knew what it was to be at anchor and he therefore counted upon the skill of his captains. Upon piercing the line the English ships could fire broadside after broadside from both batteries under the most favorable circumstances. Each ship changed its course on approach as if to head off that vessel of the enemy it desired to pass astern of (fig. 3). To sustain fire under these conditions it was necessary for the enemy to control a great angle of fire, and we know that the ships of these days were not adapted for such practice. After piercing the

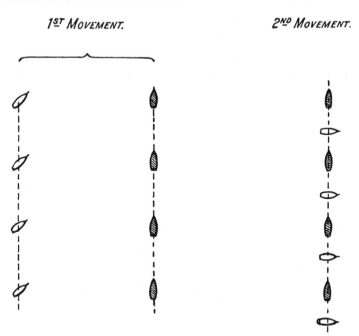

Fig. 3. Breaking through the enemy's column.

line the British ships formed to leeward, where the smoke of their guns was rapidly carried away by the wind, while the smoke formed to leeward under the lofty sides of their antagonist hung there for a long time, and prevented them from sighting their guns.

The above shows that Nelson had constituted a plan of battle in full correspondence with the conditions of the time and consequently in accordance with tactical rules as they then existed. From the moral standpoint these instructions are incomparable. In their every word he expresses trust in his admirals, his captains, and his whole personnel.

The words with which the first part of his instructions conclude, "no captain can do very wrong if he places his ship alongside that of an enemy" are superb. Referring to them

73

Jurien de la Gravière says: "At these happy words, at this simple yet deep expression of the vital principles of naval tactics, a shout of enthusiasm and pride filled the admiral's cabin of the *Victory* where were gathered the admirals and captains of his squadron." "The effect of these words," Nelson wrote at the time, "might have been compared to that of an electric shock." Some of the officers were moved to tears, and all approved the plan of attack in every particular. They found it original, enterprising, well-adapted, and capable of fulfilment, and all, from the senior admirals to a junior captain, said: "The enemy is beaten if we can only overtake him."

Having kindled by these words a spark of fire in the heart of every captain, Nelson himself at the beginning of the battle fanned this spark into a flame by his signal, "England expects that every man will do his duty," and all fought as if they felt that the eyes of their country, who now needed victory more than ever before, were upon them.

47. The battle of Trafalgar. Let us now see how Nelson's preconceived plan of battle was carried out. He had not 40 ships, but only 27, and therefore the third squadron was not formed. On the morning of the 21st of October, 1805, the wind blew lightly from the west-northwest, giving the ships a speed of about 3 knots, and there was a swell from the westward. The enemy was seen to the eastward, formed in a single line. In order to approach, it was necessary to run before the wind; the wind died down and the speed fell to 1 1/2 knots. Under these conditions the approach of the squadron was very gradual, and consequently the fulfilment of the plan decided upon presented the disadvantage that the attacking ships were for a long time unable to employ their broadside guns. Nelson had to decide whether to give battle or not. The wind was light, the speed of the enemy, in consequence of the swell, very small, so that in order to approach him a course perpendicular to the enemy's line had to be taken, whereby the ships were exposed to a prolonged fire. Under these conditions he decided to attack the enemy. History does not inform us by what conclusions he was influenced, but upon looking into the matter many tactical reasons may be found in support of his decision. Thanks to the direction of the swell and the absence of the wind, the enemy's ships constantly experienced a regular lateral roll, so that their fire was not accurate, while Nelson's ships proceeded in the direction of the swell and consequently were comparatively steady. The breaking through the line on a course before the wind was suitable for broadside firing, for the reason that all guns could be fired, beginning with those at the bow. The smoke traveled forward, so that each gun, as it came in line with the enemy's ship, was not obscured, and was therefore fired under circumstances most favorable, from a tactical point of view.

Let us see what actually happened: "Ominous silence," says Jurien de la Gravière (p. 137) "that reigned during the approach of the *Victory* to the enemy's line, was followed by continuous firing from the *Bucentaure* (which carried away the *Victory's* main topmast), and which lasted not over two minutes. The gunners corrected their sights and suddenly, as if by signal, six or seven ships in the vicinity of the *Bucentaure* opened fire upon the *Victory*, but the lateral roll imparted to them an irregular movement which increased the inaccuracy of their practice. Some of the projectiles fell short, others proved too high or passed through the rigging. The *Victory*, uninjured, approached to within 2 1/2 cable lengths of the *Bucentaure*. At this moment one ball struck her mizzen topmast, another destroyed the steering wheel, and a chain shot cut down 8 marines on the poop. The *Victory* received the fire of the whole squadron, and this ship, which, had the French fire been more accurate nothing in the world could have saved, escaped with only 50 men killed and wounded. Two hundred guns played upon it and were unable to stop it as it majestically advanced over the foaming waves and slowly approached Villeneuve's flagship."

From the above extract it appears that during the time the *Victory* was under the prolonged fire of 200 guns, while she was advancing at a speed of 1 1/2 knots, she only lost 50 men. If we consider 600 fathoms (1,200 yards) as the range of fire for guns at that day, the *Victory* could not have covered this distance in less than twenty-five minutes. In this interval each gun of the *Bucentaure* must have fired at least ten times upon the *Victory*. It is useless to attribute the fact that the *Victory* suffered so little to lack of skill on the part of the French. The trouble was the great difficulty of accurate aiming occasioned by the rolling of the ships. [This difficulty was doubtless foreseen by Nelson.]

With the old, imperfect way of igniting the charge, a considerable time elapsed between the application of the match and the actual discharge of the projectile from the gun. The irregularities of this interval, due to the impossibility of communicating fire regularly, added to this difficulty. For these reasons, firing when there was much motion of the ship was extremely inaccurate.

The English ships, after breaking through the French lines, found themselves in entirely different circumstances. They presented steady gun platforms, and the *Victory* put twenty guns out of action upon the *Bucentaure* and filled her decks with dead and wounded.

The *Royal Sovereign*, while passing under the stern of the *Santa Anna*, maintained a continuous fire against her and raked her repeatedly with every gun loaded with two and three shots. One hundred and fifty projectiles traversed the ship from stem to stern, killing and wounding 400 of her crew. Such a catastrophe is enough to place a ship hors de combat at once, yet nothing is said of the losses of the *Royal Sovereign* at this time.

We have referred here only to the losses incurred by the leading ships of both squadrons. The vessels following suffered still less on approach, while as they passed through the enemy's line they delivered broadsides no less deadly than those of the leaders.

What has been said above is sufficient to show that Nelson placed his ships in better position than those of the enemy. He himself does not state that he did this, but this does not signify that he was not aware of what he was doing. Must we not recognize, however, that a new tactical example was attempted and brilliantly carried into execution at Trafalgar, which consisted in penetrating the enemy's line, for delivering a raking fire, and then engaging from leeward.

Nelson told his crew that they must fight from leeward, so that the enemy could not retire; but this does not mean that he himself thought this. As far as relates to the obscuration of the sights by smoke, the leeward position is the more favorable. Nelson understood this, but many others did not understand it, and therefore it is useless to say of him that he violated the laws of tactics; on the contrary, he only changed conditions which others previously considered tactical.

If the English squadron were able to pass through the line of their antagonist and take up a position to leeward of him, then nothing could hinder the enemy's squadron from doing the same and from delivering a raking fire as it left the field of battle; consequently, when we assume a leeward position, we can not prevent an enemy from retiring to leeward. Nelson's orders do not show that he anticipated this. In this respect he resembled Suvorow—both put the question of morale higher than all else. Nelson could afford to do this, for his crews believed whenever he led his fleet into action the victory always remained upon his side. Perhaps, also, it was the highest tactics upon Nelson's part not to show that he was especially influenced by tactical considerations. Probably in this and in other similar actions he raised the spirits of the crews of his ships to the point which insured full success to his undertaking.

Naval tactics is the science that teaches us how to dispose our ships in the manner most favorable for effecting the destruction of an enemy. It may be said of Nelson that he dis-regarded tactics by placing his ships in disadvantageous posi-tion in respect to the enemy; but the above conclusions show that this is not so, and that there is no reason for accusing him of neglecting tactical precautions. On the contrary, he rather took the initiative in tactics than otherwise.

All naval writers do justice to Nelson in ascribing to him the ability to instill courage into his crews.

48. *Napoleon's instructions to Villeneuve at Trafalgar.* In direct contrast to Nelson, Villeneuve displayed a dejected frame of mind, which depressed the spirits of his whole squadron. Low-spirited persons are unfitted for such lively work as naval service requires, especially in time of war.

While at Cadiz, Villeneuve received instructions from the French minister of marine, which are presented below as in-dicating Napoleon's views on several matters—views that are useful to the seaman. "The Emperor's chief instructions," wrote the minister, "are to seek out of the ranks officers ca-pable of higher command, in whatever positions they may be found; but what he desires first of all is that love of renown, that eagerness for honor, which are so characteristic of the highest manhood. His Majesty wishes to do away with cau-tious timidity and acting upon the defensive, which deprive us of initiative and inspire the enemy to enterprise. The Em-peror wishes to note daring in all his admirals, captains, offi-cers, and seamen; and whatever they may do, he promises his pardon and favor to all those who exhibit this quality to the highest degree. They must unhesitatingly attack a weaker or an equal antagonist and fight him to annihilation—that is what his majesty wishes. The loss of ships is nothing to him, if these ships are lost with honor. His majesty does not wish his squadron to be blockaded by a weaker enemy, and notifies you, in case that the enemy appears in this condition before Cadiz, to attack him without hesitation. The Emperor coun-sels you to do on your side all that you can to raise the spirits of your subordinates, by deeds, by discourses, and by every act that may exalt them. In this respect nothing must be neglected—courageous example, recommendations of every kind, risky undertakings, and orders that incite enthusiasm. (His majesty wishes that commendatory orders be issued as frequently as possible, and that you regularly communicate them to him.) All means are to be employed that will instill energy and manhood into our sailors. His majesty desires to point out to them the road to the attainment of all preferences, which are to be the invariable reward of every brilliant deed. It is pleasant to me to feel that you yourself will be the first to deserve such a reward, and I deem it my duty to inform you, in all secrecy, that notwithstanding any complaint I have been ordered to make to you, his majesty awaits only your first brilliant deed to demonstrate toward you his special favor and reward you with the highest honors."

In every word of these instructions is heard the voice of the great commander, who with a skilled hand points out to his fleet the road to glory. It took Villeneuve, with his melancholy frame of mind, to fail to be incited by these great words, which had so frequently kindled enthusiasm in the ranks of a French army. It is worthy of note that the views of Napoleon in relation to the loss of ships are the same as those of Nelson. He also gave no order to be sparing with vessels, as to him "the loss of ships is nothing, if these ships are lost with honor." Remembering that all depends upon his captains, he orders Villeneuve not to be hindered by considerations of seniority, but to select men for command from the ranks.

The words of the Emperor in relation to rewards must not be considered in the sense of a bargain with his fleet, to whom he promises to pay money for the fulfilment of a contract, but rather as a promise to Villeneuve of his full support in all his recommendations. Napoleon well knew that no man could exert due influence over his subordinates without support from the central authority. The Emperor promised Villeneuve himself a reward, but this again was necessary to encourage his commander in chief, for all previous instructions had constituted in themselves indirect reproaches to him. Without encouragement he would have remained placed under a heavy restraint; for, in the Emperor's opinion, "Villeneuve is one of those men whom you have to put spur to rather than to rein in." Such a man was obviously unfitted to command a fleet in war, and the Emperor would have changed him long before if he had not been supported by Minister Decrès. Vice-Admiral Rosily had already been sent to relieve him, and had arrived at Madrid the day upon which the allied fleet put to sea from Cadiz.

49. *Extracts from Villeneuve's instructions to the fleet before Trafalgar.* Having received the above orders from the Emperor, Villeneuve exerted himself and decided to put to sea, but prepared his own destruction by the final orders that he issued to the allied fleet. "All efforts of the allied fleet," he wrote, "should be directed to affording aid to those of our vessels suffering most from the enemy's fire and to keeping as close as possible to the flagship. Captains should be guided by their confidence in their own manhood and by their love of renown rather than by the signals of the admiral, who, covered with smoke and surrounded by enemies, may not be in a position to make them. Any captain who does not place himself under fire will be out of position, and the signal made to remind him of this fact will be a mark of dishonor to him."

At the commencement of this order Villeneuve states that the end sought is not the annihilation of the enemy, but the affording aid to those of his own ships that suffered most from the enemy's fire. According to these instructions, a ship that had almost annihilated an opponent should hasten to the aid of a ship of his own side if the latter were suffering.

Villeneuve himself was to give an example how to do this. He then proceeds to describe the difficult position in which the admiral's ship wil be placed, powerless to make signals, and the very last words of his orders show how poorly he understood Napoleon's instructions. The Emperor advises him to arouse the amour propre of his captains, instead of which Villeneuve implies distrust in them, and he prematurely places a stigma upon a number of them before any had occasion to prove themselves guilty. Both Nelson and Villeneuve commanded their captains to take part in the general engagement, but while Nelson knew how to say this in such a way as to incite enthusiasm in the heart of every commander, Villeneuve, by his remarks, insults the pride of his own people just at the very commencement of the fight. It is the duty of a commanding officer to bind his captains to himself by his esteem of them, but Villeneuve expressed himself in such a way that some of his commanders must have immediately thought, "evidently the admiral thinks some of us will prove cowards, and is not well-disposed toward us; consequently there is no need of being in a hurry to place ourselves indiscriminately under fire."

Napoleon in after years, at St. Helena, referring to various manners of waging war, wrote "you must tell cowards that they are brave men if you wish them to be so." Villeneuve did exactly the opposite, and told the brave that there were cowards among them. This utterly destroyed the mutual self-esteem of his captains and ruptured whatever ties might have existed between them. No one considers his own bravery beyond all reproach, and therefore Villeneuve's words might have touched every one and made each take the reproach to himself. The battle of Trafalgar, however, bore witness to the fact that the French seamen were men of desperate bravery, for most of the French ships fought until they were completely disabled. The flagship *Bucentaure* was, after the capture of Villeneuve, retaken from the enemy. The captain of the ship *Pluton,* that was making water at the rate of 3 feet an hour and had lost 400 men of her command, put to sea from Cadiz on the following day with 4 other ships, 4 frigates, and 2 brigs, and recaptured the *Neptune* and the *Santissima Trinidad,* which were being towed to Gibraltar. Captain Jugan, of the frigate *Themis,* was also conspicuous for his energy in affording aid to injured ships and for his activity in many other ways.

These were the people to whom Villeneuve turns as to cowards, when in fact they were heroes. When all that was needed to have reversed the issue of the battle of Trafalgar was to unite all forces against the common foe, if the van of the allied fleet had displayed greater activity and had promptly worn as soon as it saw that the attack of England would fall upon the center and the rear, the battle might have been reopened; but the manœuver was performed too late, and Dumanoir, with five vessels, crossing the track of the *Bucentaure,* decided that to "attack an enemy at such a time would be a desperate deed that could only result in our total destruction."

The blood chills in one's veins at the very idea that there are people in this world who would calmly decline to take part in a general engagement. Mere approach would have inspired the allies, and who knows how the tide of battle might have turned? The victors were in a sorry enough plight; five vessels constitute a strong force, and these same ships fought with desperation a few days later.

Further comments upon this theme are superfluous, and there is no need of advancing further particulars of the influence of morale upon success in war, for the matter is self-evident. The closeness of the relation existing between the personality of the commander in chief and success in naval battle is also apparent. Place Villeneuve in the English squadron and Nelson in the French a month before the battle and the results would have been far different. The ancients did not say in vain that "a flock of sheep led by a lion is better than a flock of lions led by a sheep."

50. Napoleon. Napoleon furnishes us with the example of the despot of inexorable will who well understands how to compel all others to submit to himself. Such a man would appear to have no need of defining how he should act either in regard to individuals or in relation to the masses. Uniting within himself the power of commander in chief and of emperor, he possessed the force to make every one do as he desired; but this in itself was insufficient, and in his success in war he displayed not only the genius requisite for successfully manœuvering armies for the fulfilment of a contemplated undertaking, but unusual power of inspiring others, a result that he accomplished in various ways. Napoleon did not tell his men that the enemy were cowards: he told them that their enemies were brave men but they were not capable of opposing the French.

Napoleon was successful for the reason that when he began an undertaking he threw himself into it with his full strength and spared no effort to insure success. He said: "Before a battle it never seems to me that my army is large enough, and I concentrate all the forces that I am able to control."

Herein lies the germ of a great principle, viz, that success can only be counted upon through the employment of every means of insuring it at our disposal. Lack of energy leads to the utilization of insufficient means and the result is failure. Failure proceeds, therefore, from lack of decision. Most men do not appreciate this distinction, and, as Thiers justly remarked, "in the estimation of the rabble the only difference between genius and intrigue is that when a matter succeeds it is dubbed the work of genius; if it fails, of base intrigue." From this the proverb that "there is but a step between the sublime and the ridiculous"—success, sublime; failure, ridiculous.

We have already considered the measures counseled by Napoleon for arousing the enthusiasm of his fleet. We present below some information as to the means he usually employed to effect this end. The following extracts are taken from General Dragomirow's notes (Voen. Sbor., 1894, p. 4):[5]

"How to captivate, how to allure when necessary, and how to inspire fear," says Dragomirow, "no one knew better than he how to do these things. Many persons who were originally ill-disposed toward him underwent a complete change of mind at the conclusion of the first interview; many who were bold in the antechamber and irritated at the servility of others would become servile themselves and bend to his will when brought face to face with him. He was undoubtedly a hypnotizer. As to how he accomplished his end, little has been transmitted to us."

At the battle Lonato (August 1, 1796), which was fought upon very broken ground, the French army was spread out. Napoleon with his suite and a small convoy suddenly ran across a column of 4,000 Austrians, from whom an officer advanced to him and commanded him to surrender. "Do you know to whom you are speaking?" he said. "I am the commander in chief—my whole army follows me. How dare you? Inform the captain of your column that I demand his unconditional surrender; if arms are not grounded within five minutes I will have every one of you shot." The arms were grounded and the men surrendered. The falsehood uttered in a calm tone represented to the Austrians the whole army—the unreal for the real. Imagine under what self-control he must have kept his mind, what an actor he was, not to betray himself by a glance, by a movement of a muscle, or an intonation of his voice. "How can we help saying after this," writes Dragomirow, "that imagination is the nose by which the masses are easily led."

51. How Napoleon inspired others. At Friedland (1807) when he sent Ney to attack our left wing (Ségur, Histoire et Mémoire) he seized him by the elbows with both hands and gave

---

5. Voen. Sbor. is the abbreviation for *Voenniy Sbornik*, the army journal.

him his instructions, looking into his eyes. Dragomirow says Napoleon undoubtedly employed methods of hypnotism, now deemed worthy of the attention of science, to accomplish his ends.[6]

We fully believe Dragomirow to be right. If the science of hypnotism be ever developed to such an extent that it prove susceptible of practical employment, then the commander in chief of a fleet who first acquires power to employ it will derive therefrom an advantage in battle. The capability of employing this new means to an end would represent development of tactics and the winning of a sea fight thereby. The object sought is to win the battle, and whatever brings success is purely a tactical consideration subject to no limitations.

52. *How Napoleon endured insolence.* Napoleon was not always able to hypnotize the men upon whose support he depended, and he frequently employed other methods. Thus at Marengo, when the battle was turning in favor of the Austrians, when all of his marshals surrounded him and advised him to retreat, Desaix came up from his division and turned to Bonaparte with the following disrespectful phrase: "Battu g—— f—— que tu es."[7] Instead of becoming angry with his subordinate, Napoleon turned to Desaix, who was of the greatest use to him at this time, and calmly replied: "Battant, battu, c'est le sort des batailles."[8] After this, when asked his opinion as to the state of matters, Desaix drew out his watch, and said: "Oui, la bataille est perdue, mais il n'est que trois heures, il rests encore le temps d'en gagner une."[9] He there-

6. Hypnotism has played a serious role in Russian history (for example, its use by Rasputin), and is said to be the subject of considerable research now. That the highly scientific Admiral Makarov considered it a possible option within naval tactics underscores the differences that cultures can exert upon perception.

7. Perhaps, "Defeated, completely insane that you are."

8. "Winner, loser, that's how it is with battles."

9. "Yes, the battle is lost, but it is only three o'clock in the afternoon. There is still time to win one."

upon returned to the command of his division and wrested the victory from the hands of the Austrians. Fifteen years later, at the battle of Waterloo, Napoleon would have given much to have had this officer again, but Desaix was no longer among the living; he fell there at Marengo, at the very moment when the French prevailed over the Austrians.

Once Napoleon turned to Marshall Masséna, who, as is well known, was a great robber, and said to him, "Vous êtes le plus grand brigand du monde" (You are the greatest robber in the world). "Après vous, sire" (After you, sire), replied Masséna, and Napoleon swallowed the remark.

The fact was that Napoleon was always in need of executives, and knew how hard it was to find them. We have already seen how sorely he needed an energetic admiral who could employ the French squadron to defeat the English fleet; but, notwithstanding all the means that Napoleon had at his disposal, he was unable to find such, and was obliged to content himself with Villeneuve. People who know how to work to accomplish results understand the value of good subordinates. Nothing can be done with those who are capable of doing but little.

53. Influence of Napoleon upon the masses. In relation to control of the masses, Dragomirow says that "there is required roughness, force, and the qualities of an actor. The first means of affecting the masses is through the individual; to be able to call a man in the ranks by name and ask about the work intrusted to him, knowing well beforehand what that work is. Moralists tell us that such means are unworthy. Let them talk, for the moralists are the very ones that preach justice and require from others in life that which they themselves do not put into practice; but a man struggling in the world, who is compelled to obtain practical results, and chooses those means by which he may attain his end, pays no attention to what fools may consider a sine qua non. Are not these very moralists themselves constantly feigning in every walk in life? Are they not always telling people "charmé de vous voir," when they are not "charmé" at all, and may be disposed entirely otherwise? Flies are caught in traps by honey and not by vinegar, "et si le monde veut être trompé, il faut bien s'y soumettre."[10]

General Dragomirow's words evidently do not relate to private life, but to war and politics. If a man were to attempt in private life all that is permitted in life political, and should then display the military cunning of Hannibal, he would fail in his undertakings.

"Moralists," says Dragomirow, "revolve in the sphere of politics, and military people have to do with interests and passions; hence there is unceasing and determined controversy between the former and the latter." Catherine the Great said, in conversation with Diderot: "You work on paper and I work on human hide." Cavour said: "If we did in our own behalf all that we have done for Italy, we would have been great scoundrels."

The above may be illustrated by a tactical example. At the time of the attack of Nelson upon the French fleet at Aboukir a great many of the crews of the latter were on shore with the ships' boats. If this had been a duel everyone would have blamed Nelson for taking advantage of existing conditions, and would have condemned him for winning the battle unfairly; but a battle is not a duel, and tactics counsel us to utilize every disadvantage of an enemy and to give him no rest until he is beaten.

Besides influencing the masses through individuals, Napoleon had recourse to other methods. In the Military Laws of Napoleon (p. 65) we find the following passage, which shows that he was not unaware of what soldiers and officers talked about in bivouac:

Addresses delivered at critical moments can not instil bravery into soldiers; veterans hardly listen to them and recruits forget them at the sound of the first shot. Such speeches are

10. "and if the world wants to be deceived, let it."

only useful in prolonged campaigns, to counteract the effect of painful impressions, lying rumors, for maintaining the good spirits of the army, and to furnish subjects of conversation in the camp. Printed daily orders should fulfill these desired requirements.

We may conclude our brief remarks upon Napoleon with a description of how he usually gave battle.

54. How Napoleon gave battle. "Engagements generally began," writes General Dragomirow, "about 5 o'clock in the morning. Napoleon occupied a position not far from the reserves, whence he could obtain a general view of the battlefield; dismounted, walked about, conversed with those about him, received dispatches, gave orders whenever necessary. He supplied reinforcements only to those whom he knew did not ask for them without reason, but sometimes he refused these. The affair would drag on in its various phases until about 4 o'clock in the afternoon; he then took his seat in the saddle; everyone knew what this meant; the decisive blow was about to be struck; shouts of 'Vive l'Empereur!' resounded from the reserve and were taken up all along the whole line of battle. When this reached the enemy their hearts fell, for they knew the general advance was about to be made, and who could tell how or when he would be destroyed?"

In this manner Napoleon held his antagonist under the threat of misfortune eleven or twelve hours before making the final attack upon him—that is, he exhausted him physically and morally. Having impressed his imagination by this very exhaustion, he then by a very simple but eminently practical movement, and one well understood by his own army—mounting his charger—inspired his own men with the certainty of victory, while he impressed his antagonist with the probability of certain destruction.

CHAPTER THREE

MILITARY AND NAVAL PEDAGOGICS

55. General Hershelman upon the influence of morale on success in war. In the previous chapter we touched upon the influence of the moral element on success in war, and showed that all military commanders deemed this subject one of great importance. Besides the writers above cited, Hershelman has studied this subject deeply in recent years, and has communicated to the "Voennoi Sbornik" a series of very interesting papers upon the same. Morale constitutes actually a vast power in war, and every effort must be made to elevate naval as well as military forces to the highest degree of efficiency in this direction.

The moral element is developed through education and training. Each man receives his education and training first in his family, then at school, and finally in life and in service. The training received in family and school falls under the cognizance of pedagogics, and training in service within the limits of what is called naval administration. We shall consider in this chapter problems in naval pedagogics.

56. Problems in naval pedagogics. The science of naval education must be developed in accordance with the requirements of war. Officers and men must be trained so as to fit them for war. All other considerations are of secondary importance. General development is of course necessary, but in no case should the primary object be lost sight of.

By speaking in this manner we do not wish to imply that the general development of the officer is unimportant, but general development constitutes the self-evident part of the work, and is therefore never forgotten. On the other hand, it may happen that naval pedagogics, influenced by the desire to develop young men in every respect, overlook the matter of crucial importance, which is the development of boldness, perception, and readiness—three qualities indispensable in war. If pedagogics were influenced by the voice of tactics, such undesirable results would not be realized, and the young man upon completing his course would have been developed under conditions of naval war, which is the chief end to be sought.

Let us consider what qualities should characterize individuals trained for war. This will indicate to us the ideal toward the attainment of which pedagogics should strive. To this end we shall first call attention to qualities the leader should possess; subsequently to those which should characterize the ordinary seaman.

57. Napoleon upon commanders. All writers agree that much depends upon the personal characteristics of the officer in command. No one, however, speaks as positively on this point as Napoleon, who has expressed himself in the following words:

> It was not the Roman armies that conquered Gaul, but Cæsar; not the Carthagenian armies that made Rome tremble, but Hannibal; not the Macedonian armies that penetrated into India, but Alexander; not the Prussian armies that defended Prussia seven years, but Frederick. (On the Study of Naval Warfare as a Science, Luce, p. 540.)

58. Historical opinion upon the qualities of commanders. We must study history in order to form a clear estimation of the type of a commander or military leader. History does not present to us ideals, but true examples, and we there learn that persons who develop military genius often begin to ex-

90

hibit signs of the existence of this genius in their early childhood. Sometimes, however, when these people were young they were careless or else promised nothing unusual. We have already made a somewhat elaborate analysis of Nelson's personality. Let us refer in a few words to the qualities of other renowned military leaders.

Napoleon was a great soldier from the day he entered upon his military career. He slept upon his arms and was always occupied with the study of military matters. He spent whole hours upon the contemplation of plans and charts.

Alexander was considered from his youth destined by fate to become a great man. He is described as a nervous boy, and it is said that the temperature of his blood seemed higher than that of other persons. His nervous temperament was indicated by his passion for wine.

Plutarch says (p. 13): "With all his burning energy (from a moral standpoint) Alexander when in childhood exhibited marked self-control and equanimity under difficult circumstances."

They accuse him, however, of keeping up orgies too long after feasts. Alexander was liberal to an extreme.

Plutarch (p. 38), referring to Alexander's bestowal of gifts before the Persian campaign, adds: "When Alexander had thus expended all his resources, Perdiccas said: 'What, sire, have you left for yourself?' 'Hope,' replied Alexander."

Julius Caesar was a young man of the world, fond of pleasures, always energetic, confident in himself, but only after he had received command in Gaul did he begin to develop his genius.

We find the following in Plutarch (p. 31):

> They also relate that in Spain, in his hours of leisure, Cæsar read Alexander's history. At times he was so moved by such reading that he long remained in silence, would sigh heavily, and finally burst into tears. When his friends asked him why

he was weeping he would reply: "Why should I not lament, when Alexander at my age had already made himself master of so many conquered countries, while I can not yet count a single brilliant victory."

Cæsar was also liberal in rewards. Plutarch says (p. 53) that "he conquered his enemies with the armies of Roman citizens and recompensed the latter with the gold of the former."

Among our own leaders, Suvorow, who at the age of 15 became a private in the Semenovsk Regiment and who was advanced at the age of 24 to the grade of officer, stands foremost. He had no school education and was entirely self-educated. He was small in stature, thin, puny, badly set up, ugly; but received commendation in his first war as "quick in reconnoitering, brave in battle, and cool in danger." The example of Suvorow serves to show that persons who are not endowed by nature with high physical qualities have no reason to be apprehensive of their career. The above opinion of Suvorow when he was yet young is brief and graphic. It shows the ideal toward the attainment of which officers should strive, and he whose task it is to train officers can do no better than to make them as Suvorow was—"quick in reconnoitering, brave in battle, and cool in danger."

Among our contemporaries, Skobeleff was considered in his regiment as a poor officer.[1] If there had been no war it is probable Skobeleff would never have risen to distinction. All his brief service was spent in campaigning, but when the campaigns ended he did not know what to do with himself and succumbed in consequence of his restlessness. History has not

1. General M. D. Skobelev (1843–82) made his reputation in battles in Central Asia, where Admiral Makarov accompanied him to Akhal-Tekke, in the Turkish wars, and in the liberation of Bulgaria. Referred to as the Akhaltinsk Campaign, Skobelev's battles in Central Asia, beginning in 1879, were fought to conquer the largest Turkomen tribe. With great superiority in arms, he accomplished this in 1881.

yet spoken its last upon Skobeleff. Our personal acquaintance with him at the time of the Akaltikinsk campaign has left with us an impression of his brilliant military talent. Skobeleff knew how to inspire his command, and one glance from him was enough to fill every one with an irrestrainable desire to fight with the enemy and to conquer him. With Skobeleff in command, men rushed under fire and every one became a hero.

Every famous commander possesses along with his talents certain evident shortcomings. He is selected only because a good chief is needed, and his military qualities compel us to put up with his deficiencies. People who are talented in military matters are, as General Leer says, very rare, and war compels us to pardon them for many things. Napoleon, who was always fighting and who always needed talented people, states in his "Memoirs," written at St. Helena, that "you must take people as you find them and never listen to what others say about them. The problem in question is to win a battle, and to do this suitable persons are needed. If you stop to listen to what some say about others, you would deprive yourself of persons who might be very useful to you." This man, who appears to us the embodiment of despotism, was always in need of the services of talented persons and, as we have stated above, he even submitted to insolence from them. But Napoleon, notwithstanding all his art, was not always able to find such people. Thus, he never had a man like Zeidlitz to command his cavalry, for Murat was but a bold horseman, and Napoleon never gave him the necessary independence in handling cavalry, the result of which was, as General Leer says (Contribution to Tactics, part 4, p. 30), that in Frederick the Great's great battles the cavalry acted better than they did in Napoleon's.[2]

2. Freidrik von Zeydlitz (1721–73), a brilliant cavalry officer and general under Frederick the Great, gained great fame in the Seven Years' War.

59. The qualities a commander in chief should possess. Many military writers discuss in detail the qualities desirable in a commander, and all agree that although intelligence is an indispensable quality, yet they gave the preference to character over energy. Napoleon considers the best quality in a general to be a clear head; that is, the ability not to make fancy pictures of things, as he graphically expresses it. In other words, the capability of not being governed by his imagination and not to look upon flies as elephants. Suvorow very concisely designates this quality as perception, which consists, according to General Leer (Positive Strategy, p. 18), in the capability of estimating truly at every moment the conditions of time and distance indispensable to the fulfilment of a given combination.

Jomini says: "The most important qualities of a commander will always be magnanimity of character or the moral fearlessness which leads to great enterprises and, next to this, coolness and the ability to control one's self in the presence of danger. Knowledge only occupies a third position in importance, but it is always a strong auxiliary. To deny this is to close one's eyes. On the other hand, as I have already stated, vast learning is not required. It is necessary to know but little, but to know that little well, and especially to be deeply versed in the rules of tactics." (Outlines of the Art of War, Jomini, p. 115.)

General Leer says the following upon this subject:

By our analysis we have endeavored to indicate those qualities which should characterize the military mind. These qualities—character, understanding, and perception—are rarely found in that state of development which use in war requires, even when considered separately. How rarely do we meet them in that happy combination which constitutes military genius. History shows that in twenty centuries there have been hardly more than ten cases that can be cited—Alexander, Hannibal, Cæsar, Augustus Adolphus, Turenne, Prince Eugene, Peter, Frederick, Suvorow, and Napoleon. Nature is evidently very stingy with such people—stingier in bestowing military talent than in all else. (Positive Strategy, Leer, p. 18.)

Marmont, in his work Esprit des Instructions Militaires (p. 253, 254), defines the qualities of an officer in command as follows:[3]

Two things are indispensable to a commander—mind and character. Mind, because without it it is impossible to form a conception of any undertaking; character, because the successful accomplishment of predetermined plans can not be effected without strong and energetic purpose. But the matter is altogether one of comparative qualities and not of qualities in the absolute. This correlation constitutes in itself a very weighty element of success. If we express in figures each quality in accordance with its value, I would prefer a general whose mind corresponded to a value 5 and character a value 10 to a general with a mind 15 and character 8. When character controls understanding while the mind possesses the necessary depth, a man willingly undertakes a task, and his chance of accomplishing it is excellent. On the other hand, when the mind dominates over character the result is constant change of proposed plans and measures, for a great mind is apt to regard matters from a different standpoint at each moment. If the power of the will be insufficient to put an end to this hesitation the result will be an unavoidable balancing between various conclusions, and nothing will be undertaken (which is the very worst that could happen) and, besides, the nearer the end approaches the greater our hesitation tends to withhold us from it, and finally causes us to miss the mark.

Marshal Saxe says almost the same, viz, "that the first quality in a commander is character (bravery), without which

3. Marshal A. de Marmont was one of Napoleon's generals who first achieved fame at the Siege of Toulon in 1793. At the battle of Leipzig, 1813, he and Marshal Ney opened a corridor for the escape of Napoleon's troops retreating from Moscow, thus, in effect, prolonging the war until Waterloo.

I place no value upon other qualities, as they all prove useless. The second is understanding, and the third good health."[4] (Positive Strategy, Leer, p. 117).

As a general deduction from the above in what relates to character and understanding we may cite the résumé of Napoleon, who compares character with the base of a rectangle and understanding with its height. "If," he says, "preference is to be given to either one of these two qualities, I would prefer character and not understanding." Besides character and understanding a military leader should possess knowledge and health. Jomini requires from him still another attribute—justice. He writes:

> Unfortunately, the ability to do justice to subordinates is very rarely met. Moderate intelligences always depend upon others and are rather prone to choose their associates from people with ability no greater than their own, fearing lest the latter should discuss them and unable to realize the fact that he who bears the name of commander in chief always receives the full credit of any success, even if he takes a very insignificant part therein. (Outlines of the Art of War, Jomini, Chap. I, p. 115).

60. *Qualities desirable in commanders of fleets.* Upon this point we do not find such positive opinions as in the case of a commander on land. In general it is necessary to admit that the commander at sea should possess the same qualities as the commander on land, as far as they apply to the kind of activity that obtains at sea. The knowledge of the sea commander is totally different from that of his comrade on shore, and military perception does not suffice to enable him clearly to estimate circumstances which arise at sea.

Naval conditions call for certain special qualities in addition to the general ones above cited. We will not go into de-

---

4. Marshal Saxe led the French forces in the defeat of the British and the Austrians in the Netherlands in the War of the Austrian Succession, 1745.

tails upon this point, but will limit ourselves to stating that a commander in chief of a fleet should possess a seaman's eye; that is, the ability to estimate at a glance the position of his own ships and squadron in relation to other ships and to the land. He who does not possess a good seaman's eye will never be able fully to control his own ship, and, consequently, a squadron. This is an inborn attribute, but one which may be developed to a considerable extent by education and practice. We are personally acquainted with very talented persons who can not accustom their minds to controlling the movements of a ship, although they have developed high capabilities in technique and in administration.

By what we have above stated we do not mean that a man should not endeavor to acquire this attribute, for by effort one may overcome his faults and develop his good qualities. Anyone who is not naturally shortsighted, and who possesses sufficient keenness of vision, may improve himself considerably in this respect.

61. *The attribute of a seaman's eye and the quality of military perception.* Does it follow that what we have called the seaman's eye is related to what Suvorow has described as perception? We deem it impossible to consider them identical. Both possess much in common, but differences exist between them. For the sake of accuracy in nomenclature they should be distinguished from one another. One may be able to guide his ship at sea and yet be altogether deficient in military perception; that is, the knowledge of estimating one's position in relation to that of the enemy. If Suvorow's perception had been styled, in its application to naval matters, "naval perception," there would have been introduced a new term. We therefore decide that by the word "perception" is to be understood that which has been described by us as the seaman's eye, the capability of controlling one's own ship and of noticing at a glance, upon looking at a ship, all of her external deficiencies, which aids us in forming a conception of her other qualities.

62. Conclusions in relation to qualities desirable in commanders of fleets. Summing up all that has been said in relation to naval conditions, we may consider that a commander of a fleet should possess the following qualities:

First. Character, which includes bravery and coolness.
Second. Understanding.
Third. Military perception.
Fourth. The seaman's eye.
Fifth. Knowledge.
Sixth. Health.
Seventh. Justice.

63. Qualities that a soldier should possess. Having reviewed the qualities of a commander, we now turn to the consideration of those that should be possessed by the soldier. Napoleon states the following:

> The first quality of a soldier is manhood, which enables him to endure all the fatigues and privations of war—bravery is but a secondary consideration. (Military Rules of Napoleon, Ed. 1846, LIX, p. 63.)

Upon page 33 of his work, General Dragomirow states:

> The following qualities are required from the soldier in war:
> First. The sense of duty developed to self-denial or readiness to sacrifice himself for the deliverance of his comrades; fearlessness, skill, and unquestioning obedience in the commands of the chief in all that relates to service.
> Second. Capability of patiently enduring hardships and privations of war without becoming rapidly exhausted.
> Third. To be skilled in the use of his weapons.
> Fourth. The knowledge of how to conform his movements and actions to those of his comrades.
> Fifth. Skill in surmounting local obstacles and the knowledge how to utilize them in his own defense from observation of the enemy's firing, without depriving himself, however, of the possibility of seeing the enemy and firing upon him.

The first two qualities are determined by the soldier's education, and the last three by his training.

64. Qualities that a seaman should possess. Whole books could be written upon this subject, but we shall be brief in this regard, and but state our conclusions as based upon the opinions of the high authorities already stated and upon our own observation. The sailor should possess the following qualities:

First. Health and endurance.
Second. The habit of discipline.
Third. The sea habit.
Fourth. Daring.
Fifth. Knowledge.

65. Qualities that should be possessed by all serving afloat. We have endeavored to outline the qualities of the commander in chief of the fleet and of the ordinary seaman. All other positions demand the exercise of some or the other of these attributes, for all other persons are called upon, some to control, some to be subordinate to others. The problem of naval education consists in imparting the above-mentioned qualities to all those serving on shipboard.

66. Training received in the family. Every man receives his first training from his mother, and that which is instilled in the child in his early years remains with him through life. We observe, for example, how in Asiatic nations the idea is impressed upon the child that it is his duty to avenge his father or brother with his own blood, and the young man who has reached mature years under the influence of this idea sacrifices his life, if necessary, to fulfill that which he believes to be the obligation of his birth.

Nations are now so accustomed to the benefits of peace that military valor is beginning little by little to disappear. The wars of the last three-quarters of a century have been waged in quite a humane manner and the terrors of war are fading year by year in our national tales. Mothers are not so often found nowadays who teach their sons that it is their duty to grow and become strong to defend their birthplace and fireside from the enemy. This is now regarded as a matter of duty of the government, while it is really a social and national question.

67. Jomini upon military spirit in all nations. Let us see what men of eminent intelligence say in relation to military spirit. Jomini writes: "If the government do not strive to instill the military spirit into a nation, the best measures adopted for training armies will prove vain" (Outlines of the Art of War, Jomini, Part I, p. 124).

In the second part of his work (p. 2) Jomini returns to this question and says: "The composition and qualities of armies, the superiority of artillery and cavalry and the efficient use thereof, but above all this the moral exaltation of armies and even of nations themselves, is that which renders victories more or less decisive, and determines the significance of their results."

68. Military valor in a nation. No one would be accused of assuming the rôle of prophet who suggests that the great transmigration of nations that have occurred in the past might again repeat themselves; and if a movement of the yellow races from the east toward the west should begin, we would be the first called upon to oppose our strength to resisting the shock. Reason demands that we should anticipate this and be prepared against such an emergency, and such preparations could do no harm; they would serve to instill into the masses of the people the spirit developed in the Romans at the time of their mastery of the world and the absence of which led to the downfall of their universal empire.

There is no need of my raising my weak voice to defend these great principles. In fact, we have no reason to reproach the Russian mother with inability to train valorous sons. The recruits that we receive every year serve to prove that she supplies to the ranks of the army and the fleet those who are fully adapted to the requirements of war; men who are accustomed to work, to endurance and to subordination; who are contented with their lot and require but little. Better material would be hard to find. Discipline and respect for parental authority are to be noted in the families of the peasantry. The mother tells her son he is to grow and become strong, so as to support his parents in their old age. Thus the child acquires from the cradle the sense of duty imposed upon him. They may tell us that the peasant mother does it unconsciously, but, if so, her services are none the less therefor. But, on the other hand, she stands far above those few women of the middle class who, having the power to train their sons intelligently, supply to the nation only those of sickly constitution—moral degenerates, who, incapable of doing anything, are a burden upon society and ultimately an expense to the State.

69. *Influence of national folklore.* We think it impossible to disregard the fact that the stories heard in childhood leave traces of their influence in after life. Pushkin says that he obtained his first inspiration of poesy from his nurse's tales. In comparatively recent times national tales and legends of the past were carefully preserved, and all Petersburg has listened to their narrators. It is not uncommon to find on board of our own ships a story-teller who during long cruises will almost daily continue to tell to his comrades stories and ever new stories. Evidently our nation possesses the power of preserving ancient tales of battles and heroes, and no one can disregard the fact that these stories have their influence on the real training of the individual; whereas it is desirable that all such tales as serve to arouse the mind to the emulation of valorous deeds should be carefully preserved.

70. *School training or practical training.* The young man who wishes to follow a naval career enters his profession from

home, and the years which he has spent in educational institutions and exercises have a great influence upon his fitness for military service. In relation to school training we may turn our attention to Dragomirow's question, "What should not be taught?" It took Dragomirow to put the question in this form, but we believe that every ordinary man can realize its significance. All professors are prone to extend their courses, and it is necessary therefore that there should be a controlling voice to put its veto upon extended instruction in those subjects which are learned one hundred times more easily in practice afloat than from books or diagrams. There should only be taught in school that which it is inconvenient to teach in service.

There are, however, two systems of education—the one by schooling; the other by practice. England has always preferred the latter of these systems. To become an engineer in England a young man who has finished a course of general instructions is entered at the age of from 15 to 17 in a machine shop, where he serves as an apprentice during a period of four years. Some are sent to a special school after this, but the majority finish their training in the shop.

In the United States a young man who wishes to become a sailor or naval mechanician is, at the age of 15, upon completing his general training, sent to a ship as a sailor or an oiler (Morsk. Sbor., 1896, No. 6), and he acquires his special training in practice or from such books as he brings to sea with him. What we style a sea school does not exist, but there are sailors; while under the school system precisely the opposite is brought about—that is, there is a school, but no sailors. In America and nearly everywhere abroad, it is believed that, when the question is general education, the school is the best means of obtaining the end; but that when the matter is one of acquiring a trade to be followed throughout life, practical methods afford better results. Notwithstanding the fact that higher education is given greater privileges in Russia than elsewhere, too great a number of persons possessing higher technical training are out of place. Economy of manufacture demands in most cases simple, skilled, practical laborers rather than theorists, unless the latter are capable of applying their ideas to their trade.

The fault of school education lies in the fact that pupils see everything artificially and not naturally, and have relations not with persons engaged in the same pursuit as that which they are to follow, but with teachers; the better the teacher— that is, a man who knows how to train youth—the less he resembles the type of an able seaman or a skilled mechanic, while it is such types that the young must endeavor to imitate. Once having inspected a school-ship and seen the complete systematization of employment, distribution of time, etc., the idea involuntarily suggests itself to me, "will all this not serve rather to systematically destroy in a youth the spirit of daring and determination; will not this system produce the result that the young man will develop timidity and fear of deviating from routine in spite of himself?"

Being allowed to remain too long at school has a bad effect upon a young seaman. If a young man of 22 be kept within doors as a pupil he will develop in life into a faint-hearted student rather than a bold, capable man.

71. Conclusions. All of the above leads us to the conclusion that the personal abilities of the officers of our fleet would be improved if the age of entrance as an officer in the service were lowered to about 18 years, and if the deficient theoretical knowledge resulting therefrom were corrected by subsequent special training in officer's duties. Everyone should realize that his education does not end upon his leaving school; but that throughout his period of service as an officer he must study and work in order to obtain his advancement.

CHAPTER FOUR

SELF-TRAINING* AND SELF-EDUCATION

72. General conceptions. He who has completed his education at school must enter upon life with the conviction that he yet knows nothing and has had no military education; that he has only been made familiar with the program of studies and has only had pointed out to him the branches of knowledge in which he must personally interest himself to accomplish his education, and that all he can accomplish will result from his own labors and not from aid received from others. We consider military training above military education, and therefore we begin with it.

73. The necessity of familiarizing ourselves with the thought, "death with honor." It is a very grave question what a young man should accustom himself to consider as of fundamental importance when he adopts the military career. We find a reply thereto in Klausewitz, to whom we are indebted for many lofty conceptions. Speaking of the fact that one may be called upon to decide upon an undertaking without foreseeing favorable issue therefrom—one which is decided upon because it is impossible to do anything better—Klausewitz says:

---

*Note by the author: The Russian word *vospitanie,* translated *training,* is a very expressive word meaning the acquiring of a knowledge of one's duties so that routine becomes a second nature.

In order not to be deprived at such a moment of calmness and firmness (qualities paramount in war), which, under such conditions, are very difficult to preserve, but without which the greatest mental capabilities prove useless, we must familiarize ourselves beforehand with the idea of "death with honor." This feeling should be reverently referred to and incessantly instilled into ourselves, so that we may become completely familiar with it. Be assured that without this firm determination no great thing will be accomplished in war even under the most favorable circumstances, and still less in misfortune. (Instructions upon War, Klausewitz, p. 7.)

Klausewitz's idea, the necessity of impressing upon ourselves that it is our duty "to perish with honor," possesses a deep significance. Every living creature by force of instinct fears death, but to man is given will-power to control this instinct. We see that animals not only fear death for themselves, but they are frightened at the sight of the death of others like themselves. When an animal falls in its death agony all others that may have flocked around it run away. A man may control this feeling in himself, and he fearlessly works upon the dying to lessen his agony or to restore him to life. More than this, he has endeavored, from the most ancient times, to conquer in himself the fear for his life; and military valor, of which indifference to death is a chief characteristic, has been long held in high esteem.[1] All great commanders were personally brave. Alexander and Cæsar often fought with swords in hand, and at critical moments placed themselves at the head of their legions. The change to firearms removed the commander in chief from the line of battle, which became drawn

---

1. This indifference to death was observed with awe and fear by the Germans in World War II. It is a characteristic that accounts, in part, for the famous charges without ammunition and the unwillingness of Russians to surrender even in the face of the most hopeless situations.

out to an enormous length. It is hard to imagine to-day a commander in chief who, with drawn sword, could throw himself before his armies in an attack upon an enemy's column. But the division commander is not the commander in chief, and should be ready to place himself, sword in hand, at the head of his men, and by his example promote the general attack and the annihilation of an enemy.

General Dragomirow says that one conquers who does not fear to die; consequently he who wishes to gain a victory should determine that he will either conquer or die, as he can only anticipate a full victory under these conditions. In the moment of excitement man not only willingly sacrifices his life, but the idea of fighting to the death may seem pleasant to him.

Skobeleff, who better than anyone understood how to captivate the army and to throw them under the heaviest fire, at the battle of Geok-Tepe placed the Apsheronsk Regiment that had the day before lost its colors at the head of the storming column, and inspired his soldiers with a few words in which he congratulated them upon that "honorable death which awaits them who have lost their flag." According to the account of an eyewitness, thanks to these words, men rushed under fire with the highest enthusiasm.

With necessary preparation a man may not only render himself impressionable to exaltation, but may render himself capable of acting upon others by his own influence and example. Every military man should absorb the consciousness that he should be ready to sacrifice his life. When he first thinks seriously of this he will probably turn pale and will feel the blood throb in his veins, the second time the idea does not produce the same deep impression, and finally he becomes so accustomed to it that it seems easy and even attractive.

When the mother of an officer, killed at the post where he had been sent by our national hero, reproached Skobeleff, he replied to her: "Madam, your son has received the highest reward that war can give—he has been killed in battle. A greater honor I could never wish for."

As we know, Skobeleff, who was so often in danger, was not destined to receive this reward.

Suvorow, whom we have quoted above, did not tell his men that they would never be killed, but, on the contrary, told them to look death in the face and "die for your native land, for your mother (the Empress), and for your most holy church. The Holy Church is praying for you. Honor and renown for him who remains alive."

We know of many instances where not only individuals but whole groups of persons calmly met their death. Thus, in the time of the French Revolution, those who knew that the guillotine awaited them passed their time in agreeable conversation, as if they were facing nothing unpleasant. Often in the evening, lists were received with the names of those who were to be guillotined on the following morning, and the reading of this list would sometimes be accompanied with jests and witticisms from persons who had only a few hours to live.

74. Skobeleff's views. Skobeleff tells us that when he was carried away wounded he thought very carefully in his mind what he would say. He decided if his wound were light to say one thing, and if mortal, another. This shows that even at this very time, when wounded, Skobeleff did not fear death.

It must be borne in mind that no training is capable of overcoming natural instincts. We have cited, as an example, the case of Skobeleff, whom no one can accuse of cowardice. The author happened to be detailed for transporting by sea those wounded at Plevna and other places, and formed his opinion of Skobeleff from the tales of men who had no interest in praising him. They all, with unanimous voice, exalted him. The greater the danger the more joyful he appeared. We recall our own conversation with Skobeleff before the Akal-Ieké expedition. Skobeleff made inquiries of the author concerning certain details of torpedo attack, whereupon the author told him the whole thing was a matter of personal bravery. "I suppose," said the author, "you have never known the feeling of fear."

"You are mistaken if you think that there are any who are completely without the sense of fear," replied Skobeleff; "I do not believe that such men exist, and I think that everyone displays under certain circumstances the highest bravery and under others the most abject cowardice. In the greater number of instances a man has sufficient control of himself to conquer the feeling of fear that arises within him, but I can myself remember how I laid in the trenches and did not dare to raise my head, for it seemed to me that the whole shower of bullets was about to fall upon me. Some minutes later I conquered this feeling, and in order to punish myself placed myself under a heavy fire, but as soon as I laid down in the trenches I became the same poor coward again."

This story of Skobeleff instructs us that if anyone should feel frightened under fire he should not be astonished at this, but only make a conscious effort within himself and his self-control will immediately reappear. The greater the development of the man the more is he capable of exercising this control over himself.

Officers should understand that it is their duty to encourage their own men. In artillery instruction the battery commander gives corrections for range and other data for firing. In war he can only do this for the first shots while there are no losses, but when losses begin he must first of all encourage his men by his calmness and set an example in coolness; otherwise, errors in firing will greatly exceed the limits of correction.

There are other ways of encouraging a command and restoring it to self-possession. Skobeleff counsels in some cases to execute the small-arm manual—that is, to do that which the men in the ranks are most accustomed to do under conditions of peace training.

We are sorry that we did not write down many of Skobeleff's stories relating to his own experience in war, but we remember one that bears on the subject in point. This was at the time of the Turkish war (1877–78). A company captured some redoubt occupied by the Turks. The men advanced to attack, but in consequence of the heavy fire they did not run up to the enemy's lines, but laid down; the company commander laid down also. When his first impressions passed away he began to converse with the soldiers nearest to him, telling them that it was useless to act in this way; that they should go forward. The soldiers replied that they had been frightened, but they would go now. This conversation passed along the whole line, and the men sent word back to the commander that they all swore to a man that they would all advance and not stop until they took the redoubt, if only the captain made the signal and that not one of them would remain behind. Being thus convinced that the men had now recovered from their first impressions, the captain notified them that he would spring forward and all should follow him. What was said was done, and a few minutes afterwards the redoubt was taken. Skobeleff arrived when the whole battalion already stood in the redoubt and, being convinced that the enemy had offered serious opposition, questioned the officers and asked them to point out the one that was worthy to receive the George's Cross. The officers indicated the very company commander who had taken the redoubt. Skobeleff went away satisfied, both as to the capture of the redoubt and the man chosen to receive the reward. The same afternoon the battalion commander visited Skobeleff and stated that the officers, not having been prepared for the question as to who was the most worthy, had indicated an officer who did not deserve it. In proof of his assertion he stated how matters had been, emphasizing the fact that the officer had set an unworthy example in not inciting his own men; but Skobeleff adhered to his former opinion, for he thought that under the circumstances the officer had acted properly. It would have been worse if he had jumped up and advanced toward the fortification alone and unsupported by all his people.

75. *More than all else is it important that seamen should familiarize themselves with the necessity of meeting death with honor.* We return again to Klausewitz's proposition upon the necessity of regarding as honorable the presence of death. This is more necessary for seamen than for soldiers, as actual circumstances of battle develop gradually for the latter. Armies do not enter immediately upon a general engagement; unimportant skirmishes first take place, and the sight of the dead and wounded upon the battlefield, as well as constant information concerning losses in action, diminish to some degree the fear of death, so that people become somewhat inured to the conditions of the general engagement. Tolstoi well describes in his romance, War and Peace, the order, "Close up!" after shell or grape had struck down a few men from the ranks. The defenders of Sebastopol who remained some months in their bastions were so accustomed to the idea of death that each one of them considered it a lucky chance that they were alive, and not chance that they might be killed. Commodore Sheman, who as a young man commanded the naval battalion at the siege of Geok-Tepe, told us that he fully realized that he was left alive only after he had been severely wounded.[2]

Naval actions, however, occur under different conditions; a great battle may take place without preparatory skirmishes,

2. Commodore Sheman, then a lieutenant, was in charge of a naval detachment of steam cutters that protected the supply lines across the Caspian Sea during the campaign to suppress the Turkomen tribes at Geok-Tepe in 1880–81. The unit was so outstanding that General Skobelev changed them into a naval battery ashore, and with the help of 30,000 camels (!), crossed the desert, led by Makarov. This is a dramatic example of how Russians are not controlled by categorical definitions in their wartime use of manpower or sea power, and why they so consistently surprised the Germans, who are.

110

and that fleet whose personnel has accustomed itself in time of peace to the idea that it is the duty of every one to honorably sacrifice his life, that fleet, we assert, will possess a great moral superiority over an antagonist.

76. *Upon the training of the will.* At the conclusion of our lectures at the Kronstadt Naval Club we happened to hear the remark made that commanders and writers, in enumerating the various qualities of a commander in chief, said nothing about "nerve endurance." The commander in chief and every one in military service should possess, according to their opinion, strong nerves, without which a man would be unsuited for the task to which he might be assigned. In justification of the authorities that have been cited by us, we should say that in the term "character" they probably intended to include the capability of self-control; that is, of resisting such impressions upon the nervous system as might impair their work.

The following questions merit practical consideration:

First. Can a man so control his will as to place himself above nervous manifestations; that is, is he able to suppress within himself the sense of fear?

Second. May he make himself sensitive in a certain direction—for instance, in what relates to the movements of his own and other ships—and at the same time ignore the stronger sensations, such as the noise of firing, etc.?

Upon this point we made inquiries of a very competent man, Dr. Shidlovski, who replied to us as follows:

> The nervous systems of different people may, from nature and education, be more or less receptive to impressions from without. Diminished receptivity of the nerves is observed, in general, in undeveloped persons. Intelligent and capable persons possess, however, active nerves, and if their will power be insufficiently developed, then many nervous irritations are transformed into various forms of muscular contractions, such as shivering, pallor, trembling, weeping, and the like; that is, they develop what are called nervous symptoms. By development of the will-power the effect of nervous irritations

111

leads to muscular contractions only after their exact analysis by the higher mental activity, and in this case nervous agitation only produces muscular contractions which are recognized as useful in a given direction. We find people with very receptive nerves, but with firm characters, and the activity of such people in all walks of life is in the highest degree productive.

The susceptibility of the nervous system to outer impressions in a known direction may be developed by systematic exercises, upon which are based the education and training of persons for various special pursuits; and as we have seen that the activity of nervous persons is very useful, it is also necessary to develop in them will-power. In order that the latter may always properly control muscular contractions, it should itself be under the control of good, high, mental activity—that which is commonly called the mind. Mind is the highest gift of nature and may be developed in every direction by education; that is, by the systematization and grouping in the brain of the nervous impressions received through our organs of sense from our environment. It follows from this that the development of will power without the simultaneous development of the mind leads to stubbornness, but that the simultaneous development of the mind and will produce useful stability of character.

The seat of control of the powers of mind and will is in the human brain, whence nervous impulses are sent out through the spinal marrow for the control of all muscular contractions. All outer impressions received by our senses proceed to the brain, where, with the aid of mind and will, it is decided what muscular contraction is adapted to given conditions, or speaking in simple words, how to act. In this case, the relation between the impressions received in the brain and the order sent along the spinal marrow for the necessary muscular contraction may very infinitely—all depends upon the degree of development of the will-power. The man who has developed in himself will-power in the highest degree may die from frightful nervous or physical suffering without moving, so to speak, a muscle, without twitching his eyes, while another, on

112

the other hand, who has no control of his will, writhes, weeps, and even faints (extreme shock to the nervous system) upon the mere approach of a cutting instrument or at the sight of blood. I repeat, nevertheless, differences may be observed under given conditions—people who have personally experienced and bravely borne all the horrors of war may fall into a faint at the sight or trace of blood in their own saliva.

Man does not possess the power to change the conductivity of the nerves from the periphery to the center. For example, he may not overcome in himself the susceptibility to pain, but through the use of the will and the mind he may refrain from exhibiting muscular contractions undesirable under given circumstances; that is, he may refrain from tears, sighs, etc.

All expedient harmonious muscular contractions of the body proceed under the guidance of the nerve centers controlled by the brain. While a man is studying any complicated muscular movement (walking, dancing, playing of musical instruments) he is controlled by his mind, but as soon as he is educated, that is, when the necessary combination of the nerve elements has been established in the brain, then all those movements are performed apart from the mind-control—are done, in fact, much more rapidly and better than if the man thought out every movement. Walking becomes in the highest degree ungraceful when the man knows that others are looking at him and he wishes to bear himself better than usual. We give this fact to show that there are in our brain elements called into action by our will and by our knowledge, which act upon our nervous contractions, even when we are not thinking of them. A mother is not awakened by the moving of furniture in the adjoining room, but she hears the slightest movement of the child in its cradle. We are able to wake up at a desired hour in the night, if necessary. A great number of similar examples might be cited; and it should be said that, thanks to circumstances, the power of nervous activity in man may be developed to the highest degree and in a great number of directions. A man thinking and determining one thing, may at the same time, while completely unaware of the same, perform very complicated movements. Variations in direction of nervous activity in the mind are endless, but how to develop one or the other of them is almost completely unexplained. There is no doubt of the fact that a man may develop his own will; and in view of the vast significance of such development, both in the life of the individual as well as in that of communities, more attention should be given to the subject than is now done, although in this direction, there being insufficient scientific data on the subject, each has to work in his own way.

77. Conclusions in relation to training the will. From the above statement of Dr. Shidlovski, we arrive at the following conclusions:

First. Artificial mental development imparted at school disturbs the equilibrium existing between will-power and nervous impressionability, to which may be attributed the great number of persons with abnormally developed nerves that are to be met with among educated men. Avoiding such abnormalities, the power of developing the will so as to establish the capability of maintaining self-control under various conditions should be taught every youth—the greater the mental development, the greater attention should be turned to the development of the will-power.

Second. Man can not compel himself not to feel pain, but he may control himself to such a degree that, feeling it, he exhibits no appearance of doing so. A man can not avoid hearing the hissing of the shot flying over him, but he may train himself to such an extent that the sound does not hinder him from performing his duty, although in so doing he is called upon to exert energetic control over himself. A man can not but suffer at the sight of the wounded, but his will may force him to act under these conditions in a regular and cool manner, as if there were no such sight. One can not but feel that he is annoyed when at the time of performing any work he is constantly distracted by the questions of others, but he should accustom himself to exhibit no signs of annoyance under such conditions, for in battle a commander has to act under just such circumstances as these.

Third. In learning how to do anything, first of all every movement is performed consciously; subsequently the habit is formed of performing the work without giving a thought to it, consequently one may do one thing and think of another at the same time. It is desirable, therefore, that everything that one may be called upon to do in battle should, through frequent practice, be converted into a habit, so that it may be performed unconsciously.

Fourth. Science can not give us exact instructions as to how to train the will in every individual case, but scientific facts of science undoubtedly prove that the will may be developed to the highest limit, and to the complete subjugation of the desire of self-preservation. If a man becomes nervous he has himself to blame; he has made too little effort to control his will. In this matter, as in all others, we may take as our guiding rule the words of the Greek sage, Solon: "It is never too late."

78. *Choice of reading matter.* The development of the officer depends to a large extent upon his choice in reading. One of the great mistakes of writers of scientific educational schoolbooks is that they do not quote sufficiently authors who are authorities on the subject on which they treat, but advance each subject and proposition developed by science as if it were their own. This develops abnormal mental conditions in the scholar. Montesquieu says: "I prefer a well-made head to a very full one." If citations from the classics were presented to the student, he would acquire the necessary esteem for the discoveries that serve as the basis of the sciences themselves. If the teacher presents everything in his own words, he instructs the pupil only superficially, and leads him to regard all former productions as imperfect; he does not instill into a scholar the necessary esteem for the original, and the scholar may forever be satisfied with compilations.

Our counsel to young men is to read as much as possible from original works, and in his choice of books not to be guided so much by his interest in the subject treated upon as by the worth of the author. We mean to say that it is more instructive to read the works of a great writer, although one of a very unimportant epoch, than the works of an unimportant writer who lived in a very important epoch.

All great men have placed great importance on the study of history. Napoleon said: "Read and read over again the campaigns of Alexander, of Hannibal, of Cæsar, Augustus Adolphus, Turenne, Eugene, and Frederick; imitate them; that is the only way to become a great commander and acquire the secrets of the art of war" (Napoleon's Military Maxims, p. 79).

There is still another maxim of Napoleon in the same spirit: "If you wish to learn how to conduct battles, study 150 battles fought by great commanders."

79. *Views of General Krotkow upon how to study battles.* What has just been said may be supplemented by the advice of General Krotkow to his pupils. He considered it insufficient in studying battles to understand their general plans, and deemed it necessary to follow out all their parts—so as to penetrate to the motives actuating the commanders upon both sides. Only in this way can the study of battles afford its full share of usefulness. It is impossible to study out a number of battles very closely—a few will suffice; superficial study never produces desired results.

80. *The necessity of learning through practical experience.* Besides reading, we must acquire everything indispensable to us from life itself. It is not enough to be present at an event to derive benefit from it; we must endeavor to derive useful instruction from everything that we see.

When they told Admiral Lazarev that a certain incompetent officer had spent much time at sea, the admiral pointed to his trunk and said: "That trunk has made the voyage around the world three times, but it is a trunk still."[3]

3. Admiral M. P. Lazarev (1788–1851) was a famous scientist and Arctic and Antarctic explorer who circumnavigated the globe three times.

General Dragomirow, in one of his articles, agrees with Suvomlin's shrewd remark that the hackman who has driven 10,000 versts in St. Petersburg may not become for all that a good coachman.

Frederick the Great, in his writings, touches upon this point as follows: "To what does life serve," writes Frederick, "if it be the life of a plant; what use is it to see things only to have seen them? Vegetzie says war should be made a study (ein Studium), should be regarded as an uninterrupted exercise (eine Uebung), and he is right."

Experiments should be conducted carefully. Artists arrive at the conception of the fundamental principles (Grundbedingungen) only after careful analysis, and in moments of rest prepare new material for experiment. Such investigation constitutes the power of inquiring minds. But how rarely are such persons met; while on the other hand, how frequently do we meet those people who, possessing the use of their senses, never think of employing their minds. Reflection alone, or, to express ourselves more accurately, the power of placing our conceptions in order (to think logically) distinguishes man from the animal. The mule who had made ten campaigns with Prince Eugene was none the better tactician for it, and to the shame of man it must be admitted, in consequence of this idle stupidity (trägen Dummheit), many old (i.e., experienced) officers are not a bit better than the above-mentioned animal.[4]

Such people move when all others move, following the routine requirements of service (dem hergebrachten Schlendrian des Dienstes folgend), absorbed in the performance of their personal duties and looking for something good to eat; they move when others do; they pitch their camp when others pitch theirs; they fight when others do, and this, in the minds of many, constitutes campaigning and participation in war. Here is the source, the true reason, of existence of those masses of persons absorbed in trifles who remain in gross ig-

4. "Prince Eugene" is probably Prince Eugene of Savoy (1663–1736), a famous Austrian general in the War of the Spanish Succession.

norance of military principles, and who, instead of elevating their minds to the heavens, wallow in the dust of routine and never bother themselves to discover the reasons for their successes or failures, although such knowledge would be of the greatest value to them.

The severe rebuke which Frederick administers applies least of all to our own young officers, among whom are many constant workers—workers in the development of details; and, in fact, details are developed to the highest perfection. It would be better, however, not to study details alone, but also general aims; even when occupied in some small matters it is well to look about one from time to time. The artist at work upon his canvas turns from time to time to consider the tout ensemble, without which precaution, however good the details may be, the picture would prove a failure. It is the same with everything else.

Tactics affords the possibility of viewing the whole picture of naval operation, and not only its details; in this respect its value is beyond price.

CHAPTER FIVE

INSTRUCTION OF THE PERSONNEL AFLOAT

81. Cruising at sea in time of peace is the school for war. Let us remember, first of all, that the military fleet exists for war, and that fleet cruising, which entails such great expenditure, is performed only for the purpose of preparing the personnel for war duties; upon this assumption depends all that follows. If this circumstance be lost sight of in time of peace, then cruising does not produce desirable results. In some respects it even does harm, for the personnel acquires undesirable habits and customs, so that when war does come much has to be modified and learned over again, which is even more difficult than to teach anew. In cruising, and especially in foreign cruising, ships of war are often called upon to perform representative duties; besides this, it is necessary from time to time to permit the crews to rest from their military occupations and to give them liberty for recreation; but the chief object, which is preparedness for war, must always be kept prominently in view and must not be forgotten. The moment it is lost sight of we unavoidably enter the path of error.

The effort to realize ideal cleanliness works considerable injury to the military value of ships of war. There is no doubt that cleanliness upon shipboard is indispensable, but when exercises having for their end military efficiency begin, cleanliness and the ornamentation of paint work suffer somewhat. It is a matter of congratulation that firing exercises with guns and torpedoes are now established under such regulations that they are practiced with sufficient frequency, and it would be well if many other exercises were similarly forced on by regulations. The following are especially needed: tactical regulations relating to despatch duty, the blockade of coasts, the study of the qualities of the individual ship, and torpedo attacks; exercises in drawing of plans of fortifications while manoeuvering in time of war, etc.

It is very difficult to lay down general rules how to carry on duty on shipboard, so that each officer may be trained in the manner that tactics demands. We can only state in general terms that justice, tact, and self-control are required from the captain and his officers. Under these conditions very favorable results may be reached, if the end sought by tactics be borne constantly in mind.

82. It is necessary to learn how not to find difficulties. A matter of great importance to a young officer is to have a good example in his captain. This fact is generally recognized, and frequently, when speaking of an officer, they say he served under such or such a captain. Young men should learn from good example how not to find difficulty in any task. If a junior complains of difficulties when he receives an order, this indicates either that he did not serve under an able chief, or, if he served under an able chief, that he did not learn anything from him. The man who, having received an order, complains of the hardships of his task, makes a radical mistake in the beginning, and the sooner he is shown the proper channel the better for him. It is a significant fact that every task seems easy when its fulfilment appears to present no difficulties; work progresses smoothly under these circumstances and is accomplished satisfactorily. On the other hand, if doubt arises in the mind of him who is entrusted with its accomplishment, his powers are immediately reduced by one-half. At sea, where so much depends upon the condition of the weather, we can not apply this rule as closely as on land; it is necessary for us to allow considerable latitude to each officer entrusted with the performance of duty, but if a commanding officer remarks that the officer turns this privilege to bad use he should immediately recall the latter to a sense of his responsibilities and powers.

The author personally has always required that an officer should perform his duties intelligently, without shunning responsibility, and we remember many cases where those entrusted with the performance of difficult tasks performed feats of daring in their determination not to be thwarted. One of these cases was in the Okhotsk Sea, where Lieutenant Parominski at midnight towed eight sailing craft and pulling boats out of the river in a high wind and heavy sea, which were constantly increasing in force. The handling and towing of all these craft was far from easy, but was accomplished satisfactorily, while hardly two hours later the ship was driven towards two reefs, requiring all efforts with sail and steam to escape from the lee shore before a rising storm.

83. Opinions of various authors upon military training. In Chapter II we explained how Suvorow regarded this matter. Everyone who wishes to prepare his ship for war should follow Suvorow's advice. He should think out beforehand conditions that may occur, and give flight to his fancy in imagining various combinations of circumstances liable to arise for his command. There is no doubt that Suvorow's instructions are difficult, but Suvorow said, "Difficult to learn—easy on the march" (that is, in war), "Easy to learn—difficult on the march." (Dragomirow's Tactics, p. 40.)

Marshal Saxe is the author of the striking aphorism that "a man does in war what he is accustomed to do in time of peace." General Dragomirow says that the choice of a system of education is a tactical question. In his military notes (Morsk. Sbor., 1894, No. 4) he says:

"That which was formerly acquired by long campaigning through extended periods of service must now be acquired by a system of personal training and education, constantly pursued throughout life.

"The present is no place to expound such a system; I can only say that the fundamental idea centers in the fact that in time of peace the soldier should be acquainted with the sense of danger and be given practice in surmounting this. Under such conditions as these, manœuvers and exercises acquire importance, and without them they are but games with soldiers—very pretty, therefore much desired; nevertheless, games."

By these remarks General Dragomirow practically recommends Suvorow's system. In relation to training he reasons as follows:

"The conditions of rational training of the army: First. To teach in time of peace only that which is to be done in war. Second. To instruct progressively, so that each exercise will illustrate the purpose of some branch of training. Third. Teach more by example than by narrative.

"The scope of the soldier's training and education: First. Training; the sense of duty and subordination. Second. Education; the use of arms in conformity with movements and actions of his comrades; skill in surmounting local obstructions and in turning them to advantage for his protection, but this without interfering with the efficiency of his weapon." (Text-book of Tactics, Dragomirow, p. 33.)

On page 31 General Dragomirow says that "it is harmful to teach in time of peace anything that is useless in war," and his is the aphorism that "the more meager the instruction the grosser the soldier." He counsels us to ask ourselves the question sometimes, "What should we *not* teach the soldier?"

84. *How to apply Suvorow's system of instruction on shipboard.* The way of extending instruction afloat that most naturally suggests itself is to extend the duration of the periods allotted to the performance of routine exercises. Thoroughness in work may be greatly extended by such a method,

but there is nevertheless a corresponding loss, as readiness and those qualities that men need in war are not developed, but on the other hand are rather suppressed. It is very well to extend routine exercises for the first three or four months of the cruise, but after that other tasks should be looked for. We must remember that however varied the exercises that we perform in time of peace may be, they are in no way to be compared in variety with those that we would be called upon to perform in war. Can we count, then, upon our skill in stopping leaks, constructing booms, repairing injuries to bulkheads and steam pipes, when we have never practiced leak stopping, boom construction, or repairing injuries to pipes and bulkheads in time of peace? In fact, the usual routine exercises may develop an indifference that seems to render us less efficient in these matters. How often have we noticed torpedo boats in manœuvers firing their torpedoes in an attack at a time when they are heading in a direction from which they could not have fired at all. It used to formerly happen that guns were fired during manœuvers without sighting. Now this is almost done away with; but fire quarters and the stoppage of leaks are often conducted in an irrational manner. I once witnessed the following: An ironclad ran upon the rocks on the coast of Finland, tearing a hole in her bottom. Having been sent to this vessel by order of the commander in chief, I asked the question, "Have you put over the collision mat?" The reply was that it had been put over the side immediately, within three minutes, but that the leak had not diminished. No wonder that it had not, for they had put the mat over on the starboard side opposite bulkhead No. 8 and near the water line, whereas the injury was upon the port side opposite bulkhead No. 9, near the keel. This is the result of the performance of routine exercises without intelligent direction.

85. *We must not permit peace conditions to predominate.* The conditions of cruising at sea in time of peace are radically different from those that would obtain in war, and they may

constantly serve to incite people to perform labors which are of use only in furthering such ends as the circumstances of peace may require. This is very well shown in the anecdote of Frederick the Great's corporal, who, when he had returned to the barracks at the end of an unusually severe campaign, addressed the soldiers around him as follows: "After this you men will have to brace up. Things are not going to be as lax as they were during the campaign. Now you have got to stop your frivolity and settle down to hard work."

There is nothing more fitting, from a military standpoint, than to imitate the views of Frederick's corporal, who placed so high a value upon the peace duties of the army.

86. Practical exercises in the control of the ship. Success in battle is largely dependent upon the intelligent control of the ship, and we must study out every way to instruct officers in the manœuvering of the vessel in which they serve. First of all, we must impress upon their minds the axiom that the helm moves not in the direction of the bow, but of the stern of the ship, and that the turning point of the ship is situated well forward. Many, when beginning to direct the movements of a vessel, are not sufficiently familiar with this truth, and therefore upon entering a harbor or in navigating close waters in general they prove unsuccessful. Officers should be instructed to direct the ship so that after changing the course the vessel will remain headed in a known direction, and should not turn beyond that heading. There is nothing more useless and senseless than to allow a ship to pay off further than is necessary, and then to bring her back again to the heading required. More is said about this in paragraph 115. It is very important to impress upon the mind the idea that every vessel answers her helm badly upon shoals or in places where there is little water under the keel, and that methods that are applicable in deep water do not always apply in shallow waters. The question presents itself for consideration, in which direction does the bow of a single screw vessel turn when the engines are reversed? In still water this depends exclusively upon the direction in which the screw itself is turning. If there be a wind blowing, the bow generally pays off to leeward. If the ship draws much less water forward than aft, she will bring up with stern to wind. In this position it is easy to steady the vessel in one spot, so that if we desire to maintain her in a given heading it may be done by laying her stern to windward and giving a turn back with the engines from time to time. The author practiced this manœuver while upon the corvette *Vitiaz,* when obtaining specimens of water from the depths of the ocean for the purpose of determination of specific weights.

87. *Peculiarities of twin screws.* As a rule, twin-screw ships are capricious and do not reply promptly to the action of the helm. It often happens that the ship does not answer the helm if it be put over less than 10 degrees. Turning with the helm alone, if the helm be put over at a time when the ship happens to be paying off in the desired direction, the turn is effected readily and its first portion is a sharp curve. Under contrary conditions the turn is slow and extended. From this and other causes it is impossible to establish for twin-screw vessels that position of the helm which corresponds to a squadron radius, since it is necessary to first put the helm over and then, after four points have been covered, to so apply it that the final diameter of the turning circle may correspond to that described for a squadron. Generally speaking, it may be said that the helm of twin-screw ships is in a very unfavorable position for maintaining the ship upon its course. Twin-screw vessels steer badly, and some are inclined to attribute this irregular action to the engines; but the engines are not responsible for it. The ship is not very sensitive to change in speed of the engines themselves. The trouble lies initially in the false theory of construction of twin-screw vessels, and the introduction of a third screw is a great step in advance.

88. *In time of peace opportunities for practicing exercises useful in war must not be neglected.* Cruising affords many opportunities for exercising in manœuvering one's own vessel; but these

opportunities are frequently disregarded. Let us suppose that we desire to take a pilot on board. Usually the ship is slowed down until the engines stop, and then the engines are reversed. But why should we not reverse the engines promptly from full speed ahead? This would be very much nearer to that which we would have to do in time of battle. We are told that by so doing we would injure the engines. If this be so, let us injure them. It would be much worse if in war we went from full speed ahead to full speed astern and then wrecked them. From our own experience, if reversing the engine promptly does not cause excessive vibration, no harm is done by so doing. The pistons, cranks, and other parts are only subjected to the pressure corresponding to that of steam, and this they are designed to withstand. In the engine room it is hardly noticeable that the change is made when the engines are instantly reversed. In shallow water vibrations may become excessive, and if such vibrations are observed it may be advisable to change from full speed ahead to half speed astern or even slow speed astern. In all cases, whenever possible, progressive change in motion of machinery should be avoided. We should indicate promptly by the engine-room telegraph the change ultimately desired.

There is another objection to the unexpected stopping of the engines—the superfluous formation of steam. Such a complaint may be just. All that has to be done is to notify the engineer five minutes beforehand to close the ash-pan doors, and then the steam formed during a short delay—such as occurs in taking a pilot on board—would not be sufficient to necessitate blowing off; and if it become necessary to condense no harm would result. Such conditions would be common enough in war, and we should practice them in time of peace.

It is not unusual to hear a commanding officer say that in time of peace we should make every effort to preserve matériel; that risks are not justified by the conditions of peace cruising, but that in war we should be prepared to risk everything. This is not so. It would be hardly reasonable to attempt in war any exercise we do not practice in time of peace, and no one would risk in the presence of an enemy that which he could not make up his mind to try at other times. We have occasionally met commanding officers so cautious that they would not allow the helm to be put over suddenly or anchors to be hoisted quickly, etc. All such precautions are injurious from the tactical standpoint. The exercises that are determined upon should be performed in peace time as often as possible, for what we will not practice in peace we can not use in war.

89. Economical speed. The desire to reduce expenses compels warships constantly to maintain an economical speed entirely different from that for which their engines are built. Much could be gained, in our opinion, if auxiliary motors were placed on shipboard for economical steaming, which would result in a considerable reduction in coal consumption. Under these conditions the main engines would only be used for full speed, when they would work under the conditions for which they were primarily constructed.

90. Prolonged cruising at sea. Extended sojourns at sea are necessary to make good sailors and to accustom men to live between sky and water and to regard the sea as their home. The former cruises under sail were especially favorable to these conditions. We have for our example Nelson, who at one time did not visit the shore during a period of two years. (Jurien de La Gravière, Vol. II, p. 87.) At the present day limitations of coal expenditures sensibly decrease the time of remaining at sea. Auxiliary motors would aid the matter greatly, but until they are introduced the only way to remain at sea any length of time is to stop the engines.

Most people think that when at sea it is necessary to keep constantly under way. We do not agree with this opinion, and while in command of a squadron very frequently practiced stopping the engines for more or less extended periods of time. When engines are to be stopped the squadron must be headed so as to bring the wind abeam, and then all vessels will remain as they are placed. Different types of ships drift to leeward with different speeds, but if the line be rectified every four hours extreme dispersion will be avoided and the ships may be kept together. Torpedo boats suffer more than all other vessels under these conditions, as they roll heavily. It is preferable to bring them with the wind aft and steer before the wind after stopping the engines. Under ordinary conditions they should run up to windward every two hours, so as to keep in touch with the squadron. When ships are kept at sea at night with engines stopped, all hands may have their night's rest. This is of especial importance for the captain, who may have spent the day in performing tactical manœuvers.

91. Practical exercises in manœuvering. Our fleet instructor in evolutions, Admiral Butakov, required ships to exercise in the harbor in describing various curves about a vessel at anchor. Such manœuvers are considered useful, and in some squadrons are practiced as frequently as possible. Besides this, Admiral Butakov frequently performed manœuvers which had for their purpose the development of the seaman's eye and habit, and the establishment of rules for employment of the ram.[1] He introduced and employed ram vessels by means of which one ship could ram another without injury to either. Practical exercises in manœuvering may be divided as follows:

92. Manœuvering with one ship at will, for determining her readiness in turning at various speeds under helm alone, inclined at 10 degrees, 20 degrees, and hard over. Manœuvering with one engine stopped, or with one engine reversed with aid of helm.

1. Admiral G. I. Butakov (1820–82) authored one of the first manuals on tactics for ships with engines, titled "New Principles of Steam Tactics."

In making such manœuvers it is necessary to observe carefully, by means of watches previously compared, the rate of change of direction of the ship, and also the rate of advance of the ship, so that it may be possible to describe on a chart the route followed by the vessel, thus showing clearly the form of the curve described and the relation existing between the position of the helm and the employment of the engines.

93. *Manœuvering with one ship in relation to others at anchor.* Shallow harbors are little suited for such manœuvers with large ships, for the latter, as a general rule, answer helm and engines badly when there is but little water under their keels. Manœuvering in relation to ships at anchor consists in describing curves around each one of them and in executing turns previously determined upon. When the disposition of the ships is known, it is an easy matter, if we are familiar with the turning circle of our own ship, to decide what changes of heading may be made with the helm and when we must employ the engines.

When manœuvering in relation to ships at anchor and, in general, when in depths of less than 20 fathoms, it is well to keep the leads going and have hands stationed by the anchors.

94. *Manœuvering with one vessel in relation to another auxiliary vessel,* the latter performing evolutions previously determined upon. The method of exercise as practiced in 1877 in the "active defense" ships *Grand Duke Konstantin* and *Argonaut* may be recommended.

One of these vessels played the part of the auxiliary ship, performing evolutions previously assigned to it, and was not responsible for collision. It altered the helm and changed speed only upon a signal from the manœuvering vessel. The other manœuvered around the auxiliary, endeavoring to bring its guns to bear under favorable conditions. Such exercises may be performed progressively, practicing the simpler before the more difficult.

(*a*) The auxiliary ship assumes a speed of 10 knots, putting its helm over 10 degrees to starboard. The manœuvering ship describes an outer circle in the same direction, keeping its antagonist on a constant bearing; for example, on the bows, or else chasing it and maintaining a distance beyond torpedo range.

(*b*) The same as case (*a*), except that the auxiliary keeps its helm over 20 degrees.

(*c*) The auxiliary maintains a speed of 10 knots with the helm 10 degrees over, but the manœuvering ship describes a circle outside of the one described by the auxiliary, and while remaining beyond the range of torpedoes endeavors to hold the guns of the latter in positions unfavorable for firing.

(*d*) Same as (*c*), except that the manœuvering vessel endeavors to approach within 2 cables' lengths for torpedo practice.

95. *Manœuvering at will with two vessels* may be performed under certain limitations. To this end boundaries are laid out by lines of buoys or are determined by bearings on shore objects, and each ship remains upon its own side, so that it may have the right to perform every manœuver it desires, but not to enter into the field of action assigned to its antagonist.

96. *Manœuvering two squadrons at will.* As in the case of individual vessels, squadrons may manœuver so that one of them plays the rôle of "auxiliary," performing only such evolutions as are assigned to it by the manœuvering squadron. The manœuvering squadron is, as before, responsible for collision. The problems submitted for solution may be very varied in character, and the results of such exercises may furnish data for the determination of further evolutions. It is sometimes useful for each ship of the squadron to tow a target astern at the end of a long hawser, so that practice may be had in subcaliber firing. Last summer the author employed this method for practical firing exercises and found it very useful.

97. Exercises in evolutions. These exercises are very useful for accustoming the eye to the appearance of a moving ship; they will be discussed at length further on, under the heading of evolutions. Among those which it is desirable to practice are to be included manœuvers for surrounding and destroying an enemy's rear.

98. Conclusions in relation to ship manœuvers. In our opinion, it is indispensable to establish a progressive course in ship manœuvering. Let buoys be placed in definite arrangement and let each officer perform certain exercises—first with torpedo boats, then with light vessels, then with cruisers of certain dimensions, and finally with ironclads. In this way those whose duty it is to determine the value of individual officers in this work will be enabled to express a definite opinion upon the seamanlike qualities of each officer under instruction and to decide upon a system of recommendation for advancement upon a basis of tactical merit.

99. The study of one's own ship is a matter of the highest importance. Every means should be employed to determine the qualities of the ship and for establishing numerical tables and curves relating thereto. The following tables and curves are indispensable:

1. The relation between revolutions of engine and speed of ship.
2. The relation between revolutions and indicated horse-power.
3. The relation between speed of turning and diameter of turning circle.
4. Same in relation to the amount the helm is put over when at full speed.
5. Same for speed of 10 knots.
6. The turning circle, when the ship at a given speed puts its helm hard over and stops one engine.
7. The same, with one engine reversed.

8. Same as case 6, at 10 knots speed.

9. The same as case 7, at 10 knots speed.

10. Going full speed ahead, in how many seconds the ship loses headway when engine-room telegraph is changed to full speed astern; at the same time observe in how many seconds the engine is reversed and at what rate the ship loses headway in consequence thereof. To this end, the moment the telegraph is changed, a sector of large dimensions is thrown overboard from the stern, constructed like a log chip, and a deep-sea lead line attached thereto is paid out, the time being observed when each 10-fathom mark passes the stern.

11. After stopping the ship completely, proceed at full speed ahead and, by paying out the line attached to the sector (as described in the preceding paragraph), note the time of paying out of the 10-fathom mark, and thus determine the progressive rate of gaining headway.

12. After stopping the ship, proceed with one engine at a given number of turns (let us say sixty), put the helm over, and determine what curve the ship describes.

13. The same for full speed.

14. With the helm hard over, at the command "steady" (see terms of command, year 1890, p. 446), observe how many degrees the ship continues to pay off before proceeding in a direct course.

15. Same with the helm 20 degrees over.

16. The same, reversing one screw.

It is well to perform the above evolutions with bunkers nearly empty, half full, and filled with coal, respectively.

100. The degree of accuracy necessary to maintain in determining the qualities of a ship. The above recommended program of exercises would be an extremely extended one and much time would be required for its execution were the same degree of accuracy sought as is obtainable over a measured mile, where distances are marked out carefully by buoys. It often happens that it is not possible to perform such experiments in an accurate manner, and that they are therefore neglected altogether. However, matters may be greatly simplified if we determine our speed on steering a straight course by logs from the stern of the ship, and when turning by logs put out over the side at the end of long spars. In estimating the diameter of the turning circles we may employ the speed of the ship in turning, or we may employ range finders, by use of which the distance may be estimated from boats launched from the ship and following in its wake while the turn is being made. The above methods may be supplemented by a sketch of the ship's path taken from the masthead or from other elevated points. If circumstances will permit, we might employ Lieutenant Sim's apparatus, which will furnish us with very useful data for determining the movements of a given vessel.

101. Officers should learn how to put down upon paper the path described by their ship. When the whole program of exercises of the ship is completed, it remains to instruct officers how to describe the path followed by their ship on a given scale upon a chart. Let us assume, for instance, at 7.28 o'clock in smooth water, the ship, having a certain draft, is making 63 revolutions and steering a straight course in a given direction. Mark on the chart where she will be at 7.29. At that moment the helm is put 20 degrees aport. Where will she be at 7.30 and how will she head? The order is then given: "Steady." On what heading will she bring up and where will she be at 7.31? The helm is then put hard astarboard and the port engine is reversed. Where will she be at 7.32 and how will she head?," etc.

It is only by studying the ship in this manner and by learning to describe her course for a known combination of position of helm and turns of engine that we may make clear to ourselves the best way to use the helm and engines in battle. In the army even the subalterns are required to have a good reading knowledge of the map, and we must realize that the exact describing of the path taken by our ship is similar to the use of the war map. In what does the knowledge of seamanship consist nowadays, when sails and rigging are almost gone, if not in the exact conception of the movements of one's vessel? And this is only to be gained through the study of manœuvers such as described above.

CHAPTER SIX

ORDNANCE

102. Development. The development of ordnance is making rapid strides in advance at the present day, and improvements are being introduced affecting initial velocity, rapidity of firing, and convenience in loading.

The introduction of smokeless powder is a great step in advance, both from the ballistic as well as from the tactical standpoint. The fleet fully equipped with smokeless powder possesses a great advantage over an antagonist, and the complete change to smokeless powder for arms of all calibers is now an accomplished fact in certain fleets. This matter is of the highest importance.

The introduction of guns supplied with metallic cartridges has simplified loading and has raised its rapidity almost to its possible limit, for a 6-inch gun may now fire shot after shot at intervals of a few seconds, and we can wish for nothing better than this. A still further improvement may be made by the introduction of semiautomatic loading, where the breech is opened automatically through the effect of the recoil of the gun after each shot and the cartridge extracted. Such a system of construction has already been introduced for the 3-inch, and is very simple.

The introduction of metallic cartridge cases made way in turn for another improvement, namely, the employment of side sights so arranged that the gun captain need never leave his place, but constantly keeps the enemy covered, and the loading of the piece proceeding without his taking part therein, so that when the gun is loaded it is already sighted.

Ordinary guns may be greatly improved in the future without necessarily transforming them to the rapid-firing type. First of all, sponging must be done away with, and this is possible when smokeless powder is employed. It is only necessary to devise means of freeing the charge completely from material which smoulders in the bore after firing. To accomplish this the charge must consist of nothing but smokeless powder. While ignition charges and silk ties are employed, sponging will remain a necessity.

Besides improvements in sponging, others relating to the opening of the breech are desirable, so that it may unlock and open automatically upon discharge. There is still room for numerous improvements in other small ways, which we will not refer to here. They will be enumerated in our report upon ordnance, now in press.

103. Steam, hydraulic, and electric motors. Steam motors were employed at the time of the introduction of heavy guns, but subsequently were supplanted by hydraulic apparatus, and four years ago electric motors began to replace the hydraulic. The superiority of electric motors consists chiefly in that injuries to conductors of power are easily repaired, and therefore, for tactical reasons, it is beneficial to extend the use of electricity as far as possible.

104. What is the radius of action of guns? It is very difficult to give a categorical reply to this question. An army artillerist considers the radius of action of cannon to be the greatest distance to which their shell may be thrown. They are now introducing mounts which enable us to give guns (short ones, it is true) an angle of elevation of 45 degrees. Their radius of action is considered to be the distance to which they will throw shell when fired at this angle, for which the shell has the greatest range.

If we give guns an angle of elevation of 15 degrees, which is possible for most mounts, we shall obtain as the radius of ac-

TABLE I.
RANGE OF PROJECTILES, IN CABLE LENGTHS

CALIBER.	LENGTH OF BORE.	WEIGHT OF PRO- JECTILE.	INITIAL VELOCITY.	ANGLE OF ELEVATION.		
				5°.	10°.	15°.
Inches.	Calibers.	Pounds.	Foot. sec.			
12	40	810	2,500	36.9	56.8	69.9
12	30	810	1,870	23.9	39.6	51.1
9	35	308	2,142	26.3	40.4	50.5
8	45	214½	2,950	38.3	53.3	64
6	45	101¼	2,600	30.3	43.2	52.4
6	35	101¼	2,117	22.9	35	44
6	28	91	1,830	19.8	29.5	37.2
mm 47	(a)	3.67	2,300	16.7	25	30
mm 47	(b)	2.74 2.61 }	1,476	10.5	15.6	18.7
mm 37	(b)	1.23	1,450	9.4	14.4	17

[a] Single barrel.
[b] Five barrels.

tion of the calibers most employed by us, for the 12-inch, 40-caliber, using smokeless powder, 70 cable lengths (14,000 yards); for 6-inch, 45-caliber, 52 cable lengths (10,400 yards); for the 47-millimeter single barrel, 30 cable lengths (6,000 yards); for the 37-millimeter five-barrel, 17 cable lengths (3,400 yards).

The range table here given (Table I) for angles of elevation, 5 degrees, 10 degrees, and 15 degrees, supplies data for various tactical calculations. The quantities therein presented are only approximate for certain guns. Fig. 4 expresses these data graphically.

105. Subdivision of ranges—long, medium, short. There exists no rule by which we can distinguish long from short ranges, and in fact such a division could only be arbitrary. We propose to subdivide them by angles of elevation, as follows: One degree, elevation short; 2 1/2 degrees, medium; 5 degrees, long; 10 degrees, very long; 15 degrees, extreme. Under these assumptions we find the short range for a 12-inch 40-caliber gun to be 10 cable lengths (2,000 yards); medium

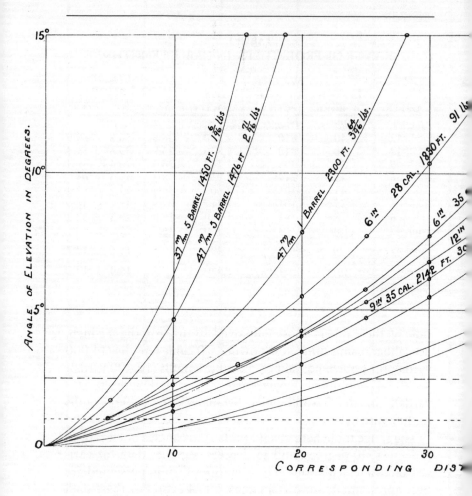

Fig. 4. Relation of distance of flight of projectile to angle of elevation.

range, 22 cable lengths (4,400 yards); long range, 37 cable lengths (7,400 yards). In applying this rule to the 6-inch 45-caliber gun, we find the short range to be 8 cable lengths (1,600 yards); medium range, 17 cable lengths (3,400 yards); long, 28 cable lengths (5,600 yards). These distinctions seem

138

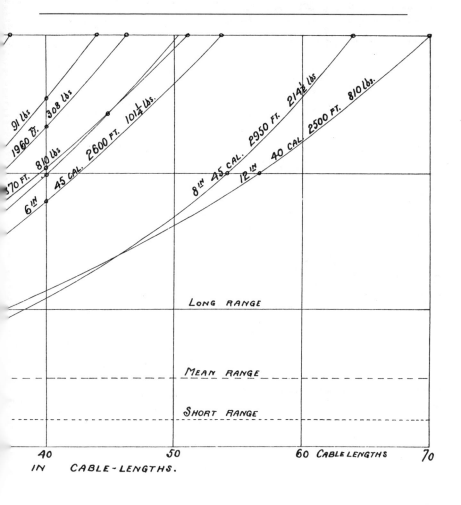

to apply equally well to the latest types of guns of medium and heavy calibers.

By the same rule the short range for the 37-millimeter is 2 1/4 cable lengths (450 yards); the medium, 5 1/2 cable lengths (1,100 yards); and the long, 9 cable lengths (1,800

TABLE II.
DIMINUTION IN VELOCITY OF PROJECTILES:
VELOCITY IN FOOT-SECONDS AT INTERVALS OF 5 CABLE LENGTHS.

CALIBER (INCHES)	LENGTH OF BORE (CALIBERS)	WEIGHT OF PROJECTILE (POUNDS)	INITIAL VELOCITY (FOOT-SECONDS)	CABLE LENGTHS.											
				5	10	15	20	25	30	35	40	45	50	55	60
12	40	810	2,500	.....	2,163	.....	1,906	.....	1,704	.....	1,540	.....	1,406	.....	1,299
12	35	810	2,090	1,934	1,788	1,655	1,526	1,412	1,316	1,235	1,163	1,111	1,076	1,051	.....
12	30	810	1,870	1,724	1,590	1,466	1,356	1,265	1,191	1,134	1,089	1,056	1,032	.....	.....
11	(a)	540	1,560	1,408	1,278	1,175	1,099	1,039	995	964	946	932	.....	.....	.....
10	45	550	2,400	.....	2,070	.....	1,821	.....	1,624	.....	1,467	.....	1,336	.....	1,127
9	35	308	2,142	1,908	1,700	1,516	1,354	1,222	1,124	1,056	1,008	976	952	.....	.....
9	30	308	1,960	1,749	1,555	1,390	1,247	1,141	1,068	1,014	978	958	.....	.....	.....
8	45	214½	2,950	2,634	2,338	2,068	1,820	1,598	1,404	1,244	1,131	1,052	1,008	974	950
8	35	191½	2,270	1,899	1,606	1,391	1,240	1,123	1,041	984	940	908	.....	.....	.....
8	30	191½	2,040	1,745	1,492	1,302	1,165	1,062	990	939	903	.....	.....	.....	.....
6	45	101¼	2,600	2,251	1,934	1,654	1,416	1,229	1,098	1,016	964	924	895	870	845
6	35	101¼	2,117	1,815	1,543	1,324	1,160	1,058	997	956	929	907	893	.....	.....
6	35	91	2,165	1,818	1,522	1,291	1,125	1,022	957	919	896	880	871	.....	.....
6	28	91	1,830	1,539	1,298	1,128	1,022	950	897	859	830	814	.....	.....	.....
4.7	.....	50	2,700	2,270	1,867	1,532	1,269	1,096	994	927	880	846	.....	.....	.....
b47	(c)	3.67	2,300	1,532	1,082	890	775	692	.....	.....	.....	.....	.....	.....	.....
b47	(d)	{ 2.74 / 2.61 }	} 1,476	.....	.....	.....	.....	.....	.....	.....	.....	.....	.....	.....	.....
b37	(d)	1.23	1,450	896	685	541	.....	.....	.....	.....	.....	.....	.....	.....	.....

[a] Model of 1877.
[b] Millimeters.
[c] Single barrel.
[d] Five barrels.

yards). These latter figures are reasonable and correspond to general conceptions.

106. Residual velocities. The penetration of armor depends upon residual velocity at moment of impact, and therefore Table II, presenting residual velocities for guns of various calibers, is of great tactical importance. This table shows that a shell thrown from a 12-inch gun with an initial velocity of 2,500 feet per second loses at first about 1.3 per cent for each cable's length traversed, and subsequently 1 per cent; and that a 6-inch shell loses from 1.6 to 1.2 per cent. After traversing a distance of 60 cable lengths (12,000 yards), the 6-inch projectile, possessing originally a velocity of 2,600 feet, retains only 845 feet, and the 12-inch, 1,290 feet. This shows at what a rapid rate velocity decreases. At this range the 12-inch shell could only penetrate armor one-half as thick as that which it could pierce at the muzzle.

107. Penetration of armor. Roughly speaking, the thickness of armor capable of penetration by projectiles is proportional to velocity of projectile at the moment of impact. The following table supplies data for general calculations, and is developed according to the formula $b = 1,462 \ v \ \sqrt{p/d}$. Table III shows the thickness of iron plate that may be penetrated. To apply this to other kinds of armor, we must multiply the quantity given in Table III by the corresponding coefficient, as follows:

	Per cent.
Steel-iron armor	87
Ordinary steel armor	85
Steel armor, high grade	73
Nickel-steel armor	60
Harveyized nickel-steel armor against armor-piercing shell with Admiral Makarov's magnetic cap	60
Harveyized nickel-steel armor against same shell without cap	45

141

TABLE III.

PENETRATION OF IRON PLATES (IN INCHES) BY GUNS OF FOLLOWING CALIBER, WEIGHT OF PROJECTILE, AND VELOCITY OF PROJECTILE AT IMPACT.

VELOCITY OF PROJECTILE AT IMPACT (FOOT-SECONDS).	CALIBER AND WEIGHT OF PROJECTILE.			
	12-INCH, 810 POUNDS.	9-INCH, 308 POUNDS.	8-INCH, 214½ POUNDS.	6-INCH, 101 POUNDS.
2,300	27.6	19.7	17.4	13.8
2,250	27.0	19.3	17.0	13.5
2,200	26.4	18.8	16.7	13.2
2,150	25.8	18.4	16.3	12.9
2,100	25.2	18.0	15.9	12.6
2,050	24.6	17.5	15.5	12.3
2,000	24.0	17.1	15.1	12.0
1,950	23.4	16.7	14.8	11.7
1,900	22.8	16.3	14.4	11.4
1,850	22.2	15.8	14.0	11.1
1,800	21.6	15.4	13.6	10.8
1,750	21.0	15.0	13.3	10.5
1,700	20.4	14.5	12.9	10.2
1,650	19.8	14.1	12.5	9.9
1,600	19.2	13.7	12.1	9.5
1,550	18.6	13.3	11.7	9.1
1,500	18.0	12.8	11.4	8.8
1,450	17.4	12.4	11.0	8.4
1,400	16.8	12.0	10.6	8.0

It is to be hoped that experts will prepare a similar but more accurate table for all calibers. Such tables are greatly needed for tactical estimates.

108. Accuracy of fire. Every gun nowadays has such precision of fire that if it be badly laid it is certain that the shell will not strike the target. The chief aim in artillery instruction is to teach men how to lay guns accurately, and no means should be neglected to bring this matter to the highest state of perfection. Courses for instruction are carefully laid out, and it only remains for us to impress others with their great importance. Of what use are our guns if shells do not strike the enemy?

109. Reserving fire. It has become possible nowadays to increase rapidity of firing to such an extent as to run the risk of wasting a greater number of shells than is desirable. This increased rapidity of fire is an advantage which we may employ when we approach to point-blank range, but at long range it is advisable to reserve the fire of the rapid-fire guns so that at the critical moment the ship may not be found short of ammunition and with crew completely worn out with fatigue. In the matter of reserving fire of rapid-fire guns, it is possible either to diminish the fire of the whole battery or else to allow one rapid-fire gun to do all the firing, and then transfer the firing to another weapon when the crew of the former becomes exhausted. We are inclined to consider the latter method preferable, as it enables us to observe the fall of each shot and constantly correct the aim. It accustoms the crews to rapid firing, and saves the strength of the other guns' crews. In time of war the men may lie down and remain covered, and the services of the most expert gun captains may constantly be made use of. It would be very interesting to determine the relative value of these methods by experiment. All that it would cost would be a few hundred shots in excess of those expended in regular firing practice.

110. Projectiles. Great improvements have recently been effected in the manufacture of projectiles. We can not but be astonished at the development of shells of such durability that they will rebound from unbroken armor when striking with an impact velocity of more than 2,000 foot-seconds.

Many improvements have also been effected in the fuses of projectiles. It is desirable that the projectile, of whatever caliber it may be, may burst upon penetrating an obstacle (in case it is able to effect penetration), whether the obstacle be thin or thick plate armor. Present types of fuses are usually set upon introduction of the projectiles into the bore, and burst either upon impact or else after some delay. It may happen that upon piercing thin armor a large shell encounters but a slight resistance, and the explosion occurs only after it has passed entirely through the obstacle and gone beyond. This would probably take place when a 12-inch shell strikes a smokestack of a torpedo boat.

In order that projectiles may burst more regularly, fuses should be so designed that they may be set, primarily, upon introduction into the bore of the gun; secondarily, upon impact; and that they may burst subsequently, after their velocity has been reduced a definite amount by obstruction. Under these conditions the shell would penetrate both a thick and a thin plate and the coal included between them, and would burst subsequently.

Upon striking earthworks, such a shell would explode when it came to rest. Upon impact upon water, it would burst on the ricochet. If it struck the side below the water line, it would pass through the water and plating and then explode.

It is to be desired that technical experts should give their attention to this problem, which is of considerable importance from a tactical point of view.

111. Choice of projectiles for use in battle. Five kinds of projectiles are used in our navy—armor-piercing, semi-armor-piercing, common cast-iron, shrapnel, and canister. With the exception of canister, all other shells contain bursting charges, but naturally the bursting effect of the semi-armor-piercing shells is much greater than that of the armor-piercing. In an attack upon earthworks the semi-armor-piercing shells should be used; while against unarmored ships common shell and shrapnel should be employed.

In an attack upon an ironclad possessing no unarmored superstructures (monitors), armor-piercing shells should be used exclusively; but when opposing battleships of modern type, which present large unarmored surfaces, both kinds of shells may be employed. Some guns should be loaded with

144

armor-piercing and others with semi-armor-piercing shells. When semi-armor-piercing shells strike armor, they do not pierce it, but when they strike unarmored parts they do more injury than the armor piercing. If an antagonist possesses no thin armor, but only heavy plates, our medium-caliber guns, which are unable to pierce thick armor, should be loaded exclusively with semi-armor-piercing shells.

Captain Yenish recommends the employment of uncharged shells for raking fire. He states that a shell will do much more harm if it passes unbroken through the whole length of the ship, and then on account of its angle of fall it may penetrate to the engines and boilers. There is much deep sense in this remark, and we ourselves think that raking fire should be with unloaded projectiles. The question arises, how forsee that we shall have a chance for raking fire? If our antagonist so manœuvers as to constantly head bows-on to us, the difficulty disappears.

Shells may explode upon impact against water. Is this to be considered a desirable or an undesirable quality? We think it rather desirable than otherwise, for if the shell falls a little short it is more probable that the ship will be struck with the flying fragments than that it would be with the whole shell. When opposing torpedo boats with guns of medium caliber, it may be an advantage in this case to fire a little short.

112. Light guns. When choice of light guns was originally made the limit was set at 37 millimeters. This caliber is about the least from which loaded shells can be fired, and was considered ample for opposing torpedo boats; but as larger-sized torpedo boats were introduced, provided with heavier plating and with Whitehead torpedoes, the 37-millimeter gun was found insufficient and the desire became manifest to change to the 47-millimeter single-barrel gun. We are not fully convinced that this change is a rational one, for the reason that automatic Maxim guns of 37-millimeter caliber are now manufactured, while the type is not yet developed for a caliber as high as 47 millimeters. We consider it highly desirable that the automatic principle be extended to all small-caliber guns. All who have witnessed the competitive trials of ordinary guns against the automatic have become convinced of the greater efficiency of the latter. The marksman need never turn his attention away from the sights, which results in a great gain in accuracy of firing, while the officers standing near by may, by following the spray thrown up by the shell, give the necessary orders for correcting the accuracy of delivery.

As far as concerns rapidity, automatic guns almost reach the possible limit, for with them we can fire from a single barrel 240 bursting shells per minute. More than this can not be desired. Automatic guns possess one marked advantage, which is, the shots succeed one another at regular intervals of time, which rather tends to calm than to excite the nerves. The effect of the ordinary firing of light guns is very much the opposite to this, and one needs to have very good control over himself who can stand in the midst of a group of four or five of such guns and not experience any inconvenience therefrom.

The 37-millimeter automatic guns have not yet been generally adopted in the various navies, for the reason that everyone is dissatisfied with the 37-millimeter caliber and is in favor of the 47 and 57 millimeter types. It is natural that the larger the caliber the more powerful the effect, but it does not follow therefrom that we should put 47-millimeter guns in places where the 37-millimeter would answer. The question is one of weight, but for the given weight we can carry three times more 37-millimeter cartridges than 47-millimeter.

It is desirable that the caliber should not be increased, but that the velocity for the 37-millimeter gun should be raised from 2,500 to 3,000 feet, and then this caliber will be ample for the required purposes.

113. Mitrailleuses. The automatic principle has been applied to gun barrels firing small army cartridges, and in many navies it is the custom to mount mitrailleuses in the tops.

There is no doubt that one mitrailleuse is better than ten marksmen, but in the army such weapons have been discarded for the reason that the point of fall can not be observed, and therefore it is impossible to rectify the fire. Such an inconvenience might also arise at sea.

Experience in war and deductions from experiment supply a rational answer to the question as to the limit to which mitrailleuses may be employed to advantage. We ourselves are inclined to declare in favor of them rather than against them, as they embody the principle of automatic fire and require from the gun's crew no work except sighting. This is the limit to which perfection in development of artillery can be carried. Much money has been spent in our navy in developing types of automatic guns. Now that the proper type has been found and the desired end attained, we should not hesitate in our progress, but should continue to advance.

114. The influence of steadiness of ship upon accuracy of artillery fire. The manœuvering of the vessel has a great influence upon the accuracy and rapidity of fire. If the firing ship constantly continues to turn, now to the right, now to the left, in relation to the position of its opponent, the aiming of guns becomes a difficult task and accuracy suffers greatly. The turning of the ship not only renders pointing in a horizontal plane more difficult, but it also affects the accuracy of pointing in the vertical plane, for in each change of position with the helm the ship alters its heel, and, as the marksman does not know when the helm is to be put over, it is impossible for him to foresee these changes, which momentarily throw out the elevation of the sight-bar. The best results in firing are obtained by holding the antagonist on a constant bearing; then the guns do not have to be sighted over again. All that there is to do is to correct the old elevation, and in this way we avoid in squadron action the very dangerous risk of firing on our own ships, and firing is continued in such a way as to occasion no loss of time in trying to pick out an enemy by peering

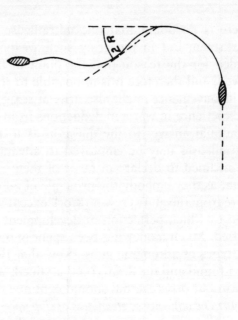

PATH OF THE SHIP WHEN, WITH THE HELM HARD OVER,
THE ORDER IS GIVEN:—

"MEET HER!"   "STEADY SO!"

2 R

Fig. 5.

through a narrow porthole and looking carefully to see that the ship aimed at is not one of our own vessels.

It is of the highest importance to employ every method to keep the enemy on the desired bearing, and this should be practiced as frequently as possible. If your ship is badly steered it is useless to count upon accuracy of fire. This obstacle diminishes by about one half the number of shells striking the antagonist.

115. Instruction in control of helm. It is to be assumed that in war, and especially in a general engagement, when ships will have to turn frequently to the right and to the left, there will probably be only three orders given, "starboard," "port," and "steady." In former times "steady" was equivalent in meaning to steady and ahead upon the course on which the ship steadies herself. The modern term of command "steady" signifies to proceed on that course upon which the ship is heading at the time the order is given. The difference is that by the first method the ship having stopped paying off proceeds on a direct course. In the second it pays off two or three points and is then brought up again to the required heading by use of the helm, so that the ship moves sinuously until it is finally steadied (fig. 5). There is a way of avoiding this, however, by giving, instead of the order "steady," the order "meet her." In accordance with this command (par. 446, Terms of Command), the helmsman should steady the ship and steer on that course on which she is steadied.

The commanding officer should give the order "meet her" in sufficient time for the helmsman to steady the vessel on the required heading and the helmsman should learn how to hold the vessel upon the exact course and not deviate therefrom. Carelessness in observing these precautions seriously impairs accuracy of fire.

116. The effect of vibration of the ship, due to movements of engines, upon accuracy of fire. The ship must be studied in this respect so as to determine the number of revolutions for which vibration and general shaking of the hull exercise the most injurious effect upon the sighting of the guns and thus diminish the accuracy of fire. The greatest vibration does not correspond to the same number of turns for all draughts in the same ship, and therefore this phenomenon must be studied under conditions presented with different quantities of coal in the bunkers.

For illustrating the effect of vibration of hull upon accuracy, besides direct observations, it is useful to make notes upon the indications of instruments placed in various parts of the ship. In the absence of such instruments, glasses filled with water may sometimes be employed, placed upon the gun platforms or near them. The engines are then given a certain number of turns, and the amount of water spilled out of each glass is noticed. Such experiments are very simple, but in spite of their primitiveness they afford results that are of more value than simple personal observation.

That speed for which hull vibration exercises the most unfavorable effect upon the accuracy of fire should be recognized as unsuitable for firing and should be avoided as far as the circumstances of battle will permit this to be done.

Some engine builders have been able to place the various moving parts of engines so that they produce no hull vibrations. All such improvements should be recognized as of the highest importance from a tactical point of view. Twin screws develop vibratory synchronisms of very marked effect. There is also a certain position of the cranks of one engine in relation to those of another for which vibration is reduced to the minimum. Designers of machinery, bearing this in mind, should require that the heavy moving parts of one engine should be in a given position relative to those of the other. Electricity has recently been widely employed by artillerists for ordnance uses, but has not yet been employed for governing the movements of the propelling machinery, yet its use would lead to the development of many appliances which, from a military standpoint, seem indispensable. Vibration at high speed in some small ships greatly impedes accuracy of fire.

117. The influence of sunlight. Sunlight may exercise a great influence when the sun is near the horizon. If the ship occupies such a position that its shadow falls in the direction of the enemy, it possesses a tactical advantage in points of determination of distances and accuracy of sighting, since, under these conditions, the enemy is seen comparatively clearly, while the observing ship turns to the enemy its dark side, and at the same time the sun prevents the enemy from estimating distances and aiming well. Such an influence of sunlight may be considerable if the sun remains a long time at a low altitude, as frequently happens in high latitudes. In action against fortifications on shore, where the fleet may choose its own time for attack, the tactical advantages resulting from choice of condition of sunlight are considerable. In a battle between ships, that vessel which is superior in speed can occupy a desired position with respect to the sun as against an enemy, and can hold the enemy in that position, even if the latter makes efforts to escape therefrom.

118. The influence of smoke upon accuracy of fire. We must distinguish between gunpowder smoke and the smoke, or more properly the gases, of smokeless powder. Our smoke has a more injurious effect upon the firing from our own ship than upon that of our antagonist, for when the side of the ship becomes obscured it is impossible to lay the guns, while our antagonist can always see some part of our vessel, upon which he fires and at which he may aim.

When the firing ship is not under way the most unfavorable conditions in relation to smoke are those of calm weather. When under way, the most unfavorable conditions are those of a light, following wind, when the smoke follows along with the ship. It sometimes happens in manœuvers, even when firing with reduced charges, that after one volley the smoke exercises such an obscuring effect that it becomes impossible to see not only the decks but also the course which the ship is steering.

Wind abeam from the direction of the firing side clears away smoke more quickly than the wind from the contrary direction, for in the first case the smoke immediately arises above the firing vessel and clears its field of vision, while in the second case the smoke is held in the eddy, where it may remain for a very long time. Some think that a leeward position is more disadvantageous, as the smoke of the antagonist then obscures our ship; but, however small it may be, the interval between ships must always be greater than the length of a vessel itself, and smoke generally disperses while traversing this space.

If we imagine a case where the smoke of the antagonist moves directly in our direction, then, inasmuch as the smoke grows thinner as it advances, it will be worse for our antagonist than for ourselves. From the above cases, as far as black or brown powder is concerned, the leeward position is more advantageous than the windward. Nelson preferred the leeward, although in doing this he emphasized his desire not to allow his enemy to run away.

Gases of smokeless powder do not diminish the visibility of the antagonist, and are injurious only for the reason that they exercise a toxic effect upon the crew. In firing smokeless powder the windward position is to be preferred to the leeward, so that the gases developed may not penetrate to the inner portions of our ship. Much used to be said of the toxic effect of these gases, but recently this matter has been dropped. Is not this change of opinion due to the fact that no one has taken the trouble to fire as great a number of rounds as would be fired in battle?

It must be borne in mind that the smoke of ordinary powder is extremely difficult to pierce with search-light beams, and therefore in night firing, when the smoke falls upon the target, rapidity of firing is diminished and, after a few shots, firing must be suspended. From this arises a tactical advantage for torpedo boats. If the antagonist does not use smokeless powder, it is better to approach him from leeward than windward.

119. Should firing be conducted by broadside or in succession. The question as to whether broadsides or firing in succession should be employed in battle is yet undecided. Some naval writers consider broadside firing impossible in action. Others divide firing into broadside and by succession, the former to be employed in a general engagement, the latter in single combat. Many experienced officers think, however, that there is a great risk in firing by broadside, for the failure of one shell to hit is of but little consequence, while inaccuracy of aim of the broadside renders useless the firing of the whole vessel. The advantages of firing by broadsides are the following:

First. Firing may be fully controlled and directed as desired. Second. The effect of smoke is much less injurious than in single firing. There is less risk in firing upon one's own ships.

The disadvantages of firing by broadsides are as follows:

First. If the officer at the indicator is nervous and liable to make mistakes, the whole firing is harmless to the enemy. Second. If electric conductors are injured, broadside firing becomes impossible, and before the conductors can be repaired valuable time may be lost.

To the advantages of individual firing may be added the fact that the gun captains take part in this practice. On the other hand, this firing requires careful supervision on the part of the division officers, so that the gun captains lay their guns accurately and do not fire on their own ships. The ship firing broadsides produces a deep impression, which can not but have its effects upon the morale of an antagonist. In military operations on land, as long as broadsides are heard one may remain convinced that matters are proceeding in a regular manner; but when irregular firing begins, the doubt arises whether some part of the force is not shattered. Broadsides in naval actions produce the same effects. When we see losses upon our own vessel and hear the broadsides of an antagonist, it seems to us that his losses are nothing, and this must have its effect upon the spirits of the men.

Personally, we are rather inclined to broadside firing; but if in war the conduct of this firing falls to the lot of a nervous officer, there should be no hesitancy in transferring the marksmanship to the gun captains. Under such conditions the latter method of firing would give better results, for, although some of the gun captains would aim badly, others would aim well, and general results would average fairly well, while volley firing under these conditions would prove altogether unfavorable. If, on the other hand, the practice of broadside firing be conducted by a cool and steady officer, the results may be valuable in the highest degree.

120. Choice of distance for battle. If both antagonists are perfectly free, the position being where shore or shoal does not impede the movements of the ships, choice of distance belongs to the vessel which under given conditions develops the greater speed. If the ship possessing the greater speed determines the position of its antagonist, it follows that it also determines the kind of combat—that is, whether with guns or with guns and torpedoes. It also determines the time of battle, for such a ship may refuse to fight, if it so desires, or may defer the engagement to a more favorable time of day or weather, or may attack its antagonist at once. From this we may perceive what a tremendous significance, from a tactical point of view, superiority in speed has, especially if such superiority can be preserved for all conditions of the sea.

The ship that possesses superiority in speed is not always able, however, to control the distance. Thus, if it is held by an antagonist in a confined position, from which there is but one exit, it will be forced, upon escaping therefrom, to surrender control of distance for a short time. Also, if the ship possessing superiority in speed is performing service (such as convoying transports, etc.), then the choice of distance will not depend wholly upon itself, although it still possesses great advantages from its superior speed.

History affords us examples of how choice of distance in a single combat promotes success in action. Thus in the battle between the British frigate *Seahorse* and the American frigates *Constitution* and *United States,* and also, as Berezim states in his Naval Tactics (p. 171), "in all other battles fought between American and English cruisers at that time," the advantages of cautious approach to an antagonist and careful choice of distance are in favor of the side possessing the heaviest ordnance.

In a battle between armored and unarmored ships the armor may prove impenetrable to the guns of the unarmored antagonist at chosen range, while, as far as the unarmored ships are concerned, the greater the distance the greater the danger of injury, for the longer the range the more danger to be apprehended from the fall of shells, which from their angle of fall may easily penetrate into the vital unprotected portions of the vessel. It may be stated in general terms that short ranges are more favorable for unarmored ships or those having only armored decks and guns of small calibers. The smaller the ship the greater reason for approaching an antagonist; but, as small vessels generally possess high speed, the initiative in single combat belongs to them rather than large ships. Consequently, when two vessels meet, the smaller ship may either decline battle or become the aggressor. In what concerns torpedoes, short range is also favorable for small vessels. Therefore, it may be stated in general terms that if a small ship determines to fight, the sooner it closes with its antagonist the better.

121. Firing at maximum ranges. If our guns can be fired at longer ranges than those of our antagonist and if we command the distance, the question arises, is it advisable for us to select that distance at which our shells will just reach our antagonist and at which his can not reach us? This distance would be from 50 to 60 cable lengths; that is, very great; consequently it would be extremely difficult to hit the enemy; but it must be borne in mind that if we actually succeeded in keeping beyond the radius of action of an antagonist we suffer no loss, and nothing hinders us, if there be no roll, from firing as accurately as at target practice, determining our distance exactly and correcting the same by the fall of our shells.

Defensive tactics in such a case should count in impairing the accuracy of the enemy's fire by constantly changing the distance from him. It must be borne in mind that it is difficult to determine at long range whether his ship is approaching us or moving away from us, therefore our antagonist should constantly change his course, put his helm over so as to turn first eight points in one direction, then eight points in another. The enemy will consider that the ship on the defensive intends to change his course sixteen points, and he will also change until convinced of his error, when he will be so close that he will enter into the area of action of his antagonist's guns, which is what the latter desires.

122. Choice of bearing in relation to angle of fire. The choice of that bearing on which it is most desirable to hold an antagonist depends upon the position of our guns and armor. In what relates to guns the most favorable bearing is that on which the greatest number of guns can be brought into use. The most suitable angle under these conditions for ships with two turrets placed in the fore-and-aft plane is the sector included between the extreme train aft of the guns of the forward turret and the extreme train forward of the guns of the after turret. The most favorable firing sector for broadside ships is that included between the train of the after guns forward and of the forward guns aft. Ordinarily this sector

156

covers an arc of from 45 to 135 degrees [from broad off the bow to broad off the quarter]. The type of ship with one or two turrets is a very common one, so that in most cases the firing sector will be as above indicated.

123. *Choice of bearing in relation to armor.* Our ship must be placed in such a position that our antagonist may have the least chance of hitting us, so that his shells may do us the least injury. The target presented by the ship is smallest when bows-on to the enemy, but errors in firing are more commonly made in the vertical than in the horizontal direction. This is due to our lack of knowledge of the distance from our antagonist, which becomes a serious consideration at long ranges. The length of modern ships is sometimes as great as three-quarters of a cable's length. Therefore, in relation to the elevation of the sight bar, if a mistake of a cable's length is made when the enemy is bows-on us we are able to strike him, while if his position be at right angles to the line of fire a mistake on our part of one-quarter to one-half of a cable's length results in a miss. In view of this, it is advisable to place our ship broadside to an antagonist.

In what concerns injury caused by projectiles, the position bows-on to the line of fire is less favorable than the broadside position, for the shell on its flight in the direction of the length of the vessel may do more injury than striking her broadside. Raking fire always used to be considered the most injurious, and must be held in the same estimation to-day.

Broadside fire does less injury, but under these circumstances the maximum amount of armor is placed in the position normal to line of fire of the enemy, and consequently is unfavorably situated for resistance. In this respect raking fire also has a disadvantage, for the thwartship armor is then placed normally to the direction of the flight of the enemy's projectiles.

Notwithstanding the above, the bow toward the enemy is considered in some naval fleets as the most advantageous for battle, and it is recommended upon the sight of an enemy to turn toward him, bows-on, and to hold this position. This is equivalent to maintaining an angle of bearing equal to zero [enemy dead ahead], and the question of control of the position of the ship is greatly simplified. Such a position possesses great advantages. In squadron action it results in the disadvantageous bows-on formation and can not be practiced in column.

We ourselves thought it was best to attack from the bows-on position when we prepared our paper in 1886, "In Defense of Old Ironclads with Modern Improvements" (Morsk. Sbor., 1886, Nos. 2 and 3). At present we consider that the bows-on position possesses great advantages, but the danger of raking fire compels us to conclude that the bearing of from 45 to 135 degrees, for which armor is placed at an oblique angle in respect to the position of the antagonist, but for which both turret and broadside guns may be brought to bear, possesses the greatest tactical advantages (fig. 6).

124. *Choice of course in relation to roll.* Rolling may exercise the most injurious effect on firing from two causes—heeling of the ship and the pouring of water and spray into ports and gun embrasures. As far as concerns spray and sea, it is more advantageous to be to the windward of an antagonist. In relation to roll, it is best to take the position where our ship rolls the least. If our ship is pursued in chase, we must bear in mind our antagonist's rolls as well as our own, and endeavor to occupy that position in relation to the sea in which our ship will be most steady and our antagonist most unsteady. It must be borne in mind that the steady ship heels most with the wind abeam and the unsteady ship frequently rolls most with the wind on the quarter or when before the wind. Knowing our ship and the type of our opponent, we must promptly decide which course is most favorable for us and unfavorable to him.

125. *Choice of course in a sea way when pursued by a powerful enemy.* If upon meeting an enemy our ship proves consider-

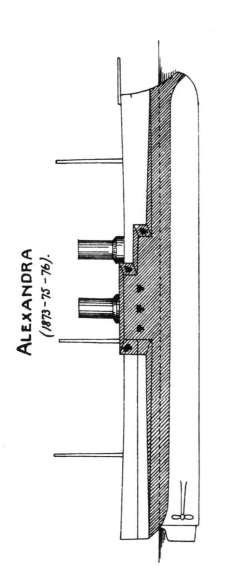

ALEXANDRA
(1873-75-76).

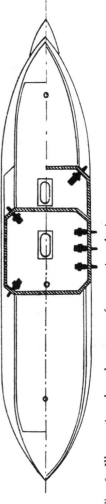

Fig. 6. Illustrating the advantage of course in relation to armor.

SHORT RANGE.

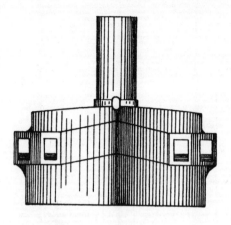
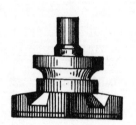

LONG RANGE.

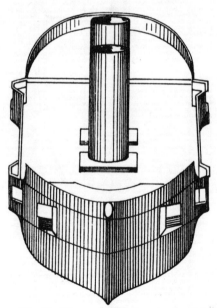
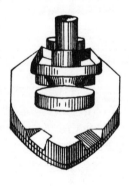

Fig. 7. View of ship for angle of fall of projectile.

ably weaker in battery, or if, having a special mission, we decide to decline combat, the question arises, what course should we choose so as to bring our guns to bear under the most favorable circumstances? There may be many reasons which would decide us to choose one direction or another; a small vessel, especially, may be anxious to approach one of its own ports or to join its squadron. If, however, there are no such reasons, it is best to take the windward course, and then our stern guns are protected from wind and spray, and may be brought to bear under the most favorable circumstances, while the bow guns of our antagonist will suffer from spray and finally may, for a time, be put altogether out of action.

Every hit that we succeed in making will render the progress of the antagonist who has the wind ahead more difficult. All this affords a great advantage, and therefore a greater chance of success. Under these circumstances the chasing ship, becoming convinced of the undesirability of its position, will endeavor to assume a course in another direction by taking advantage of its superior speed to head off the chase, who is compelled to change his course and sacrifice the advantage afforded by wind and sea. But there is a good deal of time lost in all this, and the approach of nightfall, etc., may render circumstances more favorable.

126. Where to aim. At long ranges we should aim with all guns at the center of the visible target presented by the ship. In fore and aft firing we should aim a little above the center of the figure presented by the vessel, for under the conditions of the angle of fall of the shell the actual target is as represented in fig. 7. In very short ranges we would advise firing, not at the ship as a whole, but at various objects; such as, for guns firing armor-piercing shells, at turrets or armored casemates; while guns firing semi-armor-piercing shells should aim at the unarmored extremities of the ship, endeavoring to pierce them near the water line. Light artillery may be aimed at the bridges, tops, and superstructures.

CHAPTER SEVEN

TORPEDOES

127. General review of torpedo warfare. Since the time of the discovery of the Whitehead torpedo all other torpedoes have been gradually withdrawn from general use, so that the Whitehead remains to-day as a single type of offensive weapon. This torpedo has been constantly undergoing perfection in a progressive manner, and has been improved by increasing its speed, by enlarging its supply of air, and increasing its bursting charge.

The first type of torpedo (1876) possessed reservoirs 6.4 cubic feet capacity and developed a speed at short range (400 yards) of 22 knots, with an explosive charge of 75 pounds. Later types (1894) were provided with reservoirs containing 9.5 cubic feet and possessed a speed of 26.75 knots (for 600 yards) and carried an explosive charge of 200 pounds. The increase in charges led to the adoption of blunt torpedoes. This circumstance is to be regretted, inasmuch as upon impact at a very oblique angle the torpedo may not explode, as will be described later.

The following changes have been made in torpedo-projecting apparatus. Primarily, submarine discharging tubes were employed in which air was made to force water, which in turn ejected the torpedo. This apparatus was very cumbrous, so that when above-water tubes appeared they were generally adopted. Improvements in this device, in virtue of which the torpedo developed no latent deviation upon discharge, still further extended their use, but nevertheless there is a tendency at the present time to revert to former types. The motive for this change is that torpedoes placed above the water line are in danger of being struck by the enemy's shells, which may cause explosion of their war heads and reservoirs. Submerged apparatus has been improved by the substitution of water impulse for air impulse, and by the employment of shields which permit the firing of the torpedo in the direction of the beam. Above-water tubes placed in broadside are capable of being trained in a desired direction. Stern tubes, and in general all bow tubes, are fixed. Submerged tubes are all fixed in position. In consequence of this, each ship possesses a dead angle through which air torpedoes may not be fired. This is about the way matters stand in relation to torpedoes at the present day.

128. *Inconveniences arising from the absence of all-around fire.* The absence of all-around torpedo fire is a great tactical deficiency, chiefly for the reason that in order to fire torpedoes the ship has to be placed in a certain position. On the other hand, in fleet engagements the commanding officer must make efforts to preserve his place in formation, while in a single combat he must manœuver, not for torpedoes alone but holding all means of attack in view, so that there will be intervals of time in which he will not be able to fire his torpedoes, although his antagonist may have come within their radius of action.

These are disadvantages which arise from the absence of all-around fire. Let us suppose that our antagonist has injured his engines and we wish to ram him. As we know that his bow and stern tubes are immovable, and that his broadside tubes possess but a small angle of train, especially toward the bow, we may ram him by approaching at an angle of from 30 to 40 degrees from the line of his keel, measuring from foward, without risk of being torpedoed by him. If an all-around fire were possible, a ship with injured machinery would be protected from ramming attack upon all sides.

If under-water broadside tubes permitting all-around torpedo fire were invented, we would declare in favor of submerged apparatus; but as such devices have not yet appeared, all-around firing may only be effected by means of above-water tubes.

It is an interesting question whether the results of an explosion of a charged war-head on shipboard would prove as disastrous as to require a veto to be placed upon all above-water apparatus. We had a case of explosion of an air reservoir upon the cruiser *Pamyat Azova* and the explosion of a gun-cotton torpedo upon a popovka, and both produced only insignificant local damage, the ships remaining intact.[1] If we fear the effects of an explosion of war-heads and reservoirs we must so install torpedo tubes that they are partly mounted outside of the protecting walls of the ship, and then danger will be reduced to a minimum.

In reply to the objections that the torpedo-charging apparatus may be injured at the first shot, we may cite an example in the Chinese ironclad *Chen-yuen,* whose injuries the author personally inspected at the close of the Chino-Japanese war. The ironclad was struck 464 times, but the following apparatus, situated outside of the armor belt, remained undamaged: pumps, capstan, chains, hawse-pipes, steering wheel, two 6-inch guns and six small guns; in fact, all isolated articles remained undamaged. This indicates that

1. An example of the restless Russian imagination and experimentation, the *popovka,* named after the inventor and ship designer Admiral A. A. Popov, was a perfectly round monitor. Two models were launched in the Dnepr, but their whirling motion caused the crews such dizziness that they could not perform their duties.

these objects possess a very small visible surface, as the result of which no one of the shells succeeded in striking them.

129. Firing torpedoes at long range. No exact determination of the distance at which torpedoes may act has been made. At the present time it is understood that the Whitehead torpedo will move in a perfectly straight line for a distance of 330 fathoms (660 yards), and that it will cover this distance at a speed of 25 knots. In general, all practice firings are made within this limit of range. Suppose we had 100 fathoms (200 yards) more in each case, bringing the distance up to 430 fathoms (860 yards), the question arises, may we consider ourselves safe from torpedo attack when we are 430 fathoms (860 yards) from the enemy? Specialists generally reply to this indirectly, and say that torpedoes have not been tried at longer ranges, but if proper regulating springs are used, or if the speed be reduced to 11 knots, the torpedo will cover 13 cable lengths. From this it is evident that torpedoes may cover very long distances, but we must remember that under these conditions the percentage of hits will be small, and that the angle of deviation will be very great, as the torpedo when adjusted for high speed will deviate a little toward the left at low speed. We sometimes hear it said that if people took up torpedo firing at long ranges all firing would thereafter be conducted at long ranges, and that there would be no torpedoes left for short ranges; but if the antagonist commands the range we may never be able to approach him, and if he has a large supply of torpedoes and uses them unsparingly, shall we not be at a disadvantage?

Much advantage may result in time of war through firing torpedoes at long ranges, and therefore their performance should be studied out for every distance that they are capable of covering. Preparatory experiments made last summer upon our initiative by Lieutenant Muraviev afforded the following results for normal torpedoes:

| Speed of torpedoes. | Distance covered in— | |
	Fathoms.	Yards.
Knots.		
23	330	660
18	600	1,200
14	1,000	2,000
11	1,300	2,600

We are convinced that if the condition be imposed for practice firings that torpedoes shall cover great distances at moderate speeds, their capabilities would be greatly increased. The following table is useful for other purposes:

Speed.	Distance covered in 1 second
Knots.	*Feet.*
5	8
10	17
15	25
20	34
25	42

130. Radius of action of torpedoes. The radius of action of torpedoes must be considered as the distance from an antagonist that it is possible to cover by torpedoes. In firing at an immovable target the radius of action is determined by the table given in the preceding paragraph, that is, for 23 knots, 330 fathoms (660 yards); for 11 knots, 600 fathoms (1,200 yards), but if the target be movable the radius of action changes. Let us assume the case of an antagonist on a heading parallel to our own, 330 fathoms (660 yards) ahead of us. Under these conditions, if we are both underway, and if we fire at him a torpedo set for 330 fathoms (660 yards), it will not reach him; while he can easily reach us with his torpedo, for the reason that he is running away from our torpedo while we are heading towards his. Consequently our an-

166

tagonist is not yet within our radius of torpedo action, while we are well within his.

The curve determining the radius of action of torpedoes at the speed of the antagonist assumes the same for all speeds of the ships; the position of the firing ship changes only in relation to the speed of the antagonist. Fig. 8 gives a graphic representation of the radius of action of torpedoes under conditions of parallel chase at a given speed for both our own and the antagonist's ship.

The radius of action is indicated by means of two semi-circles, the connecting line between the centers of which is the line of bearing of the ships. The circles show at a glance ships pursuing courses parallel to those of the firing vessels placed at distances corresponding to the limits of torpedo action. The position of the firing ship is shown in relation to the speed assigned it, assuming that, at the moment of firing, the ship is at the center of the figure, and at the time of the arrival of the torpedo at its limit of range the ship has moved forward to that position in which it is shown in the figure. During this time the torpedo goes directly to the point to which it is directed, and consequently the circle gives its radius of action under given conditions. If we desire to introduce into the sketch other conditions relative to one's own speed as compared with that of an antagonist, all that is necessary to do is to change the last position of the firing ship in the figure to the point where she will be when the torpedo reaches the circumference.

Fig. 8 shows us that the radius of action of torpedoes for parallel courses of our own ship and our antagonist's is greater in the direction of the stern than in the direction of the bow, and therefore a position in front of an adversary's beam is the more favorable for torpedo fire. In relation to torpedo firing, these circumstances result in a great advantage to the ship that is being chased. If we assume that the speed of the later is 22 knots, then the chaser is already within the radius

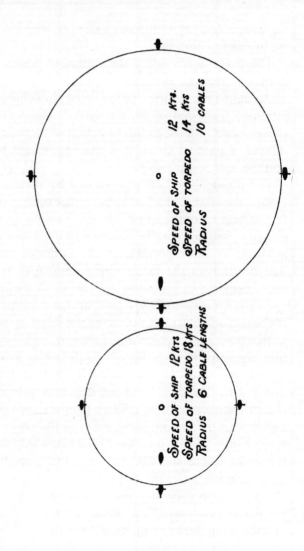

Speed of ship   12 Kts.
Speed of torpedo 14 Kts
Radius   10 cables

Speed of ship   12 Kts
Speed of torpedo 18 Kts
Radius   6 cable lengths

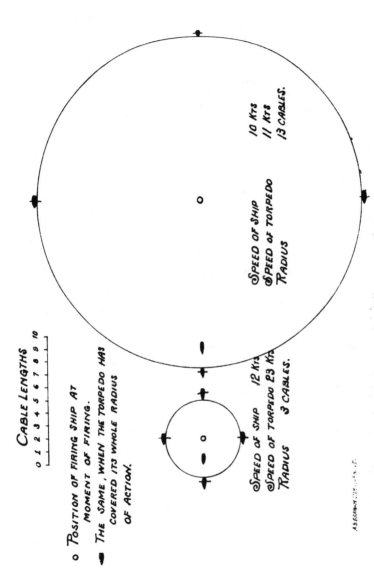

Fig. 8. Radius of action of torpedoes under different conditions.

of action of the torpedoes of the chase at a distance of 39 cable lengths (7,800 yards), while under same conditions of speed the latter enters into the radius of action of the torpedoes of the chaser only when the distance is reduced to one-half of a cable's length.

131. Torpedo firing. It is of the highest importance to form a rational conception of torpedo firing. Should we strive exclusively for exact shots, or should we, as in gunnery practice, count upon a certain percentage of hits for all shots fired? The difference between artillery and torpedo practice is that in the former we may make errors both in the vertical and horizontal plane, while in the latter vertical control is effected automatically. It only remains to give the torpedoes the necessary train. Among the disadvantages of torpedoes may be counted the circumstance that a torpedo moves in a medium which may exercise a sensible effect upon its direction. One disadvantage of Whitehead torpedo firing arises from the comparatively prolonged and uncertain time expended in the discharge of the torpedo from the tube.

Accuracy, properly speaking, in the movements of a torpedo for short ranges is very great, so that if we suppose a target 300 feet long and 200 fathoms (400 yards) distant, then under these conditions each torpedo fired makes 100 per cent of hits. If the firing occur under way, and the target, 300 feet long, moves parallel to our course, we can no longer count upon the same percentage. If the target now be moved in a direction exactly opposite to our own, then, in accurate firing, we must apply a correction for our own speed and for that of our antagonist, so that by setting the direction beforehand, we may fire the torpedo at the corresponding moment. The matter becomes more complicated if we happen to be changing the heading of our own ship at the same time. The above conditions show that there is little chance of attaining 100 per cent of hits, and that it may be considered satisfactory to attain 25 per cent. If the exercises be repeated a number of times under the same conditions, the percentage of hits increases, but in battle there will be such great diversity in the relative position of own ship and that of our antagonist that each shot must be considered as an independent one, subject to no correction from those preceding it. Besides this, in view of all the circumstances of battle above enumerated, we must apply a certain factor representing actual mental condition of the antagonist at a given time. Even in the very simple case of gun firing, morale has an immense effect upon the per cent of hits. It has been said by military authorities that each man killed in battle represents his own weight in rifle bullets expended. If the firing were conducted as accurately in battle as in exercise it would be impossible to take by open attack even the most weakly fortified places. The corrections applied in torpedo firing are far more complicated than those for small-arm practice. It is possible that the officer may apply correction for a wrong speed, or apply it in the wrong direction; or that the man firing the torpedo may make a mistake in carrying out the orders in setting the sights; for instance, he may set them at 35 degrees when he was told 45 degrees. It may happen that by mistake the safety pin is not withdrawn, or that the distance gear is set for entirely too short a range, etc. Every accident is possible under fire, and we shall have to be satisfied with a percentage of hits one-half of what is obtained in ordinary practice. Under these conditions this number is reduced for headings on opposite courses to 12 1/2 per cent. We must conclude that the percentage of hits in war for high speeds, even at short ranges, would not be even as great as this.

The percentage is less at long than at short ranges; consequently, short-range fire is preferable. The question arises, should we reserve our torpedo fire until the moment when we approach our antagonist, or should we open upon him with torpedoes at long range? There are reasons for concluding in one way and in the other. If we commence firing at long range, a few torpedoes may be expended uselessly, but we know there is some chance of injuring the adversary. If we reserve our fire for short range we will not utilize chance, and it may happen that during the whole fight not a single torpedo will be fired; while, if during this time our antagonist can fire upon our ship with his torpedoes, he has more chance of succeeding than we have. We are inclined to believe that firing should be begun at long range, in which we perceive another advantage, namely, that under these circumstances firing at short range will be more accurate, for the reason that other shots have been fired before them. If we fire no torpedoes at long range, it may happen that when we do close in upon our antagonist the torpedoes which we so carefully reserve will have been placed hors de combat.

We believe that in single combat torpedoes should be regarded as guns, to be fired slowly and deliberately at long ranges and with increased rapidity as we approach our antagonist. The number of torpedoes carried on shipboard to-day is insufficient for such firing and should be increased. It is a question of weight; but a torpedo weighs no more than a 12-inch shell, and it is easily possible to increase the number carried.

When we change from the duel to squadron action, the number of reasons for undertaking fire at long range increases, as in this case long-range firing may greatly increase the chances of success. Let us assume the easily possible conditions that two hostile squadrons of ten ships each are formed in columns with intervals of 2 cable lengths; that they meet and engage upon contrary courses 8 cable lengths apart. In one squadron, torpedo fire is interdicted for distances over 300 fathoms (600 yards) and is never practiced at long ranges; while in the other squadron, firing is practiced up to a distance of 13 cable lengths, for which distance the assumed angle of deviation is very great, say, 30 degrees. When the two squadrons arrive in positions abreast, the latter squadron fires torpedoes from abeam at the same time that it fires its guns. If we assume that each ship possesses two broadside torpedo tubes and that each succeeds in firing during the time of passage of squadrons at least 1 torpedo, then 20 torpedoes are fired at the first squadron. To miss this whole squadron, covering a distance of two miles, is impossible. The distance between ships at intervals of 2 cable lengths is two or three times greater than the lengths of the ships, and therefore one torpedo out of each group of three or four should hit; that is, from five to seven should hit out of the whole twenty—that is, one hit may be counted upon for two ships. Such results may be expected in return for the expenditure of 20 torpedoes. This shows that at the beginning of a fight torpedo firing in squadron action must be regarded as artillery firing even more than in single combat, and without waiting for the arrival of our antagonist within pistol shot we must fire upon him at all possible ranges. Has the time not arrived for regarding the torpedo as an artillery shell? It is true that they cost us 3,000 rubles, but the 12-inch shell with its cartridge costs about 1,000 rubles; and we open fire with the 12-inch without awaiting arrival at short range, where the chance of a hit becomes greater. If torpedoes are to be used at various ranges they must be adapted to ready change of speed. We do not believe that this matter will be difficult to accomplish from the technical standpoint. It is needed that tactics demand such a change, and then technique will meet the demand.

132. The influence of speed and direction upon the magnitude of the permissible angle of dispersion. There is one circumstance influencing the number of hits to which attention has not been called up to the present time. It is a fact that if an antagonist holds a certain bearing in relation to ourselves, he is easier to hit when his course is in a direction opposite to our own than when he is approaching our course. In the first case, he is chasing the torpedo, as it were, which otherwise might pass by him, and in the second case he rather runs away from

173

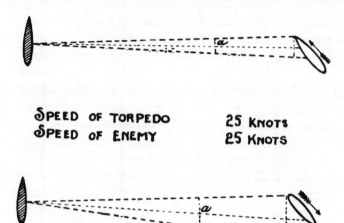

Fig. 9. Influence of speed and direction of adversary on magnitude of admissible angle of dispersion.

it (fig. 9). Captain Prestin, whom we asked to work out this problem, prepared a diagram (fig. 10) illustrating this difference very clearly. If we assume the length of the target as 300 feet, the angle between the course of the adversary and the path of the torpedo as 45 degrees, the distance 2 cable lengths, the speed of the torpedo 24 knots, and the speed of the adversary 20 knots, then, if the courses of the two ships are in the same direction, the permissible angle of torpedo dispersion is 6 degrees, and if courses are in opposite directions, 25 degrees. If the antagonist remains stationary, the permissible angle of dispersion is 10 degrees.

This circumstance must be borne in mind when firing torpedoes and when endeavoring to avoid them. It is more favorable for attacked ships when under way at fair speed to bring the enemy's torpedo-firing apparatus to bear from aft; but if there is no time to do this completely, and we bring the enemy to bear upon the bow, then as his torpedo approaches our

Curve

CONSTRUCTED UNDER THE CONDITIONS: LENGTH OF SHIP 300 FT.
TORPEDO IMPINGES AGAINST SHIP'S SIDE AT AN ANGLE OF 45°
SPEED OF TORPEDO 24 KTS
DISTANCE OF ENEMY 1200 FT.

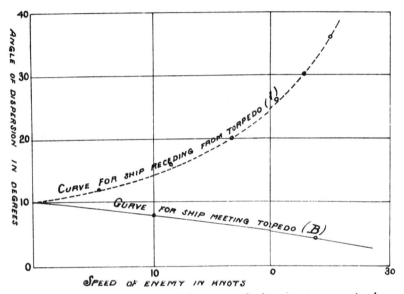

Fig. 10. Influence of speed and direction of adversary on magnitude of permissible angle of dispersion.

ship we actually aid it to hit us. Under these circumstances the ship approaches the torpedo, which otherwise would pass by it.

133. Within what angles of impact is torpedo firing effective? The latest types of torpedoes have very blunt noses; therefore, upon oblique impact, they may ricochet from the side without exploding; this fact must be borne in mind.

It is fair to assume that a torpedo striking the ship in the fore and aft direction would glance along the bows without

175

exploding; it is probable also that the torpedo would not explode upon impact within a certain angle of obliqueness. Experiments should be made to determine the least angle at which torpedoes are effective upon impact, and improvements of torpedoes in this respect are to be desired. Earlier types were much more effective in this regard than later ones, so that torpedoes have taken a step backward in this direction.

134. Is it possible to avoid a Whitehead torpedo? The possibility of avoiding a Whitehead torpedo depends upon the distance from which it is fired. Let us assume that the firing occurs at 5 cable lengths; the torpedo covers this distance in one minute and a half at a speed of 20 knots. Let us see if it be possible by stopping the ship to avoid a torpedo thus fired at us. The corvette *Vitiaz*, upon reversing her engines from full speed ahead (12 knots) to full speed astern, reduced her speed to 3 knots in one minute and a half, but as it takes fifteen seconds to reverse her engines, we must consider her speed at the end of the minute and a half after reversal of the indicator to be 4 knots. The mean speed for the elapsed one minute and a quarter will be 8 knots, and the distance covered 170 fathoms (340 yards); at 12 knots the distance covered would be 250 fathoms (500 yards). It is evident from the above that a 3,000-ton ship might, by reversing her engines from full speed ahead, reduce the distance traveled by her 80 fathoms (160 yards) in one and a half minutes, and allow a torpedo to pass; but to accomplish this it would be necessary to determine with accuracy where the torpedo is coming and also to have no vessel directly astern of us.

It is far more practical to avoid a torpedo through the use of the helm. The most suitable direction from which to receive torpedoes is from right ahead, for the reason that the target is minimized when the ship is bows-on, also that the torpedo, on account of its blunt nose, may slip along the sides of the ship without exploding, or else upon exploding only injure that part of the ship best protected by bulkheads. With firing

176

from a distance of 5 cable lengths a ship possessing good manœuvering powers may alter its course 90 degrees in this time.

From the above conclusions we may establish the rule that
in single combat whenever it is noticed that the enemy who
occupies a position forward of the beam fires his torpedo in
the direction of the attacking ship, the latter should rapidly
put his helm over so as to bring himself bows-on to the direction of the firer; if it be observed that the torpedo has deviated
or has missed the target, the helm may be quickly put over
again.

With above-water discharge a peculiar sound is heard the
moment that the torpedo is fired; therefore by paying attention we may observe when a torpedo is launched from the enemy's ship, but with under-water discharge we can only observe the white cap that is formed in certain cases when the
torpedo is fired, which it is difficult to catch sight of. This is
one of the many advantages of the under-water discharge.

Ships' signalmen may be employed to observe when torpedoes are fired, and one of them should be especially instructed in this work.

135. Firing torpedoes in shallow water will prove unsuccessful
if the torpedo touches the bottom. All torpedo apparatus do
not have similar qualities in this respect; some torpedoes dive
but little after flight; others make deep dives. Systems of firing
should be developed for which torpedoes dive as little as possible; categorical rules should be prepared for prescribing
what is the least depth and what are the conditions under
which firing may be conducted.

136. Effect of cold water upon torpedoes. It has been stated that
the Whitehead torpedo will not act in a regular manner when
the temperature of the water is below plus 4° C. [39.2° F.]. If
torpedoes act unsatisfactorily in cold water, then this is one
of their properties which must be borne in mind. If one torpedo proves accurate under these conditions and another not,
then this lack must be supplied. The fact that a torpedo may

stop its engine in cold water has some significance in war. However, experiments and improvements are needed in this direction.

Along our Siberian coasts there are many places where not only in winter, but in early summer, the temperature of the water at a depth of 15 feet is very low, and if we can not use our torpedoes in such water we may be subjected to very undesirable surprises in war time, which should have been foreseen and could have been avoided through the establishment of necessary technical instructions.

CHAPTER EIGHT

THE RAM

137. Conditions governing the exclusive use of the ram in battle. If two adversaries had no guns or torpedoes and were only supplied with rams, then the problem presented to each would be to place himself within the circle described by his adversary or to place himself astern of him at close range. The ship possessing superiority in speed should take his position astern of his antagonist so as to be able to ram him or to deprive him by ramming of helm and screws. When speeds are the same it is useless to try to ram in an open position, for to do this it is necessary to be able to chase. Conditions change when proximity to the shore or other causes compel the chase to change his course, and then the chaser should endeavor to head off his antagonist and thus reduce the distance between them. By manœuvering in this manner he may approach within ramming distance. In manœuvering in close waters, for example in Tranzund harbor, with vessels especially equipped for ramming, the one that was able to place himself astern of his antagonist succeeded in the end in ramming the latter.

It was shown in a previous paragraph (130) that the tactics of the ram are in direct opposition to those of the torpedo. In the former case it is preferable to be astern of, in the latter to be in front of, our antagonist. In general, seamanlike qualities are called into play in what relates to ramming, for upon attempting to ram it is easy to have one's own vessel rammed instead. It is very difficult to estimate correctly upon approaching an antagonist if his course is perpendicular to one's own. Under these conditions it is necessary to watch the antagonist closely. If his bearing does not change the ships will meet, and it may happen that instead of ramming him our ship will receive the blow, which is what we are endeavoring to avoid; therefore it is better for us to reduce the angle of bearing. If the angle of bearing of the antagonist diminishes somewhat, our course is a correct one; if not, we must put the helm over a little so as to cause the angle of bearing to decrease. As the antagonist will probably do the same thing, we must be ready to put the helm over at once in case the antagonist heads suddenly in our direction. In doing this it must not be forgotten that besides the helm, the two engines are at the captain's disposal. If the antagonist continues to proceed on a direct course, which does not hinder us from reducing the angle, we must try to reduce it as slowly as possible, otherwise we may pass astern of him.

When it becomes evident that the antagonist's ram will pass ahead of our own, then before collision we should put our helm over so as to recoil with the bow in the direction of the motion of the antagonist. This relieves somewhat our ram upon impact, and enables it to be withdrawn with less injury.

138. "Stand by." * Before ramming it is necessary to give the alarm, "Stand by!" which should be communicated to all parts of the ship. Upon receiving this command people should seize various immovable objects so as not to be thrown on the deck by the unexpected impact of the vessels. It is especially important that this signal be communicated to the engine room, where the decks are extemely slippery and where, upon slipping, men might fall into the moving parts of the machinery. Before ramming it is advisable to stop the engines, to accomplish which it is well to establish the rule that, before

* In Russian, "derdjes," meaning to hold on.—Note by translator.

turning the engine room telegraph to the position "stop," it will be reversed to full speed astern and then full speed ahead and then immediately to stop; that this would signify that when engines were stopped the order "stand by," is to be immediately communicated to the fire rooms. In some of our ships, bells are supplied as fire alarms; we would suggest communication of the signal "stand by" through the employment of these bells.

139. How to proceed after ramming. We must bear in mind that sooner or later the building of ships with bulkheads of insufficient strength will come to an end, and that if the fore and aft bulkheads of the wing passages be placed back 10 feet from the ship's sides and be well built (which nowadays only happens by chance), then a blow from a ram, however powerful it may be, could not sink a ship, and therefore after one blow were delivered and the ram withdrawn by going astern, it would be necessary to proceed full speed ahead and deliver a second and even a third blow. These blows, however weakly delivered, would pierce the outer plating, cause the wing passages to fill on that side and produce a heavy heel that might result in the capsizing of the enemy's ship. If upon receiving the blow the antagonist continues to work his engines ahead, it may be sufficient upon withdrawing the ram to proceed full speed ahead with the outer engines and slow astern with the inner, from which the ram would press against the antagonist's side while he is driving ahead (fig. 11). If the underwater portion of the antagonist were not sheathed with wood, our ram would rasp along the under water plating its whole length, as a result of which all of the side compartments on one side would be filled, and if the antagonist did not take immediate measures to right his ship it would capsize in a very short time.

140. How to act upon being rammed. A ship desiring to ram an antagonist should be prepared for being rammed itself, and no captain can rest assured that he will not be rammed in

Use of engines under various conditions of ramming.

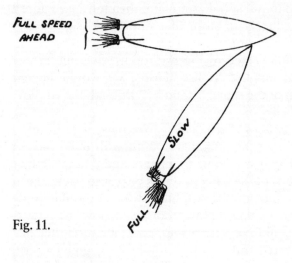

Fig. 11.

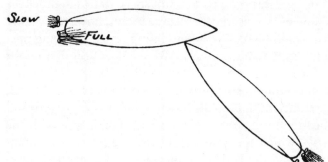

Fig. 12.

battle. All precautions prescribed by the collision rules must be observed; that is, the spread of the water must be localized, means must be prepared for stopping leaks, and additional means must be devised to keep the ship upon an even keel. These details relate to collision exercises (unsinkability).

It is the province of tactics to direct us how to manœuver after being rammed, so as not to be subjected to another blow

182

or suffer injury to the whole of the plating upon one side. The most important thing for the commanding officer of the rammed ship to do is to turn his vessel bows on the enemy, so that the second blow will not be received, which can be accomplished successfully only when the ramming vessel is handled badly. If the blow be received near the stern, full speed ahead must be maintained, so as to utilize the time during which the antagonist backs to clear his ram, and then shoot ahead of him. After this, if he succeeds in withdrawing 3 or 4 cable lengths, and the condition of the ship requires the engines to be stopped for placing collision mats, or for other reasons, one of the engines should be given full speed astern and the ship turned so as to bring the antagonist to bear on the bows and to hold him in this position by the movement of the ship. If the antagonist wishes to ram again, and our ship can not be turned, we must proceed with both engines, turn the ram toward the antagonist, and receive his blow with our ram.

We may also manœuver differently; e.g., at the moment a blow is received upon the starboard side our stern pays off to port. If, when this happens, the starboard engine be backed full speed the turn is increased, and the ship will have taken up a progressive motion to the left and will swing away from the antagonist's ram. Then, if he delays as much as ten seconds between the time of withdrawal of his ram and that of starting his engines ahead, our ship may pass ahead of his ram, for, notwithstanding the backing of the starboard engine, the rammed ship will retain its progressive motion ahead. As soon as the antagonist's ram is withdrawn, should the ship heel heavily, it is necessary to proceed full speed ahead with the starboard engine and put the helm hard aport, so as to turn the stern away from the enemy with the helm. The most important matter here is that the engines must be promptly reversed, one speed to another. If the blow be received forward, near the bow, and if the ships preserve after impact the position in which they met (as in fig. 12), it is better to give the starboard engine full speed astern and proceed slow ahead with the port, and to turn one's ship bows on to the antagonist, after which we may ram with our own ship, if it is possible to move, or prepare to receive a second blow by turning our bows toward him if he advances to ram again, or to retain him upon the bow for torpedo and artillery fire, should he choose a position rendering this possible.

If, after being rammed near the bow, the enemy retains the position shown in fig. 11, it is better for the ramming ship to proceed with his engines full speed astern. If the antagonist moves ahead, so that his bows escape our ram, we may proceed ahead on the engines and ram him before he succeeds in escaping across our own bows. If he backs and tries to retire, we should turn one engine ahead and put the helm over, so as to turn our bows toward him quickly. This is the most favorable position when the adversary is near at hand.

141. Meeting bows-on. In discussing the question of approaching an adversary we have considered what should be done if he declined to meet us bows on. If he accepts such a meeting and turns his ship toward us—that is, does what we do—the stems of the ships will come in contact.

The opinion prevails to-day that the bows-on collision of two heavy ironclads will result in the sinking of both of them, and that consequently both ships had better decline such an encounter. The commanding officer, however, who happens to be the more cautious and begins to change his bearing so as to avoid such a collision, places himself in a position favorable for being rammed, for his antagonist has only to maintain his original course to enable his ram to strike the side of the former's ship. We may therefore arrive at the conclusion that it is unwise to be prudent in this case, and it is best to maintain one's course straight for the antagonist. Let us consider, however, what dangers are superinduced by the bows-on meeting that might result in the loss of both ships. The force of the blow is proportionate to the square of the velocity; that is, a shock at ten knots is four times greater than that at five knots. If we express the vis viva in foot-tons we obtain figures so enormous that they pass our conception. Let us assume the impact of a ship at normal speed as equivalent to the fall of a body. To impart to a body falling freely through space a velocity of 5 knots it must fall 1.2 feet; 10 knots, corresponding to a height of 4.5 feet; 15 knots, to 10.5 feet; 20 knots, to 17.3 feet; 25 knots, to 27.5 feet; 30 knots, to 39.7 feet. In this manner the torpedo boat *Sokol,* moving at a speed of 30 knots, acquires a velocity which corresponds to a fall from a fourth-story window, that is, 39.7 feet. We know that people falling from this height to the pavement are dashed to pieces, and if we were to drop the *Sokol* from the same height it naturally would float no longer, as it would be completely disintegrated.

We know, however, that if a net be spread in the street so that anyone falling from a fourth story window will strike upon it, the man will be recovered completely uninjured. If the *Sokol* did not possess a very sharp bow but ended abruptly in a transverse bulkhead, like a locomotive, and ran into a granite wall, the effect would be the same as from a railroad collision. As the matter stands, however, the *Sokol* has a very sharp entrance, and necessarily less durability in the fore and aft direction than in the thwartship, so that if it struck a wall its momentum would not allow it to stop abruptly; its bow section would begin to yield, from which the vis viva of the whole vessel would gradually be absorbed. This crushing in of the bows of the *Sokol* plays the same rôle as the net in checking the fall of a person from an upper story of a house.

What has just been said in relation to the *Sokol* applies exactly to every ramming ship. If we assume two large ironclads directing their course toward one another, bows on, ram to ram, then when the rams come in contact each of the ironclads must stop, and consequently each of them will receive the force of the blow just as if it were ramming an immovable wall sheathed with some extremely durable material; the fastenings of the ram and of the bow in general, being weaker than those of the whole ship, yield first. First of all, the rivets give way and the stem is forced inward, then probably the whole bow is pressed in, while the body of the ship remains practically unhurt and does not leak, as the plating of the decks receives the shock. Then the ship's boilers, condensers, and heavy machinery would possibly be displaced, but this would occur only in case they are improperly secured.

Under ordinary circumstances the rupture of the rivets around the ram would be preceded by certain deformations of the metal of the stem, and when the force attains the necessary magnitude a rupture of the rivets will occur. The interval of time between the moment of meeting of the rams and the tearing away of the riveting is very small, but it exists, and a chronograph could indicate its magnitude. If we assume that the ship has a speed of 15 knots and that the working and yielding of the rivets is equivalent to 3 inches of the movement of the ship, we obtain an interval of 0.01 of a second, which is easily measurable by the chronograph. Let us assume, further, that the elasticity of metal and the strength of hull of one of the ships is such that this yielding takes place somewhat before the lapse of this 0.01 of a second, and that in the other ship it takes place later, then the first ram will be disrupted sooner, and this may be enough to save the second ram from disintegration. What happens is the same as when one egg is struck against another—one breaks and the other remains entirely whole. It must be remembered, however, that the meeting of ram to ram in a manner so exact that one ram does not slip off from the other is an extremely unlikely occurrence. In the first place, rams are placed at different heights, and then they may slide, one away from the other, by reason of the lack of their vertical correspondence (fig. 13). Besides this, the stems in which rams terminate may possess different cur-

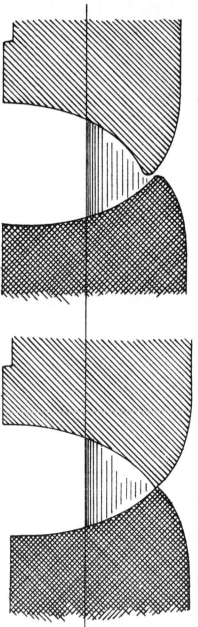

Fig. 13. The problem of rams meeting.

vatures, which serve to render the slip of one ram off from another very probable, so that a case where two ships will impinge one upon another in such a manner that their rams do not deflect would be such as to be most improbable.

When one ram slips along another the ships do not experience a shock that is disproportionate to their endurance, and it may happen that the result of such a glancing blow will cause both ships to heel in opposite directions. A moment later the round parts of their bows come together, and it is possible that two ships so placed would glance off from one another without doing more than deforming their bows near the stem. If one of the rams or both begin to tear away the other's plating, then the ships will not pass by after having delivered a glancing blow, but will continue to expend their energy in destroying the sheathing and other portions of hulls near the bows. We can not believe that impact, bows-on, is fatal for the ships in all cases, and would counsel commanding officers not to fear such encounters.

142. Improvements in rams. It may happen that one ramming ship has a narrow entrance and the other a broad one; in this case the narrow ship has the greater chance of injuring its antagonist without receiving injury itself (fig. 14). A narrow entrance, however, is undersirable, as it does not insure sufficient strength to the ram in a lateral direction. If the ram strikes a ship that is under way, then at the moment of impact it exposes itself to the lateral shock of its antagonist, in consequence of which it may yield. Such cases often occur when a ram strikes a ship under way, and in these respects not only are the rams of sharp ships weak, but also rams of ordinary ironclads with full entrance. To obviate these difficulties rams should be constructed with lateral reenforcing ribs. We would advise giving these ribs a much more solid form than they commonly receive, and also that they be constructed with teeth (fig. 15). Upon meeting bows-on, these teeth would tear away the plating of the antagonist and rip open his sides.

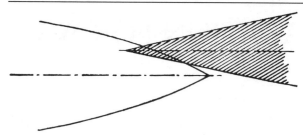

Fig. 14. Effect of sharp entrance upon results of direct impact of rams.

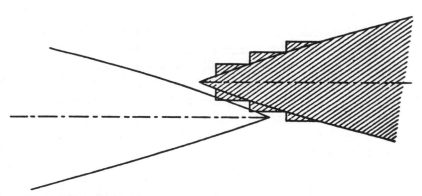

Fig. 15. Improvements in rams.

They also afford another advantage in that they tend to impart a rotary motion to one's vessel with respect to an opponent, which results in placing our ram in better position and in throwing our side and stern away from our adversary's ram. Without these teeth the ramming ships would develop a turning couple and the rammed vessel not, so that it might happen that after coming to rest the rôle of the ships would become reversed, and the ship that originally rammed its antagonist would itself receive a blow.

189

CHAPTER NINE

PREPARATION FOR WAR

143. Preparedness of ships for war. Every ship in commission must be prepared for war at all times, and the naval regulations require a vessel to be ready for action when approaching a foreign port, even in time of peace. Declaration of war may come so quickly to-day that the measures prescribed by the regulations should be rigidly enforced, especially in those cases where ships are to remain for long periods of time without telegraphic communications.

It frequently happens, however, that upon approaching foreign seaports much more attention is paid to cleanliness and outward appearance than to compressing air for torpedoes or making other military preparations. However strict the requirements for preparedness for war may be, peace conditions nevertheless engross attention to such an extent that when news of war is received great preparations for war will be called for. We must admit honestly that systematic timely preparation in all directions of this nature is not a trait of our national character, but the Russian readily sets to work when called on by the turn of affairs, and we remember with pleasure the busy days not long ago when two squadrons, under the general command of Admiral S. P. Tirtov, were put upon a war footing. The work fairly boiled and the ships vied with each other in rapidity and fullness of their preparations. These preparations may be divided into two headings: (1) Preparations for war. (2) Preparations for battle.

Preparations for war consist in doing away with everything necessitated by conditions of peace cruising only and in converting everything to the fullest degree possible into an engine of war, allowing everything to remain, however, that is indispensable to the exigencies of life afloat and to the health of the crew. It may appear that, in accordance with the fundamental principle that the fleet exists for war, nothing superfluous should be left on board. But this is not so. Human beings are always human beings, and must be taken as they are found. We therefore declare openly and frankly that a ship is not prepared for war in time of peace, and we shall enumerate those points in this regard to which attention must be directed.

It is useful to practice preparations for war from time to time during peace. War is an examination, the time for holding which does not depend upon ourselves. Preparation for war is a preparation for this examination, and if we never make such preparation we must not be surprised if, when the time comes, we make a bad showing.

144. Precautions against fire. When ironclads were introduced many said that serious fires could never occur on board of them. Practice shows, however, that this is not so and that fires are still to be dreaded. Any fire may be put out with a few pails of water when it starts, therefore precautions must be taken that in time of battle all receptacles are kept filled with water. It is also important that main fire service pipes be constructed for constant pressure, so that in time of need hose may be employed for extinguishing fire by those persons who happen to be in the vicinity without any sounding of the general fire alarm. If the fire apparatus is not constructed to withstand pressure the necessary result may be obtained by taking a few precautions. For example, a line of hose may be kept hoisted to half the height of the mast and the end let overboard.

191

If the fire pumps are kept pumping through this length, the necessary head of water will always be maintained.

145. *Throwing away articles useless in battle.* There are many articles on board of every ship which are useless and even harmful in time of war and of battle. In many vessels there are linings under wooden decks, which are only installed for appearance sake. These linings should be torn out and thrown overboard. There is no need of preserving them, for war will demonstrate their utter uselessness and afterwards they would never be replaced. Very careful measures are needed to effect the removal of all such useless articles from shipboard. Fifteen years later it is very probable that they will begin to install such things again, but this is no reason for preserving before a war such a useless collection of rubbish. It is common nowadays to install upon gun decks various cupboards and shelves for cartridge-bags, etc. These are superfluous and are but food for fire, and in our opinion should also be removed and thrown away as material liable to cause injury in a fight.

As expressed by an experienced and capable French admiral, "Le premier luxe à bord d'un bâtiment est le vide."[1] Space is in fact a luxury from a war standpoint and efforts must be made to secure it. Merchant seamen realize this, and upon visiting the deck of a large merchant steamer one is astonished at the absence of obstructions, while at the same time everything is supplied that is necessary for performing all requisite work with a small crew. When the author took command of the corvette *Vitiaz,* he sent ashore two fish-booms, weighing 6,000 pounds, and cruised three years without them, and without a fish tackle; but the commanding officer who succeeded him reinstated them in place, probably because he did not realize the force of the idea that space is a luxury.

146. *The painting of ships.* Many experiments have been made for determining the problem of the most suitable paint

1. "Space is the primary luxury aboard a ship."

to be used on ships in war. At one time seamen differed greatly in their views, and we have seen vessels painted in various shades with a view to determining the best color to adopt. We may safely conclude as follows: White renders a ship less visible in daytime against a sea horizon than black. Black is less visible against a green background than white, but against a background of rock not of a green tint white is the least conspicuous color. At night white is less visible than black in the absence of electric search lights; when electric lights are employed the conditions are reversed. Shiny paint is always more visible than a dead color. From the above reasons dead gray is the very best color that can be used. As regards the shade, whether blue, green, or yellow, the preference is to be given to the yellow, for this approximates most nearly to the color of rock and of the obscured horizon.

147. Inspection of water-tight bulkheads. It yet remains evident that necessary attention is not directed to water-tight bulkheads, and on most ships, as we have seen, the matter is neglected both from the standpoint of construction as well as that of preservation. There is no reason for surprise if a ship sink as the result of a blow received; one should rather be surprised if under these conditions the ship did not sink. In time of peace the good condition of the bulkheads is an important matter; in time of war it is of vital importance, and he who closes his eyes in peace to the imperfections of his bulkheads will have his eyes opened in war. It will be too late to make discoveries when the ship begins to fill with water.

In many cases ventilating ducts without valves capable of being hermetically sealed pass through water-tight bulkheads. The removal of these ducts in time of peace requires the consent of various administrative bodies; but when war draws near we must act upon our own responsibility and, without awaiting permission, remove the pipe joints from the bulkheads and close the openings with simple wooden sheathing. Wood swells when wet and prevents water from passing. We need not repeat here all that we have said in previous papers,

193

and especially in our work, Elements of the Fighting Qualities of Men-of-War. We shall confine ourselves to stating briefly that all bulkheads must be examined before war, and care must be taken to see that they are actually water-tight.

148. Pumping systems. The ship's pumping systems must be carefully tested by admitting water into various compartments of the inner bottom, and then pumping this water out separately by each pump and by all combined. There are always reasons why it is not desirable to admit water into the compartments; but such difficulties must be set aside and the captain should insist upon every compartment being filled with water and the water expelled out of each by the pumps. Before doing this it is well to examine the suction-pipe strainers, both for the main piping as well as for direct branches leading to the turbines, circulating pumps, condensers, etc. Inspection by officers must be made everywhere, for if the captain of the hold states that the strainers are in place, this does not mean that the suction pipes are properly supplied, but only that there actually is a little netting there, while the netting may be torn so as to admit various objects that could choke up the suction system.

In many places (storerooms, wine and spirit rooms, coal bunkers, etc.) suction tubes are placed in the bottoms of compartments, and where there are wooden decks which impede the withdrawal of water, holes are made in these decks to allow the water to escape. They are generally found covered with oilcloth, and it is necessary to bore holes in these coverings and to form gratings of wire gauze or metal bars, so that floating objects may not close the openings. The oilcloth should be properly fastened down so as not to be liable to shift in case of pumping water from the compartment.

If the ship possesses appliances for filling her side compartments for trimming ship, it is necessary to test them and ascertain whether the water enters into the compartments with sufficient rapidity. This must be determined for each compartment, for it sometimes happens that when the pipes are laid red lead collects in the inside of the pipes and more than half closes them; under these circumstances the water flows with extreme slowness.

149. Improvised protection. In time of peace articles of equipment are located in positions from which it is convenient to employ them, but before the commencement of a war it is well to rearrange them from the standpoint of use in battle, and as far as possible to employ them for purposes of protection, bearing in mind, however, that any change of weight from below upward raises the center of gravity of the ship, which is extremely undesirable.

In former times, chests, sails, etc., were used as shelters; today the initial velocity of bullets and shells is so great that chests, mats, and even wooden sheathing no longer furnish cover from projectiles; but they would all probably afford some protection from flying fragments, although in close proximity to an explosion such fragments would pierce even large beams. Chests, mats, etc., which afford no real protection, nevertheless constitute combustible material, and the question arises whether it is well to try to use such articles in this manner or whether it is better to send them all below to places where they could not be ignited by the bursting of shells. We are inclined to believe that boxes, chests (if not life-saving apparatus), and other objects of a similar kind, should be kept below the water line in war; if this be not possible, then, if time permits before the fight, they should be thrown into an empty coal bunker or other place where they could not be ignited. Chests containing cork life-preservers should be near at hand for use in case the ship sinks.

150. Secure all objects against displacement upon ramming. Ships should be so built that no object, in event of ramming, could be displaced; nevertheless, upon declaration of war it is well to examine whether boilers, condensers, and all articles of equipment, such as shells, spare anchors, torpedos, etc., are properly secured. All this is very important for minimizing injuries resulting from shock upon ramming. If it happen that any object be badly secured, it must be fastened down with wooden battens. If articles of secondary importance be liable to displacement, it does not matter; if the boilers are liable to be not properly secured, a general catastrophe is imminent, which may be avoided by apparently insignificant precautions. All this should be considered in due time.

151. *The framings of engine-room hatches,* now made largely of glass, are of great convenience in time of peace, but in battle the glass would be shivered, not only by projectiles, but from the blast of our own guns. Breaking of glass in the engine room, hatches, etc., may cause general disaster, as the falling of the fragments upon the cranks might put the engine out of action, and consequently place a ship in battle in a critical position. Not only all glass of the upper engine hatch frames, but all other glass, lights, and illuminators near the engine, should be unscrewed and removed, and tarpaulins and similar coverings substituted for them.

152. *General preparations.* After war is declared guns must be kept loaded; projectiles and charges kept in readiness; hand rails and every object likely to impede their fire removed; cartridge cases and primer boxes filled; Whitehead torpedoes charged with compressed air. It is necessary to ascertain whether the chains are ready for unshackling, and to make sure that the unshackling implements are in their proper places; the water in the main and auxiliary boilers and in the boilers of steam cutters should always be heated by means of supply pipes, and a certain pressure of steam maintained in them; ash pans and furnace doors should close well; the boilers themselves be well sheathed, so as not to lose heat. Torpedoes in steam cutters and torpedo boats should be loaded and charged with compressed air, and it is necessary to decide what doors, hatches, etc., are to be kept closed, to

be opened only under conditions of necessity for short periods of time.

153. Maintenance of the physical strength of the personnel. When war begins, constant work for the preservation of the ship at night commences. If this work is to be performed in addition to that required in peace, the whole crew will soon be worn out. Extreme exhaustion of the men is to be avoided in all manœuvers, notwithstanding that the manœuvering work is far from being as severe as that required in war; therefore, it is necessary to reduce the amount of ship cleaning and other such employments, and to establish such a routine that each man who becomes fatigued during the night may have a chance to sleep during the day. The best way of accomplishing this is to assign time for this purpose after early breakfast, and clean ship with one watch while the other is allowed to sleep. Under these conditions the general work of instruction can be carried on during the hours from 9 to 11 in the morning. Time for rest after dinner ought then to be increased by one hour, so that the men can be free from 11 a.m. to 3 p.m.

154. Alarms. Bugles and trumpets should be kept ready for quickly calling the crew to quarters, but it is still better to accustom people to repair to their quarters on hearing the sound of the boatswain's pipe, as this call may be given more quickly than that by bugle or trumpet.

155. Preparation for battle. There should be posted on each ship a list of what each man is required to do in clearing ship for action. We present a few points below which, while not covering the ground completely, call attention to some matters of importance. The following must be done:

1. The national flag must be hoisted at every masthead, whether by day or by night. This rule applies equally to torpedo boats and steam cutters.

197

2. All skylights and all openings which are of no use in battle must be closed, so that in case of the ship heeling over they will not allow water to enter.

3. All bulkheads and doors not especially assigned to be kept hermetically closed must be left open, so that there will be free access to compartments; exception to be made only in case of the spirit rooms; prisoners are to be liberated.

4. All sails and other canvas articles are to be wet down; this is important to prevent these articles from burning and for the reason that they are then more serviceable in putting out fire. Nelson, who witnessed the affair of the *Alcide* and *Orient,* considered fire one of the chief dangers of a naval combat, and before the battle of Trafalgar he ordered the hammock nettings of the *Victory* carefully wet down and the davit boats lowered into the water; in a word, that all precautions against fire should be taken.[2] To this carefulness is to be attributed the absence of sharpshooters in the tops of the *Victory,* as Nelson feared that a careless shot or explosion might set fire to sails and result in a frightful catastrophe, which actually happened in the battle of Trafalgar in the French ship *Achille.*

5. To order the men who are placed near the line of fire of their guns to put cotton in their ears. The chains are to be unshackled at the first shackle and to be secured in position by lashings, so that if the anchor does break adrift at the time of ramming it will not carry the whole chain with it, which might result in great damage.

156. How to dispose of steam and pulling boats before a battle. The following question merits our attention—should we allow all boats to hang at the davits during battle or should we

2. Both ships caught fire and blew the *Orient* up catastrophically when the magazines, improperly stowed, were reached.

lower them, as is sometimes done? At the time of the battle of the Yalu, the Chinese fleet was without boats, which had been left at Port Arthur before putting to sea. In the American civil war ships frequently fought without boats, or more properly, with a very small number of them. The presence of boats at the davits increases the area liable to be struck; consequently some shells which would fly by unimpeded strike the boats, burst, and scatter their fragments among the people on the decks. To abandon the boats at sea before an engagement would be to deprive ourselves of the possibility of using them in case of the sinking of one's ship; but it must be borne in mind that as a result of prolonged artillery fire the greater number of boats would probably be so badly damaged that it would be impossible to use them. In any case, there are weighty reasons for carrying boats and going into action with them, but there are equally weighty reasons against carrying them, especially as, in event of sinking in battle, greater trust would be put by the sailors in life-preservers than in the boats themselves. As both arguments have equal weight, the commanding officer may decide for himself whether he will carry the boats or not. The lowering of boats before entering into battle would be impossible in many cases on account of existing conditions of sea and wind.

As far as relates to steam cutters and torpedo boats there are greater reasons for lowering them than for lowering pulling boats, and if circumstances permit they should be launched with full armament of guns and torpedoes. These boats should manœuvre in time of war in the proximity of the fighting ships and use their guns so as to injure the adversary; it is best to keep them astern of their own ship, so that they may shorten the distance upon turning. Torpedo boats and cutters should realize that the fire directed toward them draws the fire of the antagonist away from the chief object of attack; therefore, every such shot is useful; but besides their passive value, such small craft may make a positive attack by firing torpedoes, and may possibly deliver a vital blow even to a very powerful enemy. When the ships begin to describe curves and to manœuver in respect to other vessels, then steam cutters often have afforded them a chance to get in their work, by which possibly a whole engagement may be decided.

CHAPTER TEN

VARIOUS OPERATIONS

157. Protection of a fleet at anchor. From the moment of declaration of war it becomes necessary to begin the defense of a squadron from the enemy's torpedo boats. The best way to accomplish this is to obstruct the harbor with booms and to illuminate protected areas by search lights placed at prominent points and defended by guns placed alongside of them. We are also in favor of the establishment, even if temporary, of projectors and guns on shore, for under these conditions the effect of both, in consequence of steadiness of platform, is greatly increased.

If the entrance to the harbor to be protected is so broad that it can not be well illuminated and covered by guns from the shore, or if it be impossible to mount guns and projectors on shore, it becomes necessary to establish a floating defense. To this end we may employ either ships, boats, or else the local craft. Our own boats possess the advantage of portability, and may be despatched and recalled at will. Local craft are still better, as they afford a space for the crew and roll less. Besides this we may, by employing local facilities, center the whole defense at one point.

Temporary defenses may be constructed by placing, say, a barge with two projectors and four guns in the center of a harbor and two barges with guns near the beach. The electric current may be furnished to the projectors on the barges either by dynamos temporarily installed on the barges them-selves or by dynamos upon steam cutters secured to the stern of the barges.

If booms be constructed, defense duty consists in prevent-ing the enemy from destroying them. If there are no booms, the purpose of the defense is to discover the enemy's torpedo boats and destroy them.

158. Illumination of harbor with ships' projectors. If there is no possibility of suitably obstructing a harbor with booms pro-tecting its entrance, it becomes necessary to illuminate it with ships' projectors, in which case beneficial results may be ob-tained only by employing some recognized system of illumi-nation. We present the instructions upon this subject included in the orders of Vice-Admiral Kaznakov to the Practice squad-ron for the year 1891.

Ships, in the order of their position, illuminate the horizon by sections, and endeavor not to allow any portion of their section to remain unilluminated. Having projected the ray on the horizon, clamp the vertical side of the search light in the desired position, and swing it in a horizontal plane.

The light discovering an enemy's vessel holds it covered with its beam, and does not change the direction toward any other object.

In the meantime the other lights continue to illuminate the horizon, but never turn their rays upon the ship that is already covered.

Care must be taken not to illuminate one's own torpedo look-out boats, as well as one's own ships crossing the beams. In this case employ a light-screen without altering the position of the light itself.[1]

1. For reasons of economy, government practice was to activate the fleet for training. In 1891 this meant, for all practical purposes, that the Baltic Fleet put to sea only the three to four months of summer. There were long cruises, however. (Note that although the Soviet Fleet operates much less than its Western counterparts—as a matter of economy and to promote endurance—it probably trains more.)

159. Should a squadron occupying a harbor whose entrance is protected remain with or without lights? It is impossible to give a general answer to this question, covering all cases. If protection with ship's projectors is unnecessary, it is safer to remain without lights, and, in order to further conceal one's position, to place a few coasting vessels in another part of the harbor and display lights from them. If, however, the harbor is well defended, the admiral may not deem it necessary to compel the squadron to conceal all lights, the accomplishment of which is naturally attended at such a time with great inconvenience.

160. Choice of anchoring ground for ships in a known harbor depends upon many circumstances, one of which it is useful to keep in mind. This is the fact, that however well a ship be defended by nets, she is nevertheless liable to be destroyed by torpedo boats. If the depth of the water under the keel be great, the sunken ship will be entirely submerged, and it will be found very difficult to raise her. If there be little water under her keel, the ship will only fill with water, and may be raised in a very short time with squadron appliances. It follows from this that it is useful to place the ships in that portion of the harbor where they will have as little water as possible under their keels.

161. The construction of booms capable of protecting squadrons from ironclads has not been, with a few exceptions, practiced in any navy, while in time of war such booms would have to be employed. It would be astonishing if a matter to which no attention has been given in time of peace should be fully successful in time of war, but nevertheless the question is one of primary importance. It is an easy enough matter to construct a boom for show, but skill is required to construct one strong enough to resist attack. We believe that this subject should be worked up and practiced during peace, and that necessary structural material should be taken afloat by the squadron for this purpose.

203

162. Upon the approach of ships and boats to a squadron in time of war. There is great difficulty in establishing such a system of signals that there may be no doubt as to whether the approaching ship or boat is our own or an adversary's. The system of reconnoitering signals should be kept secret; here we can give general directions only.

Upon approaching one's own squadron with ships or boats it is necessary to indicate one's presence from as far off as possible by signals, and not to approach closer until permission is given. Should there be a line of lookout boats one of them should advance, whereupon the senior on board, whoever he may be, should proceed to the deck of the craft and satisfy himself that it belongs to his own countryman; the lookout boat does not give the approaching boat the signal designated for that night and hour until this has been done. It is usual to forbid the free approach of boats to the proximity of the position occupied by the vessels of war. The boats of one's ships, after inspection by the patrol, are allowed to pass; but boats that do not belong to the military establishments are under no circumstances allowed to approach the ships; whatever they bring should be delivered to the commissary's boat and carried on board thereby.

163. Parole, countersign, and password. In some cases it may be found useful to establish a parole, countersign, and password, as is done in the army. The instructions of Vice-Admiral Tchikatchow, who commanded the Practice squadron in 1884, serve to illustrate this point:

> Use for the parole the name of some town or place; for the countersign, the name of a saint; for the password, a military object or term. All of these words chosen are to begin with the same letter; for example: Parole, Sebastopol; countersign, St. Simeon; the password, sword (sablya).

> The parole, countersign, and password are communicated by the commander in chief of the squadron, in a sealed envelope, to the ship's commander, who is responsible for their being kept secret by those persons to whom he entrusts them.

The parole is only entrusted to officers and petty officers performing officers' duties; the countersign to the commanders of lookout boats going the round of the fleet—those sent with orders along the line, and to the patrol; the password is given to every one performing sentry's duties, and to boats sent with orders or for other reasons from one ship to another.

The password is employed to recognize one's own people, to which end every passing boat receives the hail, "Who goes there?" Upon reply the sentries inquire, "What is the password?" "——."

Each approaching boat or sloop, on arriving within 1 1/2 cables' length of the guard boat or ship at anchor, stops its engine or lays on oars and awaits the hail, and if it receives no hail, hails itself.

The captain of the watch or officer in command of the lookout boat, upon observing that the proper password is given by the approaching ship or boat, permits it to approach. If the ship or boat approaches without giving the password, the sentry fires and the chief of the watch gives the order to sound the alarm.

A ship or boat passing by is hailed in a similar manner.

If, although the regular password should be given, there remains a doubt as to whether the hailed boat is our own, it is not given permission to come alongside, but a boat is sent to inspect it.

The countersign is employed by the officers commanding boats making rounds for passing through the line of scouts. When two boats meet, after the hail "Who goes there?" is given, and after approaching, the one who hails asks in a whisper, "What is the password?" And upon receiving the reply the latter inquires in his turn, so as to ascertain whether he has been hailed by his own boat, "What is the countersign?"

The patrol is employed by the chiefs of the various devisions of the lookout service for identifying persons arriving with orders, or upon special missions from the seniors in command, etc.

164. *Protection of a squadron at sea.* Some advise that a squadron that is to be kept at sea off an enemy's coast should ex-

tinguish its lights at night and maintain full speed, to prevent discovery by torpedo boats. Such precautions seem to us unsuitable. Conditions of weather may change, and various circumstances may necessitate communications by signal, which is equivalent to the display of lights. In our opinion it would be more practical to stop the engines at night and lower the torpedo nets. The smaller ships, which, from their light draught, do not fear Whitehead torpedoes, should be placed in a circle around the larger vessels, to protect the latter, at such distances from them that they are beyond the radius of action of light guns, the firing of which they do not hinder. In case that one's own lookout desires to approach the squadron, it should show the signal of recognition previously agreed upon for use that night. Under the above conditions the squadron may pass the night more quietly than when under way without lights.

Ships at sea in time of war should keep their guns loaded, but circumstances of weather may be such that spray may enter at the muzzles. If the guns are so situated that the tompions may be easily removed, tompions of the regular pattern may be inserted; but if the muzzles project far over the side it is useful to have light tompions and muzzle bags, so that the guns may be fired without removing tompion or muzzle bag. Firing with the ordinary types of heavy tompions causes the shell to explode in the bore, but if light wooden tompions of 1/4-caliber thickness are employed such an explosion does not occur, as the tompion begins to move from the effect of compressed air before the shell strikes it.

Care must be taken that the water which enters the gun does not wet the powder, and that there is not much of it in front of the shell before firing, as this might endanger the safety of the piece. The opinions of specialists as to how far such conditions endanger the gun are needed.

165. Protection of a squadron in an open harbor. Said protection is similar to that of a squadron at sea; this is, torpedo nets are lowered, lookout boats sent out, etc.

166. Is net protection indispensable for ships? Defense by nets was greatly extended on shipboard a few years ago; it was never very popular with naval officers, but they accustomed themselves to it as an unavoidable evil. Bow and stern nets were not provided for ships, for they reason that it was not necessary to protect from injury such small compartments as are usually constructed at the extremities of vessels. This amounts to a simple evasion, for the ironclad *Victoria* went to the bottom from the effect of a blow received near one of these small compartments; as to the stern, the presence there of the screws and helm should prove an incentive to supplying this part of the vessel with the best protection that can be devised, the installation of which might prove a difficult but not impossible task.

At the present day a reaction has set in against net defense. It is said that the German navy is doing away with them and that the French are about to take the same step; also that the cause for the change is the invention of knives capable of cutting the netting. We are fully aware that torpedoes provided with knives can cut through ordinary torpedo nets; but we are also aware that it is possible to neutralize the effect of such cutting torpedoes to a considerable extent. Besides devices already invented, there are doubtless many others not yet developed which should be studied up as soon as possible. The struggle between knife and net should be inaugurated and invention should be brought to bear to develop the efficiency of the latter. If there are no torpedo nets how can it be possible to protect ships from torpedoes? Naturally, reliance is placed upon water-tight bulkheads; but thus far no ships have been constructed which possess immunity from destructive effects of torpedo explosions. If any nation possessed such ships nothing would be easier than to prove their qualities. Practical results from such experiments would open our eyes. It might happen that the result of the explosion of a torpedo would not only be a large hole in the ship's bottom, but also that steam pipes subjected to the enormous pressure of

200 pounds per square inch would burst. The bursting of pipes under full pressure might result in a most frightful catastrophe, which, it is natural to suppose, would in some cases result in putting the ship out of action. Therefore, even if ships were strong enough in point of unsinkability, they would have to be protected just the same from the explosion of torpedoes, from which might result not only the bursting of pipes, but also the shattering of the engines, boats, plates, turret bases, and various hydraulic appliances in which enormous pressures are also maintained.

Last summer, when in command of a Practice squadron, the author succeeded in making a number of experiments for determining whether torpedo boats could approach a squadron practically unperceived. Experiments were also conducted for establishing the accuracy of the light rapid-firing guns when attacking torpedo boats under way by means of movable pyramidal targets. All precautions were taken to render firing accurate, and as a result, after having witnessed one night attack, the author was fully satisfied; but when the targets were hoisted on board it was discovered that no one of them had been struck.

The result of night attacks by torpedo boats indicates that they may in many cases approach an enemy almost unperceived. How, then, can an admiral protect his squadron from such an attack in places where there are torpedo boats if the ships be not provided with net defense? He can only cruise every night without lights and at full speed. This is extremely exhausting to the crews and requires a great expenditure of coal—so precious in time of war—but may be done in fair weather. In bad weather, with fog, rain, or mist, it will be then almost impossible to cruise the whole night through upon various courses without lights, at full speed, and at the same time manage to keep the ships together.

Net defense affords an admiral the possibility of acting as has already been explained—that is, to exhibit his lights, to remain in the position he happens to be, and to pass the night quietly, with a minimum expenditure of coal, and find himself at daylight upon his field of action. If the squadron is blockading a port it will be enabled under these conditions to continue its work. If it is bombarding fortifications, then at night, by use of its guns and lights, it may hinder the enemy from repairing his works. If the squadron is engaged in protecting a transport fleet it may continue its protection throughout the night, etc.

All of the above-enumerated advantages should be carefully considered before deciding to do away with torpedo nets. If a ship be without nets the near approach of boats at night will cause confusion, and by mistake parts of our own torpedo boats may be taken for those of the enemy, which leads to false alarms and even to firing upon one's own people.

167. Boarding. If any seaman be asked to-day whether an enemy's ship at anchor could be taken by boarding he would reply that such a thing would be almost an impossibility; but should the question be framed differently, and if he should be asked if his own ship possesses immunity against boarding, we would receive the reply that a ship is not totally secured from boarding by an energetic adversary. Seamen nowadays have given up the idea of hand-to-hand combat on a ship's deck, which in former days was a common enough occurrence. We ourselves believe that the capture of a ship at anchor by boarding is possible. Therefore it is necessary to practice such tactics both in what relates to attack as well as to defense.

168. Should steam be maintained. Let us assume that war is declared, and that from strategical considerations we are expecting the appearance of an enemy upon our coast at any minute. Regulations now in force in all navies require that a considerable interval of time be allowed for the formation of steam in cylindrical and locomotive boilers. This interval is so long that it may greatly impede the movements of the commander in chief of the squadron. Two conclusions may be arrived at. Either the commander in chief does not believe in the

209

necessity of observing this precaution and may order steam to be formed without holding to the regulations; or he may order steam to be maintained continually, which will result in two inconveniences: first, the expenditure of coal, which is a very precious material in war, and second, the strain upon and wearing out of the boilers. If the chiefs of squadrons, without observing the regulations, would order steam formed quickly, under these conditions it could not be raised in less than two hours.

This interval is an extremely long one, and it is impossible to remain satisfied with it. Means should be devised for raising steam in all boilers from one boiler and for rapidly starting fires. These considerations are very important from a tactical point of view, both for ships' boilers as well as for those of torpedo boats and steam cutters.

169. *Scouting service.* Scouting begins with the declaration of war. What should be done to render the service efficient? We often hear it said that it is impossible for an admiral properly to dispose his forces if he knows nothing of the position or the intentions of the enemy. There is a certain amount of truth in this remark, but nevertheless there are limits beyond which we need not pass.

First of all, we should do all in our power to increase the limits of our own horizon. To this end a crow's nest should be constructed at one of the mastheads for signalmen, with sufficiently convenient means of entrance. Besides this it would be well to experiment with aerostatic appliances, to determine how far they may be useful in time of war. Particular attention is paid to this matter in the French navy.

170. *Observation stations.* Observation stations connected with telegraphic cable along the different capes of our own coast are indispensable, so that when an enemy appears news of his whereabouts may be immediately communicated to headquarters, whence they may be communicated to the admiral commanding the fleet.

It is also indispensable to have all observation stations supplied with visual apparatus for receiving messages from passing ships as well as for communicating to the latter necessary orders.

171. Reconnaissances by ships and torpedo boats. Stations are not enough to furnish all necessary information concerning an enemy. Scouting service conducted with our own ships and torpedo boats is indispensable. Scouting service may be subdivided into near and distant service. By the term "near service" is implied the service in performing which the ship does not go out of signaling distance from the admiral. It may be direct or progressive. In the progressive way a number of ships are extended in series so as to remain within the limits of signaling distance from one another, and the admiral may thus receive information from vessels that are invisible from his own.

Distant service may afford an admiral much useful information, but its maintenance is attended with great risk of loss of the scouting ship. It must be admitted that an enemy possesses ships as fast as our own, and therefore should a scout fall in with a whole squadron it would be destroyed by the superior forces of the enemy. Do the advantages to be gained from the employment of such scouts justify the risk of their destruction? We are inclined to think that it is wise to avoid such a risk as far as possible. Ships should only be sent on distant service which possess greater speed than the very best ships of the enemy. Under these circumstances it is better to send out, not a strong squadron, but a single swift vessel whose engines and seagoing qualities may be relied upon. One ship is better for fulfilling such a task than two. Two scouts offer twice the risk of a capture on account of the double chance of injury to machinery.

172. Distant scouts. Ships sent out as scouts should endeavor to see everything and at the same time remain unperceived. To this end precautions should be observed and

211

measures taken that the combustion of coal be smokeless. The best way to prevent the formation of smoke is by using anthracite or good Cardiff coal, and good fires should be kept up so that the coal is completely consumed. Forced drafts carry off unconsumed coal dust, and some torpedo boats show fire from their stacks, so that forced draft should only be employed by vessels upon scouting service whenever their visibility is not a very important consideration. Smoke from vessels may be observed at a very great distance, and therefore it is very important to devise and install upon ships of war apparatus for obviating the formation of smoke.

It must be borne in mind that it is very difficult to recognize a ship when it is protected by a shore background, and therefore if our ship is near land and sees another ship, this does not signify that we have been observed. If, however, we see another ship projected upon a background of the land, our ship, in all probability, has already been sighted if without such background herself.

In relation to a clear or cloudy horizon the following may also be stated: Visibility is much greater in the direction of the clear than of the cloudy horizon. Clear and obscured horizons may be attributable to the low altitude of the sun; moreover, when the sun is high, clear and obscured horizons are caused by meteorological conditions: the clear horizon is upon the side of the clear sky; the cloudy, upon that of the clouds.

When a vessel is sighted we inspect it to determine what it is and whither bound. In order that we may be less readily perceived, and to determine more exactly in what direction the ship is bound, the best thing to do is to put the bow or stern of our ship in the direction of the discovered vessel and stop the engines. Having ascertained as far as possbile what the ship appears to be, we must decide, in accordance with circumstances, how to proceed. If there is reason to suppose that the discovered ship is a vessel of war weaker than our own, or else a merchant ship subject to seizure or search, we must endeavor to head it off. There are several theoretical methods for determining the course to be taken by our ship at a given speed in order to approach another ship as soon as possible. The true course to take is that for which the distance from the pursued vessel diminishes and its bearing remains constantly the same. We will assume that the commanding officer makes no great mistake if he heads off 30 degrees from the bearing of the chase and then observes whether the angle of bearing of the latter increases or diminishes. If the angle of bearing increases it must be diminished to the point for which it remains constant. Let us assume that the chase bears originally north 45 degrees east, and that the chaser proceed on a course north 15 degrees east. If, after the lapse of a certain interval of time, the chase appears nearer and bears about north 48 degrees east, our course should be changed 10 degrees to the right; but if the chase shows a bearing of north 42 degrees east, we should head off 10 degrees to the left and head on a course north 5 degrees east. The change of course is continual; the bearing of the chase remains constant.

Having captured a merchant vessel it is necessary to proceed in accordance with international law and follow our instructions. Should the captured ship carry troops, all weapons should be confiscated and taken on board our own vessel. If there is no time to do this they must be thrown overboard.

173. Should scouts engage an enemy? The commander of the scouting vessel should be acquainted with the opinions of his admiral as to how he should act upon meeting an enemy's ship. Differences of opinion exist on this point. Some assert that a scout should not under any circumstances give battle, if his task be the collection of information. Others consider that a dispatch vessel should not ordinarily give battle, but if circumstances are such that a dispatch vessel can do an enemy much harm he should not lose the chance.

Suppose that a scout approach a port: it should send out its steam cutter to ascertain whether the enemy's squadron is there or not. Upon entering the harbor the cutter may be favorably placed for torpedo attack. Without taking advantage of this it should leave the harbor unnoticed. If it fire torpedoes, although it might do much injury to the enemy, it would nevertheless at the same time indicate our presence, and it might follow that, although the enemy lost a ship, yet the cruiser would be taken in the chase that would ensue, and the admiral thus deprived of all news concerning the enemy.

Let us assume another case: that a scout meet weakly protected troop ships: if he should immediately turn back and convey this information to the admiral as quickly as possible there is no doubt that he would have performed his duty as a scout exactly. If he threw himself in the midst of the transports, destroying them with guns and torpedoes, he might inflict an enormous loss upon the enemy, although there is a chance that he would be sunk himself without conveying the news of the landing expedition to the admiral. Judging from a theoretical standpoint it would be better not to prohibit a scout from undertaking military operations, and we assert that such men as Nelson, Suvorow, or Napoleon would have praised the scouts who undertook such work, even if beaten without conveying the necessary information.

174. Opinion of Suvorow on reconnoitering. Suvorow was not greatly in favor of scouting duty. In Colonel Orloff's work (Suvorow) we find the following:

> One fine morning Suvorow gave a good lesson to Shulter, who suggested performing reconnoitering duty—a favorite occupation of the Austrian commanders, who wish to show their activity without accomplishing anything serious. Suvorow cried out in exasperation: "Reconnoitering! I wish none of it. Such work is only good for cowards to forewarn the enemy. Whoever wishes can always find the enemy without it. Concentration—bayonets—cold steel—attack—charge—that is my way of reconnoitering."

175. Information conveyed privately. Besides news received publicly, it is necessary to provide for the receipt of information from private sources. The best way to secure this is through the use of spies, and the fleet in which this service of espionage is widely and systematically organized possesses great tactical and strategical advantages over an adversary. In the late war in the far East one of the contesting parties widely utilized this means, and its agents were to be found in every port. The Government not only knew what ships carried contraband goods, but even in what parts of the vessel such material was stowed. It is only in this way that we can account for the success that its cruisers had.

The service of espionage should be at least partly organized in time of peace. If the necessary measures be not then taken to complete this, the organization will be difficult to effect after war breaks out. Want of such an organization may deprive us of many advantages which perhaps may be at the disposal of more cunning antagonists.

176. Destruction of the enemy's telegraph cables. If the empire or colony against whom war is waged occupies an insular position, its telegraphic connection with the world is maintained by telegraph cables. The cutting of these cables may work great injury, and therefore it is necessary to carry appliances for this work upon some of our ships. This matter should become part of the regular naval practice, and while it may not exactly pertain thereto, naval tactics should nevertheless retain control of the subject.

The work upon telegraphic cables is performed by special steamers. The latter carry two or three stout sheaves at the bow and stern with winches (fig. 16). When it becomes necessary to raise the cable from the bottom a stout five-pronged grapnel is put overboard from the bow of the ship at the end of a wire hawser (fig. 17). The grapnel engages the cable; this is observed from the deck, where the tension of the hawser is carefully watched. When the grapnel has engaged the cable the engines are stopped and the cable is carefully hoisted. If the water is shallow the cable may be brought directly on

215

Fig. 16. Steamer for raising telegraph cables.

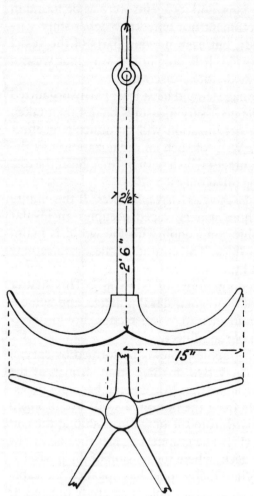

Fig. 17. Grapnel for raising telegraph cables. Dimensions approximate.

board; if the depth be great, however, and the strength of the cable be insufficient, then it is raised to a certain height and a buoy capable of supporting it is fastened to the hawser. After this is done the cable is engaged at another point, some distance away from the first, and again hoisted as far as possible, and a second buoy is made fast (fig. 18). Then the cable is finally raised to the surface between the two buoys and is brought in over the bows; it may then be wound in until the damaged section is reached. Sometimes when the cable is brought on board it is secured to the ship at two points, between which it is cut, so that telegrams may be sent in one direction or the other for verification. It is also possible, without cutting the cable, to tap it and telegraph.

All this work requires considerable skill, but we are informed that grappling a cable in 1,500 fathoms in fair weather is not a very difficult matter, and that every year telegraph steamers succeed in doing this a number of times, as cables chafe in places were the bottom is stony.

Cutting a cable does not require as much skill as repairing it. Hawsers and grapnels are alone needed. If the grapnel line be not long enough, we may use for depths of over 100 fathoms a wire hawser, and further extend it with a rope cable. In our opinion it is better to lower the hawser and grapnel from the bows. The catching of the cable is the most difficult part of the operation, as its position is not exactly known. When the telegraph cable is seized the line is taken to the winch and hove in. When the cable is raised to the surface (fig. 19) the ends must be secured, the cable cut, one end thrown overboard and the other hauled on board, hove in for a certain distance, cut at intervals and the pieces thrown overboard. After doing this over an extent of some miles, the cable should be secured to the ship, which turns short around by backing, and after dragging back the end some distance finally throws it overboard. If there is no time to perform all that has been described, then, when the cable has been raised to the surface

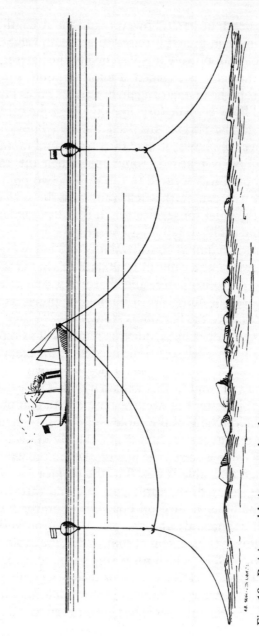

Fig. 18. Raising cable in great depths.

Fig. 19. Rupture of telegraph cables.

and secured firmly enough to the vessel, the latter is turned in another direction, so as to bight the cable around in that direction, and then by backing the ship it is still dragged in the opposite direction until it breaks on the other side. The ship then carries away the intermediate part on one side and throws it overboard. Any warship may perform this in depths less than 200 fathoms, but in great depths it is impossible to accomplish it without the aid of a vessel especially constructed for such work. It must be borne in mind that two cables are always laid, and the destruction of one cable by no means settles the matter, but that it is necessary to discover and destroy the other also.

During the time of performing this work the ship's position must be determined hourly, so as to establish where search has been made, and avoid a repetition of the search in the same place or lead us to hunt for the second cable in the place where the first was found.

Ships searching for cables should carry a telegrapher and a telegraphic apparatus.

We present below a description of the telegraphic drag given in the Mittheilungen aus dem Gebiete des Seewesens (1895, No. 6, p. 579).[2] It is stated that this drag works better on a stony bottom than the form usually employed, but in soft ooze the simple type would probably be preferable:

> Drag for engaging submarine cables. (Invention of Claude Johnson.) This drag consists [as shown in fig. 20] of five claws which are supported by pivots in such a manner that they may turn a little. In their usual position they are pressed downward by springs and when the drag is hauled over a stony bottom the two lower claws retire in the recesses formed in the casing of the apparatus. This circumstance does not prevent them from grasping the cable lying beneath, as the drag rebounds

2. *Mittheilungen aus dem Gebiete des Seewesens* is a journal of seamanship.

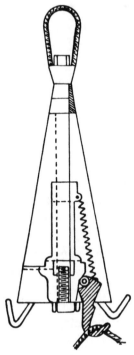

Fig. 20. Perfected telegraph grapnel.

over the stony ground. The elastic action above referred to may be easily and definitely regulated.

Drags with fixed claws present the inconvenience that when towed their claws catch in the bottom, which causes much trouble. In towing the drags of the above type over the soft bottom, the cable is seized by two of the claws.

Experiments, as far as have been conducted up to the present, indicate that this type of apparatus works well not only upon stony bottom but under all circumstances.

221

CHAPTER ELEVEN

SINGLE COMBAT

177. Nomenclature. For the sake of brevity and clearness of expression it becomes necessary to establish a few brief definitions:

"On the bow" signifies the direction nearest the bow upon which the broadside guns may be brought to bear. "On the quarter," the same with reference to the stern. "Giving chase," any position for which the antagonist is forward of the beam. "Taken in chase," any position for which the antagonist is abaft abeam. The "attacking vessel" denotes the one of the antagonists who takes the initiative in battle; "the defense," one by whom the initiative is not taken.

178. It is necessary to endeavor to have all advantages upon one's own side. A naval battle is not a duel or an affair of honor in which all conditions must be the same for both combatants; on the contrary, one must strive to secure all possible advantages for himself and to put all the disadvantages upon the side of his opponent. This is the chief end of tactics, and the more completely it is fulfilled the fewer the losses will be, or, as Peter the Great expressed it, "Victory will be secured with little blood." We must carefully consider the question of what is favorable to us and unfavorable to our opponent.

179. The initiative in battle belongs to the ship having under given conditions of wind and sea the greatest speed. The solution of the problem whether to give battle or to refuse it depends upon the ship possessing the initiative. General conceptions upon this matter should be in accordance with the general strategical plan of action included in the instructions given to officers commanding ships by the commander in chief. We shall enumerate below only the general conditions.

180. Under what conditions does battle become obligatory? Fighting is obligatory only when we are called upon to hinder the antagonist in doing that which he deems his duty. Let us suppose that a cruiser of a nation possessing an extensive commerce meets a cruiser under orders to destroy commerce. It is obligatory upon the former to fight, even if he is weaker than his antagonist and has but little hope of success. Nevertheless, he will be able to weaken his antagonist to some extent and hinder him from further destructive activity.

Another example is supplied by a ship or ships convoying transports. Upon sight of the enemy the former are forced to hinder the latter from destroying the transport ships; therefore they are compelled to give battle at once, even if it be unfavorable for them to do so.

Ships protecting torpedo defenses are compelled to give battle in order to prevent the enemy from destroying these defenses, even if this work is undertaken by a force considerably greater than that of the defenders.

181. Relative strength of ships. Speaking in general terms, it is advantageous for a strong ship to give battle to a weak one, for the former possesses a chance of utilizing his superiority at the beginning of the fight by weakening the fire of the antagonist, annihilating him or forcing him to surrender.

The question as to which of two vessels is the stronger and which the weaker is a very complex one. In former times, with sailing ships, the power of ships was proportionate to their displacement, and consequently the larger vessel was always stronger than the smaller—the weaker. To-day we may also consider the strength of the ship to be proportionate to its displacement, whether the displacement be represented by great speed and light armor, or whether by less speed and heavier armor. As a general thing, superiority in protection upon one's ship offsets the greater speed of another, so that the strength of fleets may still be measured by displacement. Experiments have been made for the purpose of determining each quality of a ship by a numerical expression, so that the sum of these expressions may express the ship's total value. The idea is a good one, but as all such coefficients are arbitrary, the general summation is more or less arbitrary, and therefore its value is open to discussion.

Detailed estimate of the strengths of ships under all conditions is a very complicated matter. For example, in squadron engagements a rapid cruiser, being unable to utilize her high speed while ships are kept in the formation, loses her superiority and becomes weaker than her relative displacement implies. It is just the same with ironclads in certain cases where they are rendered incapable of performing their work on account of their slow speed and can not prevent their swift antagonist from declining battle.

In some cases strength of ships may be so altered by circumstances that a small vessel becomes stronger than a larger ironclad. Let us take for example the simultaneous cruising of the ironclad *Resolution* and the torpedo cruiser *Gleaner*.[1] This ironclad rolled so heavily that she was almost unmanageable, and under these conditions her heavy guns could not be used, while the small ones were unable to hit anything. The *Gleaner*, however, had no such roll and could fire her torpedoes, and, consequently, from the war standpoint, under these conditions the *Gleaner* was a better vessel than the *Resolution*. If these two vessels had happened to be antagonists the *Gleaner* would have been fully justified in assuming the offensive. From this it may be concluded that in a heavy

1. The *Resolution*, built in 1892, could make 15 knots; the *Gleaner*, built in 1890, could make 18 knots.

sea, where large ships roll heavily, small vessels with torpedo armaments are the stronger. It was stated then that a small-draft ship possessed the advantage in torpedo warfare, as torpedoes would pass under its bottom, consequently the conditions of strength above referred to apply especially to light-draft vessels.

From the above conclusions the tactical rule may be established that for a large ship it is not advantageous to be in a position where she rolls heavily. Under these conditions it is preferable, if possible, either to approach the shore, so as to diminish her roll, or else to keep a long distance off the coast so as to be less exposed to an attack from the smaller vessels of an enemy.

Foggy and heavy weather in general favor a small ship armed with torpedoes, for by the time a large vessel sees the small one the former has come within the radius of action of the torpedoes of her antagonist, who is able to fire her torpedoes and vanish without suffering to any great extent from gun fire.

Dark or foggy nights in general favor small vessels, for even when projectors are employed and the small ship can not be discovered at a distance of over a mile or two, and under many circumstances she will not be discovered until at a distance of about 5 cable lengths, and, consequently, when able to employ her torpedoes.

From the above we may arrive at the conclusions:

(1) In fogs, at night, and in heavy weather, light draught ships with fair torpedo armaments are more powerful than large ships. (2) In what relates to strength, battle is favorable for that ship which is the stouter under given conditions of weather.

In most cases in daylight the strong ship is the large one; but at night, in foggy weather, or in a heavy sea, the strong ship is the small one possessing a heavy torpedo armament. As small ships are best able to give battle in fog, at night, in stormy weather, or in a heavy sea, they should be exercised under these conditions so that they will be able to perform their work effectively under such circumstances.

182. Advantageous or disadvantageous conditions of battle. If other circumstances do not hinder, it is better for vessels in danger of attack from torpedo boats to remain in shoal water or near shoals, so that if they be sunk they will not sink below the level of their upper decks. It is more favorable for torpedo boats, however, to attack ships in deep water, so that in case of sinking them the loss may be total. Other conditions being equal, it is better to fight in the vicinity of one's own ports than far away from them, as in case of receiving injury it is easy to retreat to a protected harbor where repairs may be made. It is better to give battle near one's own squadron, where aid may be offered, than to fight near the enemy's squadron, that may bring aid to its own ship.

183. Choice of kind of battle. When an antagonist is sighted it is necessary, in accordance with what has been stated above, to decide whether battle is to be given at once or to be deferred for a certain length of time, or to be declined altogether. As soon as it is decided upon to fight, some plan of action must be decided upon. As the battle progresses much will depend upon the actions of your antagonist—upon his losses and your own, etc.; but before the fight begins it is useful to establish some plan or predetermined scheme of action—whether to fight at long or short range, whether to use torpedoes and ram, or whether to do neither.

184. Subdivisions of single combat. When considering conditions of the employment of the ram, we assumed what was exclusively a ramming contest; but in fact a combat exclusively with the ram or exclusively with the torpedo could never be expected; every ship possesses guns and torpedoes; therefore when two ships approach for ramming each enters within the radius of action of the other's torpedoes; as for guns, they always play an important rôle. It could happen, however, that a fight would be exclusively with artillery. In this case the ships would keep outside of the range of each other's torpedoes.

From the above it follows that when ships are beyond the radius of torpedo action the fight is with guns; when they approach within torpedo range the battle is with guns and torpedoes, and when the ships approach nearer, within pistol shot, the fight is with guns, torpedoes, and rams.

The following constitute the chief reasons for determining the kind of battle that is to be given. If our ship possesses a powerful torpedo armament and is weak in gun power, and if, in addition to this, she is of such small draught that she runs no risk of being struck by Whitehead torpedoes, then the best thing to do is to close in as quickly as possible within torpedo range. If, on the other hand, our vessel possesses a heavy battery while our adversary has but a light one, it is to our advantage to keep beyond torpedo range so as to destroy him by utilizing our superiority in battery and injure his torpedo apparatus before he approaches within short range of us. As a usual thing, large ships carry heavy guns and small ships a powerful torpedo armament; therefore, approach for the purpose of firing torpedoes is more favorable to the latter than to the former. If ships were not provided with torpedoes, the handier and the swifter ship might ram, but as torpedoes are installed at the present time upon almost all vessels, he who decides to use his ram exposes himself to a great risk of destruction from torpedoes and might be sunk before he succeeded in delivering a blow.

185. Ships approaching. After deciding upon the nature of the battle it becomes necessary to approach our antagonist. In some foreign navies ships are directed to turn their bows toward their enemy's ships and approach him directly, but it is possible to adopt different tactics, as discussed in paragraphs 188, 189. If an antagonist also desires to approach us, the vessels close in upon one another with great rapidity, so that from the moment of deciding to give battle to the time of its actual commencement the time may be counted, not by hours, but by seconds.

In support of this statement the following circumstance developed not long since in Kronstadt at a naval court in connection with the collision of the cruiser *Razboinik* with the bark *Dorade*. The full line in fig. 21 shows the course of the *Razboinik,* striking the bark in the bows, carrying away part of her rigging. If the helm had been put over five seconds later both ships would have collided bows on; if it had been put over ten seconds sooner than it actually was the ships would have entirely cleared one another. The whole matter was a question of five or ten seconds for the insignificant speed of 7 knots.

Let us assume another case: Two ships pursuing intersecting courses may ram one another; the ship A (as shown in fig. 22) rams B amidships, but if at the beginning of the manœuver A had been his own length in advance of his former position, he himself would have received the ramming blow.

The following table shows with what astonishing speed ships approach one another:

DISTANCE BETWEEN SHIPS (IN CABLE LENGTHS).	SPEED OF EACH SHIP.			
	10 KNOTS.	15 KNOTS.	20 KNOTS.	25 KNOTS.
	Min. sec.	*Min. sec.*	*Min. sec.*	*Min. sec.*
40	11 50	8 52	5 55	5 5
30	8 52	6 39	4 26	3 49
20	5 55	4 26	2 57	2 32
10	2 57	2 13	1 29	1 17

The special table shows that two ships approaching one another, each at a speed of 20 knots, cover a distance of 40 cable lengths in five minutes, fifty-five seconds. If 40 cable lengths be considered as the distance at which firing is opened,

Upon the importance of seconds of time in ramming.

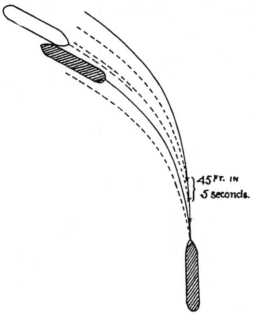

45 FT. IN
5 seconds.

Fig. 21.

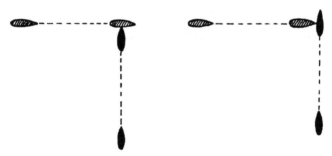

Fig. 22.

then the interval from the beginning of firing to the moment when the ships meet bows-on is less than six minutes.

If we assume that the ships see each other at the distance of 15 miles, which is an extremely long range, and both desire to approach one another at a speed of 20 knots each, they will meet in twenty-two minutes. Such rapidity leaves very little time for preparation for battle. In former days comparatively few preparations were made and the times of approach were long; nowadays great preparations must be made and the time of approach is very short. In consequence of this, the knowledge how to prepare ships for action in a short time is of the highest importance.

187. May ships manœuver in battle? Some think that manœuvering of ships in battle will be extremely difficult and that no manœuvers will be made; our opinion is entirely to the contrary. We know that in many single combats ships have been manœuvered under sail. The whole of Nelson's method of giving battle centers in the fact that the ships of his squadron forced their way through the antagonist's line. Perhaps this is not a very difficult manœuver, but how about when it is to be done within pistol shot of the enemy?

In the engagement March 14, 1795, in the Gulf of Genoa, Nelson repeatedly manœuvered his ship, the *Agamemnon,* sheering off to deliver broadsides against the enemy's ships and heading up again to close in with them.

In the battles of Sinope, Navarino, Aboukir, and Copenhagen, we have examples of ships at anchor under heavy fire veering around by use of springs from astern.

If ships manœuvered under sail in former times, when it was necessary to haul upon a hundred complicated purchases, why should it be impossible to manœuver a ship to-day, when the whole control falls upon two handles? We believe that manœuvering in battle may be conducted with the same regularity that characterizes it in time of peace. We even have an example of this, namely, Admiral Kornilov, who witnessing the fight of the steamer *Vladimir* and the *Pervaz Bachri,* wrote of the captain of the *Vladimir,* G. I. Butakov, that "he handled his ships as if on drill, and maintained at the same time a rapid and regular artillery fire."

188. Meeting of two ironclads of equal strength. Let us examine the case of meeting of two ironclads equal in strength as to guns and armor, which are disposed in the usual manner, namely, one turret, containing two guns, at bow and stern, and in the center, between these, broadside batteries of 6-inch caliber. The ships being equal in strength, it will be well to open the engagement with artillery fire, and to this end it is necessary to approach firing and to bring the enemy to bear upon the bow. If the enemy assumes an opposite heading, it is unimportant, as far as concerns wind and weather and other circumstances, what course we select, whether to starboard or to port, as, from the desire of both antagonists to maintain an artillery fire, both ships circle around one another, so that their position in respect to the sun and wind is constantly changing. If the enemy's ship takes a parallel course to our own, so as to use his battery, under these circumstances we should seek to avail ourselves of such advantage as relates to sun and wind.

In both cases the antagonist is to be constantly held upon our bow, so that we may use our turret guns and present our armor to him at an oblique angle. If the antagonist holds us upon his bow, both ships describe circles as shown in fig. 23, rapidly approaching until they come within torpedo range. If at this moment our antagonist is worse off than ourselves, or if part of his guns have been silenced, it is best to decline coming within torepdo range, but to hold him upon our quarter at a distance of six or more cable lengths and continue firing upon him. If our ship has been punished more than our adversary's, we should endeavor to approach until he comes

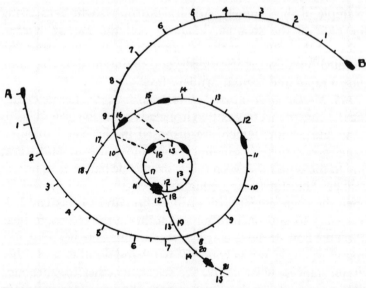

Fig. 23. Duel in which A holds his antagonist on his beam and B holds A on his bow.

within torpedo range of us, and then turn bows on to him to fire the bow torpedoes or employ our broadside tubes, if this be possible.

189. The case of an antagonist approaching our ship bows-on. The beginning of the fight is the same for both ships as in the preceding case. Our ship holds the adversary upon a bow bearing (fig. 24), firing with our broadside guns, and at the same time he is approaching and using his bow guns. If we consider the bow-bearing position more favorable than bows-on, we should try to hold him in this position as long as possible. However, we must not forget that when we approach within torpedo range the enemy possesses the advantage that we present to him a greater target than he to us, and therefore as soon as torpedo range is reached we should turn

232

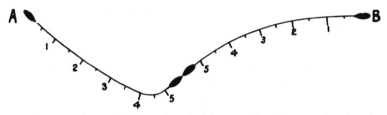

Fig. 24. Duel in which A first holds B on his bow and B heads straight for his adversary.

at once bows-on to the enemy and thereafter maintain this bearing to him.

The forward guns of the unengaged broadside, which are as yet unused, are kept loaded and ready to fire the moment we head directly upon the enemy. After this we may fire our bow torpedoes at the proper time and head directly for him, so as to maintain a favorable position for ramming him. If it should happen that the enemy does not head directly for us, desiring to pass close to us upon one side or the other, we should manœuver as if we desired to pass upon his opposite side, but then immediately afterwards head our ship for him so as to ram him in the side, or at least to carry away one of his screws. By so doing we not only ram him, but we protect our screw in case he should try the same thing. If the enemy heads directly for us and avoids direct collision at the last moment, we should utilize this fact to put our helm over so as to ram him in the bow or side.

If we desire to decline a bows-on meeting, we must begin to turn in ample time. At a speed of 12 knots, the enemy advances 2 cable lengths in one minute; at 18 knots, 3; and therefore, if our ship describes half a turning circle in two minutes, then by beginning to turn at a distance of 6 cables from him with a speed of 18 knots, we shall have our antagonist close aboard at the end of the turn. Therefore, we should begin to turn at a distance of at least 9 cable lengths. If the turn is not begun in time it is useless to attempt it, for our ship will inevitably be rammed. If we prefer to turn around in time, and if we possess the superiority in speed, it would be better not to turn sufficiently to bring the enemy completely astern, but keep him on the quarter in order to open upon him with guns and torpedoes.

190. *Meeting torpedo boats and small craft in general.* Upon meeting vessels of small displacement, which endeavor to approach us, we should either manœuver as in combat between two ironclads (that is, hold the antagonist upon our bows, then head directly for him), or, if the difference in speed be small, to place him upon our quarter. In this latter position we may thus gain time for a chance to destroy the adversary with our guns before he comes within torpedo range. At the moment when he arrives within torpedo range of us we should turn our stern to him.

If circumstances prevent our placing a torpedo boat upon our quarter, we should first bring him to bear upon our bows, firing with the broadside guns from distances of 10 cable lengths, and then turn bows on to him and endeavor to maintain this position the whole time he is approaching, as it is the most favorable for receiving torpedo attack. If the torpedo vessel does not use his helm he will meet us bows-on, but if he puts his helm over pursuit should begin.

191. *The necessity of written instructions to all persons occupying positions of command on board ship.* Each ship has its peculiarities, which in time of war must be considered, and therefore each captain should give written instructions to every officer for the purpose of determining what he may do himself and what orders he should receive from other persons; what he should report and upon what he should ask instructions. In carrying out these instructions each officer should bear in mind Turenne's advice, "outre ça, messieurs, je vous recommande le bon sens" (beyond this, gentlemen, I recommend you to use your common sense).

It would be a good thing for officers to remember the simple truth that in battle everyone should do his duty and not bother himself as to what concerns others. We will not expatiate here upon other circumstances and will conclude with instructions for officers commanding batteries.

Officers commanding guns should remember and should call the attention of gun captains to the fact that guns possess, to-day, such a high degree of accuracy that the shell will not hit the target if the gun be not brought to bear upon it when it is fired, and therefore gun captains should be prevented from firing without sighting. Such fire does more harm to our ship than to the enemy, for the smoke caused thereby prevents other guns from being sighted and the delivery is useless. The best way to lose a battle is to fire without aiming. He who permits such firing in peace time does not work in his own behalf, but in that of the enemy. The chief duty of an officer in command of battery is to encourage his own men, so as to inspire them with energy and confidence. The wounded should be removed to appointed places, and the dead put aside and covered. Blood stains make the deck slippery, and therefore the decks should be strewn down with sand. Sand should be kept ready for this purpose; this precaution was never overlooked in the old days.

Battery commanders, while encouraging their men and inspiring them with energy, should remember that their own losses are always visible, while those of the enemy are invisible, and therefore they should, from time to time, notify their men of the visible or supposed losses of the enemy. From time to time the captain of the ship should send to the guns news of the enemy's losses. Such news, which ought to be loudly communicated to the battery, is followed by encouraging hurrahs and by a well-directed fire on the enemy.

The guns' crew of the unemployed broadside, and all persons in general who are not at work, should lie down. Officers in command of batteries should remember that when the crews of one broadside are tired out the fresh crews should be shifted over from the other side, and that losses should be filled up whenever required.

For the use of the crew, water should be kept near the guns in pails and buckets. The wounded, particularly, frequently ask for water. Water should be kept in abundance in the surgeon's quarters.

CHAPTER TWELVE

GENERAL ACTION

192. The annihilation of the enemy's squadron may prove of vast strategical and political significance, therefore it is very important to do everything possible to insure that, upon the meeting of two squadrons, ours shall prevail over the enemy. The problem presented by naval action is that of shattering an antagonist so as to force him to yield to our desires. Destruction of ships, one at a time, produces a forcible impression, but the loss of ten ships in as many fights does not have the same moral effect as the loss of a squadron, although the number of the ships in the latter may be much less than in the former case; therefore, everything that relates to squadron action should be very carefully studied out and every precaution should be taken that the evolutions of squadrons when cruising in time of peace, as well as in war, should be developed to the highest state of perfection.

193. Napoleon and Lloyd upon instructions for battle. It is very difficult to lay down exact rules for conducting a sea fight, but even if such rules were possible, they could not be complete enough to insure success. Napoleon makes the following statement upon the subject: "Can rules be given for writing Homer's Iliad or one of the tragedies of Corneille? It is self-evident that the matter is one of inspiration. The same may be said concerning the practice of our art of military combinations (operations)."

"The art of war," said Lloyd, "closely resembles that of poetry and oratory.[1] Many know their rules but very few possess the talent to employ them. If such people write anything, their compositions, which follow these rules closely, are cold and bare and lack that divine fire, that heavenly enthusiasm, which are the unmistakable signs of genius. The same may be said concerning our art; many know its rules, but when they attempt to put these rules into practice they can not find their way. They try to find the rules learned from books, and here they fall back upon the rudiments, and are surprised that the woods, mountains, and rivers do not yield to their imaginative (theoretical) plans, but on the contrary, such plans are subject to them."

The above extracts serve to show that natural inborn talent is required for the successful waging of war. A man instructed in all the rules of war may prove very much out of place in the matter of commanding in battle, but a talented man who has never studied the subject in any way is also as fully out of place. It is only by union of talent with the moral force, knowledge, and wisdom, that the needs of war can be supplied.

194. The value of decision in military questions. A military commander must establish plans and take measures. It is well to see how great people regard the matter of arriving at conclusions in such cases.

Nakhimov said:

> One wise man is good—two are better—but call together a hundred and they all begin to cry out, to jest, to talk nonsense, and then they scratch and tear each other to pieces, so that the whole thing comes to naught. As for me, count me on the sick list the day of the council of war. (Menikow's writings.)

1. Henry Lloyd (1720–83) was a Welsh military historian and strategist who served in many continental armies during the Seven Years' War and others. He argued for formations in column and defined many terms such as "the basis for military operations."

Admiral Nakhimov's words are pregnant with meaning. It is certain that a council of a great number of individuals leads to no results, but that consultation with one able man is always useful; for by conversing with him we outline more clearly to ourselves the very plans that we have determined upon in our own mind. Besides this, it is useful to hear what another man says, as he may throw much light upon the matter from another standpoint. It is far from a fact that every able man aids matters by counsel. We possess many examples of capable persons who do not give themselves the trouble to listen to what has been said, but who only endeavor to explain their own ideas, which are sometimes very brilliant, but altogether out of keeping with the subject in question. If the individual selected unites positive knowledge with a desire to afford aid to the subject under consideration his advice may be of the highest value. In councils in which many people assist energetic and talented suggestions are never accepted, and it most frequently happens in such a case that, if the president does not possess the necessary ability, matters take the form of what General Dragomirow calls "Councils of the twelve wise men."

Jomini says upon this point:

> What would be decided in a council of war where Napoleon had proposed the movement upon Arcola, or the battle of Rivoli, or the passage of the St. Bernard, the movement upon Ulm, or that executed by him at Gera and Jena? Such movements would have been considered impossible, the plans audacious to such an extent as to be absurd. Others would have found a thousand difficulties in the way of their accomplishment. All Napoleon's counsels would have been rejected.

Klausewitz (Instructions upon War, p. 6) gives the following shrewd opinion:

> People who are capable of only ordinary undertakings consider everything possible only after it has been achieved. All

239

great undertakings while unfulfilled always appear impracticable to those who are not capable of performing them. Those who have performed great deeds are distinguished from others by being the first who perceived the possibility of execution.

Napoleon said (Rules of War, p. 67):

The long-drawn-out meditations, the pondering and discussions of councils of war end, as the histories of all ages have shown us, in the adoption of some bad decision, which in war is always characterized by its pettiness or timidity. True wisdom generally consists in the knowledge how to make an energetic decision.

Klausewitz, in his counsels upon the decisive moment, says:

A great part of war consists not upon deciding what is the best thing to be done, but upon deciding upon something to be done, provided that something be energetic and promptly carried out.

Rocquancourt says: "The very worst that we can decide upon in war is not to decide upon anything." Marshall Ney tells us that "indecision in war, if exhibited upon approach of the enemy, is a capital offense in a commander.[2] No time should be wasted in prolonged consultations. Whatever is to be done should be decided upon at once."

General Leer (Positive Strategy) says: "The study of data from which plans are to be developed should be a matter of steady, prolonged work, of careful observation, analysis, and deliberation by many persons, but the formation of the plan itself, as based upon known data or information—that is, adoption of a decision for given premises—should be the momentary task of a single mind."

---

2. Marshal Ney rose from a clerk to become the "Prince of Moscow" during the battle of Borodino, which proved a Pyrrhic Victory. He was noted for his aggressiveness and daring, qualities that Admiral Makarov shared.

Napoleon said: "Any undertaking is well planned if two-thirds of the plan is based upon calculation and one-third upon chance. He who wishes to take no chance in war had better not undertake anything." Frederick the Great comes to the same conclusion in analyzing this question. "In war," said he, "skill and good fortune are indispensable. There are to be found," he further informs us, "those unhappy occasions where the whole burden of human foresight and rational calculation has come to naught. In this way war, not being a subject for exact mathematical analysis, retains the character of a game, the chance of winning depending to a greater or less degree upon the ability of the player."

Klausewitz writes (p. 8):

> In the choice of measures to adopt in a given case, and in determining what measures to avoid, we are always called upon to decide upon the boldest or the most prudent. There are persons who imagine that theory always counsels prudence, but this is not so. If theory advises anything it would be the most determined and the boldest deeds, as corresponding most nearly to the character of war, but theory calls upon each commander to act according to his spirit of enterprise and his confidence in himself. Therefore, choose in accordance with the strength and the force that is within you, but do not forget *that those chiefs accomplish most who know how to dare.*

The above quotations show that a commander should always decide and then carry his decisions energetically into execution. In this connection we must remember the words of Klausewitz (p. 54), that the present always produces upon weak men an impression incomparably greater than the future, even if the future be very near. The most usual source of error is too great fear of the present and not enough for the future.

In deciding every question we must think only of the matter in hand, boldly assume responsibility for our own deeds, use

241

our own common sense, and keep attendant circumstances in view. Napoleon said that in war, circumstances control, and judgment based upon common sense affords the greatest chance of success.

195. *Before putting to sea, or before battle, the admiral should bring his commanding officers together.* This is useful not only for consulting with them, but to personally impart to them the necessary energy and confidence in success. Mutual support in a navy consists principally in the strong belief of everyone that all strive together in every part of the field to destroy the enemy.

196. *The utilization of one's whole strength in securing victory.* All authorities agree that full force must be brought to bear in the effort to win a battle. No precautions should be overlooked which may increase our chance of success, and we should always strive that our means be considerably in excess of apparent requirements. This advice should not be taken in the sense that nothing is to be attempted with small means, but when a task is undertaken, and we are able to add to our strength in one way or another, it is naturally advisable for us to do this.

Klausewitz (Instructions upon War, p. 37) says: "The first and most important principle that must be borne in mind in order to accomplish our ends is that we must exert our strength to the utmost. Every weakening of our efforts diminishes our chance of accomplishing our ends. Even if success be probable, it would be in the highest degree foolish to spare any endeavors to make matters as certain as possible."

Napoleon (Rules of War, p. 37) says: "He who desires to give battle should make it an invariable rule to assemble all his forces: sometimes a single battalion decides the issue of the battle."

He also said that he never considered before a battle that his army was too large, and always concentrated all the forces that he could. It was also Napoleon's rule that the whole task of a commander is to distribute his troops for subsistence and to reunite them for battle, "Se diviser pour vivre et se réunir pour combattre."

197. *Composition of a squadron.* Various opinions exist upon this subject. Most authorities consider that a fighting squadron should be composed of ironclads exclusively, which, on this account, are designated squadron ironclads. This opinion is based upon the practice of former times, when it was thought proper to form the line of battle from ships only, frigates and other smaller vessels being kept apart. The views that formerly prevailed must be regarded as just to-day, for size determines strength. The battle ship has been at all times more powerful than the frigate, and therefore there was no occasion to place the frigate in the center of the line and so weaken one portion thereof. In relation to vessels of small dimensions, such as torpedo cruisers and torpedo boats, the same arguments may be applied, but it is a question in what way large ocean cruisers should be regarded, and where they should be placed in squadron battle. In the old days frigates and other small craft were regarded as cruisers, but nowadays many cruisers approach ironclads in displacement.

The designation cruiser seems to us a narrow one, for by this term we understand a ship performing a special service as a cruiser, while the same vessel could, in our opinion, successfully participate in an artillery engagement. We believe that it would be more accurate to divide ships into armored, partly armored, and unarmored. Under the first heading would be included ships with vertical armor, protecting the water line and a portion of their batteries; under the second, ships whose guns are not protected by armor; and under the third, ships without vertical armor, but with a protective deck covering the machinery, boilers, and the vital parts below the water line. This nomenclature we shall hereafter employ.

If a separate division be formed of unarmored ships, we derive advantage from their greater speed but at the same time the difficulty of control of general forces is increased. Let us assume that the commander in chief of a squadron himself leads the squadron of ironclads into action and that his second in command controls the cruisers. It becomes necessary either to grant the junior admiral complete freedom in movement, or, while permitting him freedom in details, to indicate to him the duty assigned to him, or by means of signals to retain complete control of the actions of his division. We assume that smoke and other impediments will render signaling very difficult in battle. It might happen that the chief of the squadron would be unable at the critical moment to communicate his signals to his junior in command, whence, in case the cruisers are formed in a separate division, it is best to give the junior commander full freedom in movement. He should follow the actions of his commander in chief, endeavor to anticipate his movements, and so employ his own division as to strive for the attainment of the common end, at the same time not interfering with the movements of the ironclads.

However competent the commander of the division may be, there is always a risk that he will interfere with the operations of the squadron, and the commander in chief may, in certain cases, forbid him to execute such movements as would, in his opinion, cause the divisions to collide. There is nothing more difficult than to manœuver even with one ship in a place where there is another vessel that is also manœuvering. If any one has any doubt of this, all he has to do is to lay out two floating targets near to one another and allow two ships to manœuver freely about them. The captains of both manœuvering vessels will be placed in very difficult positions, for they will lose sight of the chief end in view and will strive only to see that their vessels do not collide. For the purpose of avoiding such inconveniences, would it not be better to place all unarmored ships at the rear of the fore-and-aft column, where they will not interfere with movements in any way and whence they may be controlled by signal at any time when it is desired to employ them to chase the enemy's ships or for other purpose. Personally, we are inclined to think that it would be better at the beginning of the battle to keep all unarmored vessels in the general column.

198. *Choice of formation.* It has been stated that different views have been held at different times upon this question. The tactics of the ancients were those of ramming only, which required line abreast. When the ram was abandoned and sea fights were decided by artillery, the formation of ships of war in line ahead was introduced. The introduction of steam did not change the conception of formation in battle, but the successes of the ram of the *Merrimac* again established preference for the bow formation. The echelon formation appeared later than this. Admiral Tegetthoff led his ships into action at Lissa in this formation, which in fact was the line abreast with the ends bent back.[3] Tegetthoff's antagonist, Admiral Persano, formed his fleet in line; and although this line was broken at the beginning of the fight and a mêlée ensued, many said, nevertheless, that the Italians had lost the battle on account of the formation they had chosen. This opinion is unwarranted.

At the battle of the Yalu, Admiral Ito divided his squadron into two divisions, each of which was formed in column.[4] The signal by which Admiral Ito indicated the movement of the second division was misunderstood, which inclines us to the belief that very little dependence can be placed upon signals in battle. Why Ito was led to form his ships in column we do not know, but we believe he was actuated by the idea that no reliance was to be placed upon successful signaling, and

3. In 1866 Austrian Admiral W. von Tegetthoff led the Austrian Navy to victory at Lissa in the first battle between steam-powered ironclads during the Austro-Italian War.

4. In this sea battle (1894) during the Chinese-Japanese War, the Chinese, who used such outmoded tactics as the line abreast—a position for using the ram—lost.

the single formation that he could control without signaling was column. This reason is a very weighty one, and notwithstanding what advantages other formations may possess, column seems a very practical one, and one well suited for battle. We can not see how an admiral will be able to control a battle if his squadron be formed in any other way than in column. Change of formations may be indicated by signals, but before fighting begins. Signals are also possible during battle, but only those that are not too complex. If any vessel could not decipher an ordinary general signal, this would not result in a catastrophe, and the signal could be hauled down even if part of the fleet did not understand it. On the other hand, evolutionary signals must be kept flying until every ship answers, otherwise collisions might ensue.

In view of what has already been said above, we are led to believe that the only formation capable of being maintained in battle and from which the movements of the squadron may be controlled is that of column. Besides this advantage, it possesses others of less importance:

First. Guns are generally mounted so that the greatest fire is delivered from broadside and the least in the direction of the bow and stern. When in column, our ships are placed fore-and-aft with respect to one another, so that broadsides with the greatest number of guns are completely free to be employed against the enemy.

Second. When in column of vessels there is less risk of firing upon our own ships, which is no small advantage in war.

Third. When in column it is easy to preserve distance, and the commanding officer will be less occupied with this matter and will be freer to give his attention to employment of his guns and torpedoes.

Fourth. One ship following another in column protects its mate in front from ramming attack, for the reason that he himself is able to ram that ship which attempts to ram his mate. This proposition is almost self-evident. The ramming ship, after delivering her blow, loses her speed for a considerable interval of time, while the mate astern requires only one minute of time, at a speed of 12 knots, to cover a distance of 200 fathoms. In this manner any ship observing that its mate ahead has been rammed should, without hesitating a second, so direct his course as to pick out the enemy from the two entangled ships and ram him.

To penetrate the fore-and-aft line of ships at intervals of 200 fathoms (the distance between the centers of the ships) is an extremely difficult manœuver to perform. If the vessel attempting it rams one of our vessels and does not succeed in breaking through our line, he will be rammed himself in turn by our ship following next in order, after he has delivered his blow. If the rammed ship happens to slip through the interval between two ships, he runs a great risk of being rammed. The distance between ships with intervals of 2 cable lengths hardly exceeds 2 ship's lengths, consequently the ship whose bow he desires to pass, by proceeding at full speed ahead and changing his course a little, has a good chance of successfully ramming him.

199. The post of the commander in chief. In sailing days naval etiquette required the commander in chief to hoist his flag upon a three-decked ship, and the admiral naturally chose for himself such a vessel. Usually he placed himself at the head of the line, but sometimes took up his position in the center. If the admiral wishes to utilize the advantages of column formation in fleets of to-day and to control the action of his squadrons without signaling, he should place himself at the head of the column. Many think that an admiral should select the most heavily armed vessel, which is best able to withstand the effect of the enemy's fire. There is no doubt that the enemy would concentrate upon the flagship more than upon other ships, and therefore it is logical that the admiral's ship should be the best protected; but the matter may be considered from various other points of view. Would it not be more practical for an admiral to place himself upon a swift torpedo boat or torpedo cruiser and assume, in this small vessel, his place at the head of the line? All that would be required from his ship under these conditions would be to possess masts sufficiently high to enable signals to be made with large flags. In what concerns personal danger to the admiral there would be no very great difference, for the admiral can not properly occupy an armed tower from which he can see nothing, therefore in this regard the armor of an ironclad presents no protection to the admiral.

The advantages to be derived from placing the admiral upon a light vessel are as follows:

First.   The admiral could at any minute, by hoisting the signal, move out of position and inspect his line.

Second.   The flagship, on account of its small size, would not receive as many blows as a large one, and therefore the admiral would remain in relatively greater quiet upon a small ship than upon a large one.

Third.   If the ship chosen by the admiral were of light draught he would be insured against being sunk by torpedoes.

Fourth.   Small ships have fewer guns, consequently firing would interfere less with the admiral upon a small vessel than upon a large one.

Fifth.   If the enemy should concentrate his fire upon the flagship, which from its size would incur a relatively small risk of being injured, the fire upon the heavier ironclads would be considerably weakened, which in itself is a great advantage.

Sixth.   If the enemy disregard the flagship and concentrate his fire upon the leading ironclad, and the latter be put out of action, no mistake would result, for the admiral would continue at the head of the line.

Seventh. In case the admiral desired to change the heading of his squadron 16 points and the rear thus became the van, he could utilize his great superiority in speed to take his place again at the head of the column, and again lead. He might start for his new position at the time of hoisting the signal, then the signal would be properly understood and the admiral could so time his movements as to be at his place at the head of the column just as the turn of the ships was completed.

Eighth. If the flagship be badly injured the admiral is able to transfer his flag to another ship, which would be much easier to do by changing from one small vessel to another than from one large vessel to another.

In view of all the above facts, we are disposed to think that the admiral, in most cases, would make no mistake in shifting his flag before battle to a small rapid ship, but if he intends to do this in time of battle he should practice the manœuver in time of peace.

200. The employment of the semaphore for urgent signals. Wherever he may be placed the admiral should possess the power of making certain very important signals very quickly, so that the signals could be rapidly and exactly interpreted in each case.

The masthead semaphores may be useful in this regard; besides the capability of signaling all phrases in alphabetic characters, they offer a possibility of making very rapid signals. Far more time is consumed in signaling with flags than in setting the vanes of the semaphore in a desired position; besides this, more time is required to pick out flags than in choosing certain semaphore combinations, and it is therefore very important to set apart the most important battle signals for communication by semaphore. When the index is placed horizontally this signifies ordinary semaphore signaling, and when placed in the upper or lower inclined position this may signify war signals. Fifty-six such signals may be made. The signals selected for such communication should be the most important ones, each of which should be provided with clear and exact instructions as to what should be done under existing circumstances.

201. *The fighting order of the squadron* appears to us as follows: All large ships to be in column, of which the swift ships are to constitute one part, let us say the first division, and ships of moderate speed the second part (second division). We assume that it is better to divide the ships according to speeds and not according to the caliber of guns and thickness of armor. Ships of displacement under 1,000 tons are assigned for repeating signals and are posted upon the side of the column away from the enemy. Ships assigned to this duty may be permitted to pass through the columns and should be instructed how to perform this duty without creating confusion. Torpedo boats constitute a separate division and should be formed on the side away from the enemy to attack the latter in accordance with the instructions they have received from the admiral. The ship so injured that she can not maintain such speed as would enable her to maintain her place in line should leave the line, two torpedo boats being left to protect her.

202. *General mêlée.* Many assert that a squadron may be kept in formation only at the beginning of the fight, and that afterwards, when the squadrons interlace, a general mêlée ensues which will be a ship to ship fight in which both antagonists possess no plan and present no possibilities for control. Such an assumption seems to us irrational, for the movement of each ship is impeded by the movements of other ships on their own side. We remember how difficult it is to manœuver within the radius of action of another ship whose intentions are unknown to us. In this respect ships of our own nationality are more impeded than those of the antagonist.

It seems to us that a rule should be established according to which the ship or ships who leave their places in the line should endeavor to recover them as quickly as possible, irrespective of order or of numbers. Let us assume that after the meeting of two squadrons all ships have left their places to avoid ramming or torpedoes, and that the line has been completely shattered. The commander of each ship, as soon as he sees that he is free to manœuver, should immediately turn toward his admiral's flag and endeavor to place himself, as soon as he is able, astern of him or of some other vessel that has already gotten astern of the admiral's ship. The squadron will be thus re-formed and the ships will no longer prevent each other from manœuvering, will not interfere with one another's fire, and the admiral in command will be able to resume the control of his squadron in accordance with determined plans for attacking a certain part of the enemy's forces.

We must remember Nelson's rule, which is included in his instructions before Trafalgar, to look upon the flagships as the points of union.

203. Choice of object of artillery attack. In our choice of object of attack for our guns we should bear in mind, first of all, that the chief thing to do is to hit our adversary, and we should therefore fire upon that vessel which presents the best target to us, that is, the nearest. If we neglect this rule we run the risk of obtaining no results from our fire, and in addition to this we should remember that the penetrative effect of fire at short ranges is very great. We should therefore direct our fire upon a group of ships (if the ships of the antagonist for any reason approach one another). It is well to remember that one ship at short range is a better target than a group at a long range.

Besides the principal conceptions relating to the object of attack, there are also secondary ones. It is useful, for example, to concentrate our fire upon the leading ship, or the flagship. In relation to the destructiveness of fire, it is useful to fire upon that ship which turns its bow or broadside toward us; firing upon ironclads diagonally placed in respect to ourselves is, in our opinion, disadvantageous; the chief point to be remembered under such conditions is the best chance of making a hit.

204. May we place an antagonist under a cross fire? In former times efforts were made to place an antagonist under two fires, which sometimes led to firing upon one's own ships. Nelson, in his instructions issued before Trafalgar, calls attention to the fact that "Shots will carry away the masts and yards of friends as well as foes." The occurrence must have been a common enough one in those days. The question arises whether it is better, nowadays, in a squadron engagement, to place an enemy under cross fire without being restrained by the fact that a portion of our shells may strike our own ships.

Technique has undergone a change, owing to the fact that modern shells are elongated, and therefore, on account of revolution around their axes, they ricochet irregularly, while the balls formerly used ricochetted quite regularly, which argues against placing the enemy under cross fire at the present day.

There is still another modification; that is, the introduction of bursting shells. If we fired at ships entirely with loaded shells, and had fuses so arranged that the shell bursts upon impact upon the water, we would do away with ricochets altogether. Under these conditions we might place an antagonist under cross fire at a distance of 10 cable lengths and run no risk of striking our own ships. If the question relates to two of our own ships firing against one of the antagonist, it is more advantageous to keep both upon the same side of that antagonist. All questions as to how to place an antagonist under cross fire, as has been stated above, relate to squadron action.

205. Concerning intervals between ships. In an artillery engagement it is very important to maintain close intervals between ships. This strengthens the fire of the line and gives us an advantage over the enemy whose intervals are extended.

Small intervals, however, develop the disadvantage of a greater chance of collision. Ships usually proceed to-day with intervals of about 2 cable lengths, counting from the centers of the vessels, and it seems to us that it would be well to preserve these intervals in time of war, as they are practical and the personnel is familiar with them.

206. *Should the formation in column be rigidly adhered to?* Ordinarily, vessels are compelled to follow exactly in the wake of their leaders, but under these conditions it is hard to read signals from even the third ship astern, while it is quite impossible to read them from the fifth. By maintaining an exact fore-and-aft position we insure great exactness for every change of formation, but sometimes it is useful for ships to purposely leave their position to obtain some advantage by use of their guns, etc. If such a departure be permissible, rules should be established to inform each ship in what direction it may deviate. Let us assume that a squadron meets an enemy's squadron by heading directly for it. Then the second ship from the van may be accorded the right to sheer to starboard a distance equal to its own length; the third, the same to port; the fourth, 2 cable lengths to starboard; the fifth, the same to port; the sixth preserves its position in column; the seventh sheers as the second, etc. This disposition of ships affords the first five ships the possibility of seeing the adversary and firing upon him. It also lessens the chance of the enemy hitting us. If a ship be left behind, it should endeavor to recover its position in line as quickly as possible by steering directly for that position upon every turn of the fleet, irrespective of maintenance of its position in line.

207. *Attack upon an extremity of the enemy's column.* A squadron should be manœuvered in an artillery fight so as to obtain an advantage over some portion of the squadron attacked. To this end it is useful to concentrate one's forces either upon the enemy's van or rear, or upon one of his flanks, if the enemy be found in line of vessels. This may be accomplished by suc-

cessive change of direction of the vessels in one's own column; but the concentration of force in some cases is highly satisfactory and effective if each ship from a given moment holds the rear of the enemy upon a given bearing. A description of this manœuver, which the author has put in practice a number of times in his peace exercises, is presented below.

Let us assume two opposing squadrons proceeding upon opposite courses (fig. 25). The leading ship of our squadron, when it finds the rear of the enemy's squadron bearing 45 degrees from its own course, begins to sheer in, so as to constantly maintain the rear vessel upon this course angle, or bearing. The vessel following the leading ship also heads in a similar manner with respect to the enemy's rear, and by so doing no longer proceeds in column, but describes the arc of a curve of diminished radius. The third ship from the van proceeds in an arc of less radius than that of the second, etc.

In performing these evolutions the course of each ship is determined by the course angle, the distance covered being different in each case. Thus, for an original distance between the columns of 10 cable lengths and between ships of 2 cable lengths, and with an original speed of 10 knots, if the leading ship assumes a speed corresponding to the speed upon turning of 12 knots, the second should proceed at a speed of 11 knots; the third, 10 knots; the fourth, 9 1/4 knots; the fifth, 8 1/2 knots; the sixth, 7 3/4 knots; the seventh, 7 knots; the eighth, 6 1/2 knots; and the ninth, 6 knots. This speed should be assumed from the moment of the commencement of the turn by the leading ship. In turning, the interval diminishes from 2 to 1 1/2 cable lengths, which is advantageous in relation to the concentration of fire upon the enemy's rear. The following rule should, in relation to speed, be observed:

When the leading ship begins to turn, the ships following should regulate their speeds as follows: The leader increases his speed 20 per cent; the second ship increases speed 10 per cent; the third maintains the original speed; the fourth dimin-

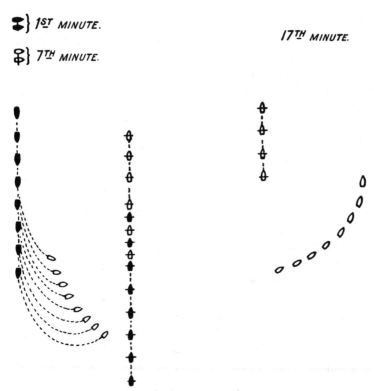

Fig. 25. Attack on rear of adversary's column.

ishes speed 7 per cent; the fifth diminishes speed 15 per cent; the sixth diminishes speed 23 per cent.

As all ships do not lose speed alike upon turning, and as differences in speeds become greater when the distance between columns is less, each ship should be careful to approach within not less than 1 1/2 cable lengths of its mate, with a course angle of about 35 degrees. Each ship observes the other one in front of him and is responsible for collision therewith. From the beginning of this evolution all ships concentrate their fire upon the rear of the enemy's column and upon those of his ships that are nearest thereto.

When the enemy's line has been completely flanked, the leader uses his helm so as to maintain himself at a suitable distance for artillery fire. The remaining ships gradually resume position in column, each ship increasing its speed as soon as it observes that the interval from its leader begins to increase.

If it be desired to pass the rear of the enemy at a closer range, it may be done as in the preceding case, with the difference that the course angle is maintained, not upon the rear ship of the enemy, but upon the second from the rear. In case the rear ship under these conditions should not fall within the angle of fire of the broadside guns it may be fired upon with the guns aft. Upon flanking the enemy's column its rear is exposed to the fire of all the ships of our fleet. In case of attack upon his rear guard the enemy should act as has been explained above. The best thing for him to do is to perform the same manœuver and attack the rear guard of the attacking squadron. He may also turn all his ships simultaneously a given number of points and advance to the attack, or assume a more favorable position in some other way. In general, after the squadron turns twelve points from the enemy the leading vessel should employ its helm accordingly and assume a course parallel to the enemy's rear. The remaining ships should in this case regard themselves as out of position and should endeavor to take gradually their places in the new line.

208. *Attack of the enemy's flank.* Let us assume that our squadron is formed in column and perceives the enemy ahead in line formation (fig. 26, beginning of action), and that the leading ship is distant 40 cable lengths from the enemy. If the latter now begins to hold the flank of the enemy upon a bearing of 55 degrees, then, as the squadrons approach each other, the leader and some ships following will be in a position to attack the enemy's flank and the ships next thereto with all broadside guns. In twelve minutes the leading ship flanks the enemy's line, and the squadron occupies the position shown (fig. 26, twelfth minute).

256

FLEET ATTACK.

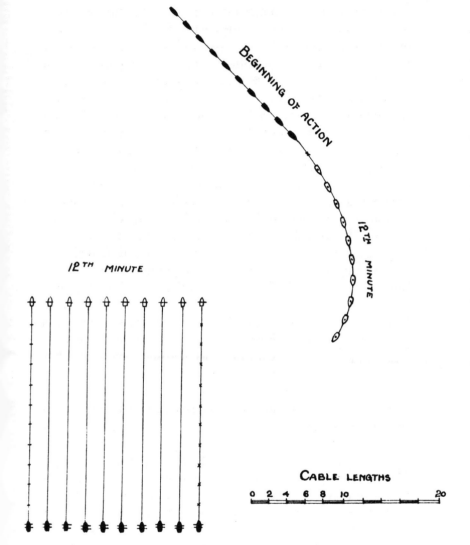

BEGINNING OF ACTION

12TH MINUTE

12TH MINUTE

CABLE LENGTHS

BEGINNING OF ACTION

Fig. 26.

During all this manœuver the position of our vessels is more favorable than that of the enemy, for we are able to use our broadside guns and hold a part of his squadron at a short range, while only his right-flank ship can fire upon us from this range. The moment especially favorable for each ship to fire is when it passes the line of bearing of the enemy's ships, remembering that the ricochets incline to the right. In case of firing shells that do not burst, in the case represented in fig. 26 it is advantageous to fire a little before passing the enemy's line of bearing.

Each ship as it approaches the enemy's flank is very favorably placed for firing its torpedoes at long range. Torpedoes should move parallel to the front of the enemy, so that if they do not strike one ship they may strike another. When the enemy observes the discharge of our torpedoes, all that he can do is to turn his ships by signal, which requires considerable time for execution. There is no doubt that our antagonist may fire his torpedoes, but if he wishes to use them at long range he must give them a low speed, and in such cases firing across the bows of his own ships is out of the question. In general, when ships are formed in line, firing from broadside tubes across bows is dangerous for our own ships.

Returning to the position occupied by the squadron at the end of the twelfth minute, it becomes necessary to either turn the whole squadron simultaneously 16 points to the right (fig. 27), or else to proceed without changing the course, so as to retire. In our opinion it would be better to change the course 16 points to starboard and remain in column of vessels, gradually assuming a course parallel to that of the enemy and concentrating our fire upon those of his ships nearest to us.

Turning our squadron 16 points when vessels are disposed in the arc of a circle requires watchfulness upon the part of a commander in chief, for ships approach one another in turning; to avoid danger, every ship should commence the turn only when it observes that its mate astern has already put its

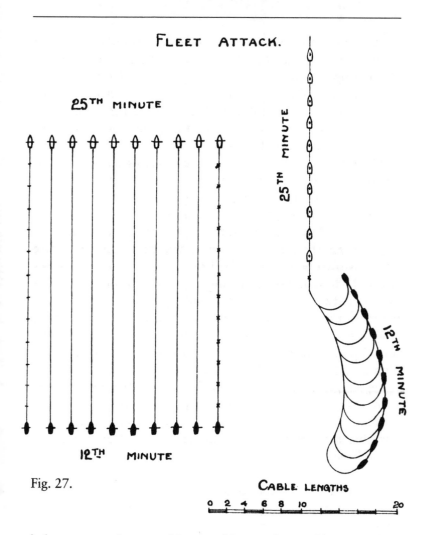

FLEET ATTACK.

25TH MINUTE

25TH MINUTE

12TH MINUTE

12TH MINUTE

Fig. 27.

CABLE LENGTHS

0 2 4 6 8 10 20

helm over, and every ship should consider itself responsible for collision with its mate astern. We assume that during the whole time of the evolution the enemy's squadron does not change his formation. If he should turn suddenly 8 points to the left, we would have to begin the above-described manœuver of attacking the end ships of the enemy's squadron. If

259

he turn suddenly 8 points to starboard, it would be better to lay our course parallel to his own, endeavoring to place part of our ships in advance of his van. By so doing we have no advantage over our antagonist, but we will not be in a disadvantageous position, and if the head of his column begins to change its course we may be able to surround the leaders in a circle and concentrate fire upon them.

209. *Interception of a portion of the enemy's squadron.* Let us assume the same conditions as before—that is, that our fleet is formed in column and our adversary's in line, and that we desire to cut off a portion of his squadron. In this manœuver our leading ship is subjected to a concentrated fire of the antagonist. He should hold the third ship of the enemy's flank upon his own bow, and he will then pass approximately between the fifth and the sixth ship (fig. 28). It is useless for the intercepted ships of the enemy to maintain the same course as before, for in line formation they do not protect one another from ramming as they do in column. If the intercepted ships turn 8 points to the right to avoid meeting our column, our own squadron begins its attack upon the rear ships of the intercepted group.

In this combination, our own ships are exposed, as already stated, to the concentrated fire of the antagonist, and generally this manœuver is far from being as advantageous as might be supposed.

210. *Forming a ring around the enemy.* If we have a long fore-and-aft column and the force of the enemy is comparatively limited, or if, in consequence of possessing fewer ships or for other reasons, the enemy lessens his speed and his ships approach one another, it is very advantageous for us to surround them in a ring, with no intervals in our own formation through which he may escape. In occupying such a position we are in a very favorable condition for the use of our guns. The enemy's ships will have no room to form line in a short time, and we must utilize this circumstance for concentrating

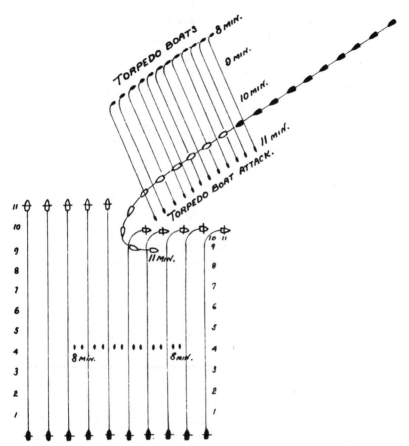

Fig. 28. Interception of part of the enemy's squadron.

our fire. Each inaccurate shot of the enemy will miss its mark, but some of our misses will strike other ships of the enemy; besides this, the enemy's ships being close together will interfere with one another.

The tactics of surrounding an enemy consists in forming an outer ring around him, without respect to order or numbers. Each ship endeavors as quickly as possible to take up a course

261

parallel to the enemy's. The enemy should form column and endeavor to break through the line and escape from the inner position.

To this end any one of the surrounded ships that happens to find the greatest interval in the enemy's ring opposite to himself, hoists the necessary signal and heads for this point, the other ships following after him in one column. The outer ring will have to yield, evidently, to the column of vessels at short intervals.

211. *The rôle of torpedo boats in squadron warfare* may be twofold, as follows: To attack the enemy's ships, and to oppose attack from the enemy's torpedo boats.

The torpedo-boat division should have its chief, around whom the flotilla is grouped. If the torpedo boats are numerous, there should be two or three groups of them of eight torpedo boats each.

Torpedo boats take no part in fights at long range, and should be kept out of the enemy's fire; near enough, however, to the place of action to be able to appear promptly when their services are required. Some consider that it is more favorable to retain torpedo boats in rear of one's own ships, near the sides. Is this so? Would it not follow that the torpedo boats behind the ships would be screened so far as their capability of seeing anything is concerned, yet not screened from the fire of the enemy? All projectiles which happen to burst upon impact against the superstructure of the ironclads would scatter their fragments in the very places where the torpedo boats happened to be. It would be much safer to place them in a very open position. We must avoid grouping vessels too closely together, and placing them behind one another develops this condition. We are therefore opposed to concealing our torpedo boats behind large vessels.

Torpedo boats can easily pass through the fore-and-aft line, and consequently may be kept at some distance from the line of their own ships, until the moment of attack. When the signal of attack is shown, all torpedo boats proceed in line to attack part of the enemy's squadron, endeavoring to maintain as high a speed as possible, and dressing upon their leader. The moment of attack should be indicated by semaphore signals; and, besides, the direction toward which torpedo boats are to turn after firing their torpedoes should have been determined beforehand. Torpedo boats should remember that their small size is their best protection from the enemy's guns, as they are very hard to hit; and, therefore, after firing one torpedo they have the chance, without being too hasty, of firing a torpedo from the second apparatus; and they should only consider their work completed after they have fired both torpedoes, after which they may retire to a safer position, out of range of the adversary's guns.

Some of the torpedo boats may, however, be regarded differently, and may be employed to weaken the enemy's squadron before we engage the latter with our artillery. Torpedo attack is naturally much more difficult under these circumstances, and it is probable that many of the torpedo boats would be destroyed; but the result might still be the actual weakening of the enemy's squadron. Such tactics would be fundamental in cases when, on account of the sea, the enemy's ships roll heavily, or when foggy or rainy weather diminishes the chance of the torpedo boats being sighted. Let us assume that the enemy adopt such tactics, and that a division of his torpedo boats precede his squadron and attack our own. Should we send our torpedo boats against his or should we defend ourselves against his torpedo boats with our guns? This question may be decided as follows: If there is a chance of attacking his torpedo boats at a great distance from our squadron, we may or may not send out our own boats, according to our desires. If time does not permit our meeting them at a great distance, it is better to send our torpedo boats as quickly as possible beyond the line of ships, so they will not interfere with the fire of our own guns. Such a manœuver should be signaled by semaphore.

When attacked by torpedo boats the squadron may either simultaneously turn their sterns toward them or maintain their former course, or turn with their bows toward the approaching flotilla. If time permits, the best thing to do is to turn stern to them, so as to gain time for firing upon them. If the torpedo boats are near at hand and it is easier to turn bows-on to them, this should be done, although the manœuver is far from being as advantageous as the former. If only one torpedo boat attack, turning bows-on toward it is almost a guaranty of immunity from explosion, on account of the narrow entrance of modern vessels and of the blunt form of the torpedo head. When attacked simultaneously by a number of torpedo boats, turning bows-on toward one of them will not prevent the others from delivering their fire under the most favorable conditions. The same will be true in the case of a torpedo-boat attack upon the whole squadron. The torpedoes should be discharged against those ships that are not turned bows-on to them. If the ships remain on their original course, they may either alter their speed and trust blindly to their guns, or, having reversed their engines simultaneously from full speed ahead to full speed astern, lower their torpedo nets.

Of the above-described manœuvers we give preference to turning stern toward torpedo boats if there is sufficient time and the squadron is able to maintain a fair speed. If the torpedo boat attack is sudden, the best thing to do is to back the engines and lower the nets. This manœuver requires only two minutes' time to perform, after which the ships remain stationary and their nets become efficient. This manœuver is one that should be indicated by the semaphore.

212. Is a reserve desirable? In our opinion there is no need of a reserve in squadron action. It weakens our own strength and affords our enemy the chance of defeating our squadron by sections. It is better to reinforce our column. Then, as above stated, the end ships will constitute a reserve for the main force, which may take a more active part in battle.

213. General conclusions on squadron action. As was stated in paragraph 193, it is impossible to give exact directions how to fight a squadron. Much depends upon the tactics of action of our adversary. But in general we may state that we should endeavor to concentrate a superior force upon some part of his squadron, and after annihilating it to attack the other part.

214. How should a battle be concluded? The results of a squadron engagement are complete only when they result in the complete annihilation of the enemy's forces. Frederick the Great said in relation to pursuit: "Nothing is done well when anything remains to be done." Blücher said that "there is no need to advance with complete brigades or battalions in conducting a pursuit.[5] It is self-evident that an enemy beaten and running away offers no resistance." Nelson said: "I am ready to lose half of my squadron to annihilate the French." He wrote to his wife after the battle in the Gulf of Genoa: "If out of eleven of the enemy's ships we had taken ten and allowed one to escape, having the possibility of capturing it, I would not have considered the day a good one."

From the above follows the incontrovertible rule of the necessity of pursuing and annihilating a beaten enemy. We must not consider our own losses, but continue to attack until he is completely annihilated or until he escapes. To allow a defeated enemy to escape from our hands is to diminish the value of the results of victory, for however great his losses may be in matériel or in personnel, his ship returns to its own ports and is repaired, and its loss to his squadron is but temporary.

5. Probably G. L. Blücher (1742–1819), a Prussian field marshal who, among other actions, took part in the defeat of Napoleon at Waterloo.

CHAPTER THIRTEEN

NIGHT TORPEDO ATTACK

215. Historical note. The first torpedo launches possessed such a low speed that they could not overtake any war ship, and torpedo outfits consisted therefore of towing devices, to employ which it was necessary to lay one's ship alongside an enemy. Torpedo boat attacks were undertaken exclusively at night, and at the time of the American civil war (1861–64) some successful attacks were made. These successes were probably regarded as fortuitous, for they led to no general armament of steam cutters of large vessels, and did not lead to the creation of a type of torpedo boat for some time.

The Franco-German war of 1870–71 produced nothing new in this direction, but the matter was further developed as the result of successes obtained by our steam launches in the Turkish war in 1877. The Russian sailors on the Danube, notwithstanding the absence of war ships, did all that the progress of military operations required. By means of the torpedo defense they limited the radius of action of the Turkish ships of war as far as was required, and they defended the line of torpedoes with steam cutters and thus impeded the action of the enemy's fleet.

In the Black Sea the proposed appliances for hoisting and lowering steam cutters fully armed and equipped for torpedo service, their outfit not interfering with their being successfully hoisted or lowered.[1] The steamer *Grand Duke Konstantin* was fitted out so as to be able to hoist four steam launches, being able to convey these boats to the desired port of the enemy, so that they could deliver a night attack and return to the steamer at dawn. The hoisting of the cutters was quite a simple matter, and so well arranged that all steam cutters with full equipment and armament, and also with steam up in boilers, could be lowered at once. In exercise they made a speed of about 6 knots. They were hoisted one after another, but on account of the weakness of the steam winches they could not be raised from the water with their full supply of coal. It was necessary to throw the coal overboard before hoisting, so they did not meet requirements in this respect. The hoisting of all four cutters from the time of the order "all hands on deck" to the command "pipe down" took about seven minutes, and could be performed when the ship was rolling considerably.

The success of the torpedo cutters in the Black Sea and the Danube served as a stimulus to the whole subject, and led, in 1877, to the establishment of a type of torpedo boat. Efforts were immediately made to develop devices for suitably hoisting and lowering steam cutters on very large ships. Besides this, some navies have built special steamers to transport torpedo boats, as the *Grand Duke Konstantin* did, only larger ones.

216. Torpedo warfare as related to the character of the Russian seaman. Torpedo attack closely resembles guerrilla warfare, and therefore well suits the disposition of the Russian seaman. We may not possess the powers of systematization that characterize other western nations, but when war begins, the Russian knows that lack of organization may be replaced by personal initiative in the commanders. This is a quality which is priceless in a torpedo attack.

1. Here Admiral Makarov refers to his invention of the torpedo boat, which eventually led to the invention of the destroyer.

The spirit of personal initiative was widely manifested at Sebastopol, and this and nothing else prevented the allies from occupying this point, unfortified up to the time of the war but strongly fortified then.

At the time of the Franco-German war the French fleet remained off the German ports for long periods of time, but nevertheless the idea of torpedo attack was never developed. They say that at this time the German fleet possessed no torpedoes: but we had none at the time of the declaration of war with Turkey; they had to be invented, and the first torpedoes were kegs filled with powder and suspended from buoys. There was no lack of steam cutters and light boats in Germany, while we, in our war with Turkey, had to take what we could lay our hands on. One of our cutters, bearing the great name of *Navarino*, that took part in all torpedo attacks, was about as large as an eight-oared barge and had one diminutive steam cylinder.

The explanation of this is to be found in the difference existing between the national character of our neighbor and of ourselves. His renown lies in his system, in his organized preparation for war; we can afford to neglect nothing that temporary organization may offer in war, and in this the spirit of initiative possessed by our leaders is largely displayed.

217. Designations of torpedo boats. In paragraph 57 we presented the views of Napoleon as to what constituted a commander in chief. He said: "It is not the Roman armies that conquered the Gauls, but Cæsar; not the Carthaginian armies that made Rome tremble, but Hannibal," etc. Naturally much depends upon the captain and his capabilities, and possibly such a conception led to the naming of the bastions of Sebastopol after different commanders. The defense of Sebastopol was established provisionally, and consequently the idea of naming the bastions after commanders was not a bad one. Peter the Great often ordered certain regiments to be named after their colonels. Subsequently he changed this, but by ukase of Paul I, 31st of October, 1798, regiments were ordered to bear the names of their commanders. This did not prove practical, for a regiment is a definite unit and the change of names upon the change of commanders is not desirable. We believe, therefore, that it would be unwise to name ships by the names of captains.

For torpedo boats the matter is different, and we believe it would not be a bad idea to do away with the individual number by which they are designated and call them in tactical and other exercises by the names of their captains. The torpedo boat possesses the character which its commander imparts to it, and when occasion to give special duty arises, first of all suitable captains and not suitable torpedo boats are sought. Thus, in working torpedo boats in pairs, although it is important that they should be as nearly as possible of the same qualities, it is more important that they should conform to the qualities of the commanding officer. We believe that torpedo boats should be named after their captains. Even now it often happens that when an admiral sends out an order or signals to a torpedo boat he applies to it the family name of the captain and not the boat number, as: "Signal Yakovlev to be ready;" "Signal Seelman to take dispatches," etc.

218. Increase in dimensions of torpedo boats. The general tendency in late years toward increasing dimensions of ships of all types is repeated in what relates to torpedo boats. They advanced from steam cutters of 6 tons displacement to torpedo launches of 20 tons; then they began to build boats of the *Batoum* type of 60 tons, while at the present time torpedo boats usually possess a displacement of about 100 tons.

The increase in dimension was effected for the purpose of supplying them with greater speed and a greater radius of action, and if the cost of all these types had been the same the change might have been deemed fully rational; but as five small boats can be made for what it costs to build one large one, then, when deciding upon increased dimensions, we must bear in mind that the number of vessels will be diminished. Besides this, it happens that the best defense for torpedo boats against projectiles is their small size. Nowadays torpedo boats have so increased in dimensions that much of quality has been lost.

As far as relates to the superiority of one type over another for night attack in the open sea, the large torpedo boats are as good as small ones; but in night attack in the enemy's harbor, where good turning power is indispensable, the ordinary steam cutter is almost as good as the torpedo boat. It must also be borne in mind that the steam cutters can be hoisted and do not impede the movements of ships, while torpedo boats and launches, under certain conditions of weather, retard the movements of ships and sometimes cause delay.

In view of what has been said above it appears to us that torpedo boats of over 100 tons dimensions, which are intended for distant cruising, will not replace the 20-ton boats which are capable of acting in the proximity of the enemy's coasts and ports. Such vessels will not replace steam cutters that can be hoisted on board, which, for convenience of hoisting and lowering in a sea way, should not exceed the dimensions of 7 tons displacement when fully armed and equipped.

219. Preparatory manœuvering of torpedo boats should consist in occupying a favorable position in relation to that of the enemy. A good situation is one from which one can approach quickly and occupy a position suitable for firing. If the enemy heads upon any particular course, the most favorable position is that ahead of him, but as he may change his course when he notes preparations for an attack, when the number of torpedo boats is sufficient the manœuver should be so executed that, at the moment of attack, the torpedo boats should surround him upon all sides. Such a manœuver becomes possible when there are several flotillas of torpedo boats, but where there is only one the attack can proceed from one side only.

In assigning the position of each boat for torpedo attack, it is better to indicate the bearing of attack without reference to the actual heading of the enemy.

Manœuvering torpedo boats at night without lights is extremely difficult, and the fact must be borne in mind that torpedo boats may, under these conditions, lose touch with one another. Steam cutters may keep nearer to each other than torpedo boats, and are easier to keep together. Nelson advised towing ships and boats one behind the other in night attacks. We believe that it would be a good thing to do the same thing with steam cutters advancing to an attack in the enemy's harbor. Plans may be frustrated by the separation of the boats, and we believe Nelson's counsels to be very practical in this respect.

220. Torpedo boats in divisions or in pairs. The possibility of dispersion by night would be awkward in controlling a large number of boats at night, and this suggests the question whether it would be better to send out torpedo boats for night attack in flotillas or in pairs. In the latter case, if the captains understand one another well, it is possible to proceed secretly, so that the enemy will notice nothing; in handling large groups of torpedo boats full secrecy should not be attempted, and some signals should be made with lights. We prefer using large groups of these vessels, but we also think that torpedo boats sent out in pairs may do good work. We think the number of boats in each group should be limited to eight.

In manœuvers the boats should proceed in column with the smallest possible intervals between them. The second boat should keep a little to the right of the first; the third to the left; the fourth in the wake of the first, etc.

221. Secrecy of night attacks. In preparatory manœuvering, when endeavoring to preserve the utmost secrecy, it should be borne in mind that if the enemy throws his search light upon one of the torpedo boats this does not signify that he sees it. It is a very usual phenomenon for those on board the torpedo boat to imagine themselves discovered, while in fact they may not have been seen.

If the sea horizon is brighter on one side than on another it is more favorable to approach from the side of the dark horizon. When the moon is up it is preferable to approach from the side of the moonlight, so that the unilluminated side of the boat will be turned toward the enemy.

When in the proximity of an obscured coast line it is best to approach from the direction of the shore, but not to intercept lines of lights from the shore or fishing sloops, as skilled signalmen from a low position on shipboard immediately notice when a light is obscured by the passing of a torpedo boat, and may even thus count the number of them. In windy weather it is more favorable to approach from to leeward. If the enemy employs electric projectors, black paint is preferable for the hull; if he does not employ them, light gray. In all circumstances the paint should be lusterless and not shiny.

If we desire to paint a torpedo boat so as to render it quite invisible, we would counsel the use of a lusterless black color and cover it, when necessary, with old trapaulins or worn-out sails. As long as the projectors do not illuminate the color of the sails the latter constitute the best protection, but when the projectors begin to discover them remove the tarpaulins and leave the black sides, as this is the least visible color under the illumination of electric rays.

222. Destruction of booms. When proceeding in divisions of flotillas of torpedo boats in the enemy's harbor we must count upon meeting boom obstructions. Sometimes it is possible to jump over booms, but in doing this one runs no small risk of losing screws and rudder. It would be better to remove the obstructions, which may be done in two ways, either to destroy them by torpedoes or to sink them by weighting them. The latter seems to us preferable. For sinking booms it is necessary to bring along a rowboat filled with pieces of ballast secured together in pairs, or lumps of coal similarly secured. Weights thus prepared are thrown across the boom until the latter sinks under the water. The torpedo boats or the steam cutters pass through the breach, and the rowboat remains to indicate the point of escape from the harbor.

223. *The last moments of torpedo attack.* When the division of torpedo boats has approached the enemy upon the desired bearing, it is necessary to make the signal of execution; e.g., a few long flashes with the signal lantern. Upon this all the torpedo boats put their helms over and proceed to attack the enemy's front at full speed. When the attack has once been begun it must not be interrupted, no difference what happens. A heavy fire must be looked for or an attack from the enemy's torpedo boats, or the enemy's ship may put helm hard over and retreat from our boats. All these conditions should serve only to increase the energy of the attack, which should never be relinquished until brought to a successful conclusion. Having approached within torpedo range of the enemy, this position must be maintained until all torpedoes are fired from the loaded tubes. It is very difficult to determine the best moment to discharge the torpedo. The distance always seems closer at night than it actually is, and therefore it is preferable when attacking a ship under these conditions to get somewhat nearer than is deemed necessary for the attack. If the attack is upon a whole squadron, it may be preferable to stop at a greater distance, say 6 cable lengths, while the torpedo boats are not yet discovered, and discharge the torpedoes from this position.

224. *The moral element in night torpedo attack.* The moral element is of the highest importance in relation to the success of a night attack, and if those in charge of the boats possess nerves of steel the attack will prove a complete success. Persons who possess full self-control may overcome difficulties, while the weak will of an executive and the lack of endurance to the necessary degree will militate against favorable results.

The conditions of night attack are very trying, and to make this matter clear we present a comparison. It is a known fact that more self-control is required of field artillery than of infantry. The soldier who exhibits the necessary firmness when he stands shoulder to shoulder with his comrades in his company is not so steady when stationed behind a gun. Artillerists are trained to the idea that it is their duty to die at their guns, and this is a matter that it seems necessary to frequently refer to, as we often hear how artillerists are exhorted by their chiefs upon the necessity to firmly maintain their ground. In this relation Kutousow's advice before the battle of Borodino is worthy of note. "Assure all field batteries on my behalf that they are not to change their position as long as the enemy does not ride over the guns; tell the captains and all officers to stand up boldly against grape; fire at short range, so not to yield one foot of ground to our enemy; the artillery should be prepared to sacrifice itself; they may capture your guns, but fire your last round in their faces, and the battery which is thus taken does an enemy injury fully compensating us for the loss of the guns."

There is a greater difference between the position of the guns' crews upon a large ship and a torpedo boat than there is between infantry and artillery on land. On shipboard people face one another, and there is a very just Russian proverb that "It is a fine thing to die in the presence of others." On torpedo boats there are but few persons, and they are scattered, so that they do not see one another. The captain of the torpedo boat feels his isolation perhaps more than anyone else. The desire to approach the enemy secretly increases the strain of the situation, which all regard as a very trying one.

These are conditions that must be counted upon, and the question may well be asked, do the advantages that are to be derived from concealment balance the disadvantages arising from the mental sensations derived therefrom? Would it not be better, then, to make a night attack openly, so that the torpedo boats can see one another? Would it not be better for the crews to shout out with hurrahs, and at the moment of attack to afford one another that mutual support which is possible in a simultaneous general attack? In our opinion the secret method of attack has its good side as well as the open, but we are inclined to give the preference to the latter.

Let us assume that four divisions of torpedo boats have left the harbor to attack an enemy's squadron. One division of the torpedo boats is directed to be to the northward of the enemy at a given time; another to the eastward; the third to the southward, and the fourth to the westward. At the hour agreed upon the signal is made by a rocket, this signal is repeated by all the boats, and, showing their stern lights, invisible from ahead, they advance at the same moment to the attack, without uncovering their distinguishing lights but at the same time employing such lights as are necessary for the proper preparation of the torpedoes.

It is useful, when advancing to the attack, to throw overboard in the water floats with lights upon them for the purpose of drawing off the enemy's fire. From the moment of signal for torpedo attack there should be no attempt not to give orders in a loud voice; let the men shout out among themselves all that they choose. In this way we think that the spirits of the men on the torpedo boats will be raised and the dejected frame of mind which is produced by extreme efforts at concealment avoided.

Suvorow said: "Light your matches, throw yourselves upon the guns; they are firing over your heads." In a torpedo attack it will be just so; the shells and projectiles from rapid-firing guns will pass over your heads. The marksmen of the enemy's ships are just the same as ours. They will be in no very calm frame of mind; but even if they are calm, night firing upon approaching torpedo boats can not be a success, for only a few of the boats can be lit by search lights, while the others must remain in darkness. The distance of the torpedo boats covered by the search lights, as well as those that are not, remains unknown, and it is impossible to correct fire by watching the fall of shells, for no gun captain can tell which shells are his own and which those of another.

From the above we conclude that secrecy should be observed while we remain at a long range from the enemy, to prevent their torpedo boats from interfering with us; but when the moment of attack approaches, superfluous concealment should be thrown aside and we should approach boldly, for "God helps the brave."

CHAPTER FOURTEEN

INSTRUCTIONS UPON VARIOUS NAVAL SUBJECTS

225. The rôle of the tactician in relation to naval science. Naval tactics, which, as we have already stated, stands at the head of all naval sciences, should indicate to each one of them how it should strive, and may sometimes point out the means best adapted for obtaining desired ends. If tactics does not undertake to define the end sought, every naval specialist will develop matters as he sees fit, and thus may start off upon a false road. Besides this, naval tactics should determine all branches of naval technique, so that everything required in war may take its assigned place, and no subject remain unclassified. This is especially necessary, not to increase the dimensions of each branch, against which we have already declared ourselves, but to show what branch is to develop each subject.

Convenience in instruction may serve as a basis for the distribution of special subjects between the branches of naval technique. As the author is not especially posted upon this matter, he will not enter into its discussion, but he believes that it would be very useful if someone well posted upon existing courses of study would declare how certain branches of our profession which have not yet been given a definite scientific status should be classified; for example, unsinkability of ships; signaling; net defense against torpedoes; stoppage of leaks; investigation of the qualities of one's own ship; construction of booms; dragging for the repair or destruction of telegraph cables. Should all these branches relate to seaman-ship, or to other departments of naval science?

226. *Instructions upon evolutions.* The movements of ships in squadrons should, in our opinion, constitute a separate sci-ence, which may be called "evolutions." This science should investigate the laws of the movements of ships and the means of investigating the qualities of each ship. It should also deal with the rules for manœuvering squadrons, and establish rules for changing the formation and for re-formation. At the present time, evolutions do not constitute a special study. Ad-miral Butakov, in his work, New Principles of Steam Tactics, develops this subject exclusively and applies laws thereto, but calls it "Steam Tactics." As tactics is the science of war, all that pertains to victory becomes its subject. According to this definition, not only evolutions but also ordnance may be comprised under the head of "tactics," but this would lead to increased dimensions of the tactical beyond limits of practical control; so that we believe it would be better to separate the laws of movements of ships and squadrons into a special study—"evolutions."

226a. *Change of formation.* Butakov first proposed moving ships in circles and straight lines during changes of formation, as this affords the possibility of making these changes in an extremely regular manner. This method of change of forma-tion, however, has its disadvantages, owing to the fact that each change requires much time and that squadrons which execute the change ought to be left to finish it, and no other manœuver can be begun. In some fleets this inconvenience is considered so serious that evolutions are performed by oblique movements. Such evolutions require proportionate reductions in speeds; and directions are given in the signal book how much the speed of each ship should be lessened or increased. In some fleets both systems of evolution are employed.

Apart from the question as to which kind of change of formation preference should be given, there is also another important question: should the order of ship's numbers be observed in evolution, or should it be disregarded? If the order of numbers be not observed, the evolution of circles in oblique lines may be simplified. Even in Admiral Butakov's method, by which systemization is as complete as possible, flanks so change sometimes that the rear becomes the van; the right flank the left flank. In consequence of this and in order to simplify evolutions, we would prefer not to maintain the order of numbers, but to have signal books for evolutions in circles as well as for evolutions by oblique movements.

We called attention above to the fact that while changing formation the fleet remained in a state of change for a long time, and the admiral could then undertake nothing without risk of being misunderstood. At such times it is impossible to hoist the most important signals relating to simultaneous changes of heading. There might be a case, however, when the change of formation would have to be stopped during its progress to enable all vessels to make such a simultaneous change to avoid torpedo attack. Brief signals would have to be made in order to accomplish this, and we propose that upon exhibiting the flag "S" (steady) all the ships should as quickly as possible assume a course parallel to that of the admiral, and thus afford him the possibility of manœuvering.

227. Re-formation. In some fleets manœuvers are attempted by which each ship strives to attain its place in the new formation by moving in the most convenient direction, observing at the same time general rules relating to collision. Let us assume that a fleet is formed into two columns and that it is desired to convert it into a wedge, headed in a given direction. The signal is hoisted, "form echelon." When it is hauled down the admiral heads in the new direction, and all other ships occupy their new positions as quickly as possible. This manœuver is called re-formation, in distinction to the previous methods, which are designated "change of formation."

Re-formation is a quick way of changing from one formation to another, and although the possibility of collision of ships is greater than in the previous case, it is probable that in time of war re-formation would be employed more frequently than change of formation. Formations will be destroyed in battle, and when they are broken re-formation is a quicker way of regaining established order. In general, when the fleet is scattered and the ships do not know what to do, the easiest thing to do is to put themselves in a position parallel to the flagship and endeavor to take a position astern of the flag.

228. *Torpedo-boat evolutions* should be very simple, for it is impossible to perform evolutions in circles, displaying the signal of execution, etc. The proper thing to teach torpedo boats is how to maintain line abreast and how to change front to the right and the left. In changing front the torpedo boat upon the flank toward which the change is made stops his engines; the torpedo boat on the opposite flank proceeds at full speed, and the remaining boats maintain a speed which, corresponding to their position, enables them to preserve their dress.

Torpedo boats must also be taught to change front upon signal by whistle; one long whistle, "steady so;" two whistles, "right turn;" three, "left turn." Upon turning, glance at the chief of the division and turn the same way that he does. When the chief of the division "steadies," he blows his whistle that the dress is to be taken upon his boat. I have exercised torpedo boats by this method and have found it fully practicable.

229. *Deductions of Flag Engineer Afonasev relating to the elements of speed and turning power.* Regularity in evolution depends largely upon the properties of the individual ship. In paragraph 99 we showed how necessary it was to investigate all properties of those ships in which we are placed. Although each ship has its own peculiarities, there are, nevertheless,

general laws applicable to the individual vessel in a greater or lesser degree. Upon this subject no one has done as much as V. I. Afonasev, who has gone to the trouble of collating all the data that he has been able to collect, and has established general deductions therefrom. Upon our making application to him he very kindly furnished us the data necessary for our work. He gives results expressed by formulas, but practical men have no fondness for formulated expressions, and when they observe formulas in a book they pass over these places without examination, thereby depriving themselves of the chance of utilizing very important material. The present book is written for practical men, and therefore we deem it more proper and suitable to present Mr. Afonasev's work in its most simple form, in doing which he himself afforded us aid. The general deductions made by this eminent writer are given below:

Upon increasing or diminishing the displacement of a ship 5 and 10 per cent, the speed upon a direct course at a given indicated horsepower is diminished or increased correspondingly 1 and 2 per cent.

Upon increasing or diminishing the displacement 5 and 10 per cent, the indicated horsepower necessary for maintaining the ship at same speed upon a direct course is increased or diminished 3 and 7 per cent.

As the effect of the fouling of the ship's hull, the following diminish as follows: Speed, 8 per cent; number of revolutions, 10 per cent; indicated horsepower, 12 per cent.

Torpedo nets at high speeds, when they float, diminish the speed of the ship 25 per cent. At comparatively low speeds, when they remain sunken, they diminish the speed up to as high as 50 per cent.

Upon increasing or diminishing the displacement 5 and 10 per cent, the time required to complete a full turn is increased or diminished correspondingly 1 and 2 per cent, and the diameter of the turning circle undergoes hardly any change.

230. *The relation between speed, indicated horsepower, number of revolutions, and coal burned* for the same cut-off is shown in the following table, in which full speed is expressed by the number 100 and the remaining elements in corresponding percentages:

Speed.	I. H. P. of engines.	Number of revo-lutions.	Quantity of coal burned per I. H. P.	Quantity of coal burned per hour.
Per cent.	Per cent.	Per cent.	Per cent.	Per cent.
100	100	100	100	100
90	70.8	89.1	113	80
80	48.7	78.7	131	63.7
70	32.4	68.7	154	50
60	20.6	59.1	184	38
50	12.4	49.9	227	28.1
40	6.8	40.8	305	20.7
35	4.8	36.3	361	17.3

This table may be very simply employed. For example, in line 6 we find that if the ships' speed corresponds to 50 per cent of full speed, this requires a development of only 12.4 per cent of the indicated horsepower that is observed for full speed; requires only 49.9 per cent as many turns; calls for the consumption of an amount of coal per indicated horsepower of 227 per cent of that consumed at full speed; while the total quantity of coal burned per hour is 28.1 per cent of that required for full speed.

231. *Diameter of turning circle.* In relation to the turning capacities of ships, Mr. Afonasev gives the following tables, which have been expressed by us for general convenience by a system of percentages:

SPEED BEFORE TURN-ING.	NUMBER OF REVOLU-TIONS BEFORE TURN-ING.	POSITION OF THE HELM.					
		HARD OVER.	90 PER CENT.	80 PER CENT.	70 PER CENT.	60 PER CENT.	50 PER CENT.
Per cent.	Per cent.	Per cent.	Per cent.	Per cent.	Per cent.	Per cent.	Per cent.
100	100	100	111	125	143	167	200
90	89	97	108	121	139	161	194
80	78	93	103	118	153	155	186
70	67	89	99	111	127	148	178
60	57	84	93	105	120	140	168
50	46	79	88	99	113	133	158

This table shows that for 50 per cent of full speed the number of revolutions is 46 per cent of the number developed at full speed; the diameter of the turning circle, with the helm hard over, is 79 per cent of its diameter at full speed; and with the helm 50 per cent over, the diameter of the circle becomes 158 per cent of the diameter of the circle with the helm hard over at full speed.

232. Table of turning intervals.

SPEED BEFORE TURN-ING.	NUMBER OF REVOLU-TIONS BEFORE TURN-ING.	POSITION OF THE HELM.					
		HARD OVER.	90 PER CENT.	80 PER CENT.	70 PER CENT.	60 PER CENT.	50 PER CENT.
Per cent.	Per cent.	Per cent.	Per cent.	Per cent.	Per cent.	Per cent.	Per cent.
100	100	100	103	107	111	117	123
90	89	111	114	118	123	130	137
80	78	125	129	134	138	146	154
70	67	143	147	153	158	167	176
60	57	167	171	178	185	195	205
50	46	200	206	214	222	234	246

The employment of this table is similar to the preceding: with 50 per cent of full speed and the helm put over 80 per cent of its full angle, the time of completing the circle is 214 per cent of the time required for its execution at full speed with the helm hard over.

Mr. Afonasev considers the latter tables based upon insufficient data, but until more thorough experiments are made they must be taken as they are given.

233. *Equalization of speed.* Regularity in evolution is only to be obtained through maintenance of necessary position in line. This condition is of the highest importance; nevertheless straggling is a common enough occurrence. No one wishes to approach too close to his mate ahead, and in consequence of this he holds back. Admiral Butakov constantly emphasized this deficiency, and every admiral finds himself placed under the necessity of frequently reminding his captains that they must observe their distance.

Regularity of maintenance of distance in the fleet depends greatly upon the capability of regulating speed. To do this we must count not upon knots, but upon the number of turns made by the ship's engines. There is no way of exactly equalizing speed of vessels, for conditions change with every gust of wind, but we are always able to regulate the number of turns exactly. For this purpose they employ in the French navy Valése's device,* by means of which a clock is set in motion at a velocity corresponding to the required number of turns. Having set this apparatus for a speed corresponding to a given number of turns, all that has to be done is to see that the dial at the engine and the dial of the mechanism show the same figures. This appliance affords the possibility of moving the ship ahead or astern, with relation to the position of mates in front and rear, any required distance. The only way to maintain distance is by the use of such an apparatus.

* Morsk. Sbor., 1895, No. I, 12.

234. Signaling by night and by day. Signaling should, in our opinion, constitute a special course, to be accorded as much importance as sail drill, and to be generally developed. At the present time, mast semaphores have been introduced into all fleets, as they afford the possibility of increasing the range of visibility of signals and allow messages to be sent without reference to the signal book. The semaphore possesses one great advantage for use in war—it may be used to make fighting signals with great rapidity. It affords the possibility of making fifty-six such signals, and this is very important, for the semaphore does not require flags to be sorted out, made up, and bent, or hoisted. Such signals may be made in a few seconds, and they may be annulled with equal rapidity.

235. Note upon navigation. Navigation puts into the hands of naval seamen no more data than it supplies to those in a commercial fleet, but while a loss in speed for a commercial fleet implies only insignificant material losses, the loss in speed of a war ship or squadron may mean loss of a battle.

In clear weather we possess the necessary means for manœuvering by day and by night; if any channel is not adapted for navigation at night, we may establish temporary illumination by lanterns placed upon boats, and by this means pursue a desired course.

236. Determination of position in foggy weather. Fog presents the greatest impediment to the accurate determination of the ship's position. Fogs are not very frequent in the Baltic or in the Black Sea, but in the Japan and Okhotsk seas they prevail; in fact, at Vladivostock in the late spring and summer fog is met more commonly than clear weather. Usually the sun is seen above the clouds, but the horizon remains obscured, and seamen are thus deprived of the ability to determine their position by the observation of the height of the heavenly bodies. It is desirable to obtain a method for determining such altitudes in times of fog. Scientific investigation should solve this question. The fact that the fog does not obscure the sun clouds shows that the height of the fog belt is not very great. The author has experimented while in a fog in throwing overboard empty barrels or similar objects to determine the density of the fog from the observation of the time taken by them to disappear. Under these conditions, when the sun was easily seen, the object became obscured at a distance of 2 cable lengths. The visibility of the sun cannot be compared with the visibility of a simple unilluminated object, but as stars of low magnitude are similarly visible, their degree of visibility may be thus compared.

In view of the fact that the fog belt possesses no great height, we assert that the use of balloons under certain circumstances may prove very useful in foggy weather for determining the position of the land. We are strengthened in this opinion by the fact that we have sometimes been able to get our bearing by observing the tops of mountains from the crosstrees at times when it was impossible to see anything from the deck. For this purpose, as well as in general for observing ships and land, it is useful to construct at the top of each mast a crow's-nest for signalmen and to make the necessary arrangements for easily entering and leaving it.

The fleet that is first able to distinguish the land and determine its position in a fog will possess a great tactical advantage. The recent discovery of the Rœntgen rays, which are capable of penetrating bodies heretofore considered opaque, suggests the possibility of the future discovery of some light capable of penetrating a fog. If such rays are discovered, it will afford an additional means of defense, for one may use his lights only when he sees fit. Consequently, from the tactical standpoint, the subject should be worked up, for such lights will afford the same possibility in relation to a fog in the daytime as at night when there is no fog.

237. Surveying fortifications. There is still another problem which pertains to navigation—the surveying of the enemy's fortifications. All ships should be provided with apparatus for this purpose, among which should be counted special photographic outfits. Such exercises are extremely useful. The matter was practiced by us to some extent last summer. Further development is needed, however, for it is of great importance in relation to the attack of shore fortifications by fleets.

238. Shipbuilding. We must bear in mind the chief purpose of tactics—namely, to maintain a fleet in condition for war. If we regard the matter from this point of view, we shall make no mistakes, but if we assign too great attention to peace conditions we shall evidently remain unprepared for battle. War ships should be built as if war were to be declared to-morrow. If we do not take this ground, we shall have to alter much that has acquired for itself a right of existence in prolonged periods of peace cruising. The opinion of the French admiral cited above by us, that "le plus grand luxe du bâtiment est le vide," has a very deep meaning.

239. Dimensions and types of war ships. Another question in shipbuilding is the dimensions of ships. Our views upon this question were expressed in our work, Elements of the Fighting Qualities of Men-of-war. We present here only the following deductions from Jurien de la Gravière (Part II, p. 6):

> At this epoch the English hoisted an admiral's flag on a three-deck ship only. This was one of the requirements of the official etiquette which the English observed at all times. Thus the desire to afford admirals suitable flagships was one of the chief reasons why England preserved a great number of vessels of this type, heavy and clumsy, whose slowness and unhandiness Nelson so much deplored.

We believe that in future years admirals in time of war will speak just as unfavorably of the present type of heavy vessels. Two-deck ships proved generally satisfactory before bursting shells were introduced.

Frigates and large corvettes were built with a view to increased speed as well as to establish large guns in open battery, where bursting shells would not do great damage. In later years all fleets have striven to improve bursting shells, and the effort to protect the guns' crews from flying fragments have recently led, in some navies, to the construction of shields around the guns upon the upper deck. This leads us to reflect whether the servers of the guns are in any greater safety upon open decks than behind thin armor. If this question be answered in the affirmative, the most suitable type of ship would appear to be small vessels with an armored deck, with their vital parts protected, and with the whole gun and torpedo armament upon the upper deck.

It is easier to hit an area than an object, and the author was convinced of this by his own eyes when, on examining the *Chen-yuen* after the battle of the Yalu, her whole sides were found covered with holes and dents, but unprotected objects that had been used in the fight were completely uninjured. Thus, two 6-inch guns with their mounts placed at the bow and the stern remained intact; six rapid-firing guns upon the upper deck; the capstan at the bow, with the steam pipes connecting; chain pipes, chain stoppers, pumps, etc.—in fact, every isolated article—remained uninjured, and the ship continued her fire until she had no projectiles left.

240. *The battle of the Yalu has been misinterpreted.* The fact that the ironclad *Chen-yuen* and her mate *Ting-yuen* survived the fight of the Yalu successfully is considered as a victory for armor. The author himself saw the *Chen-yuen* and perceived that it was not a question of armor but of projectiles. The Japanese had poor shells, and the Yalu fight confirmed the long-known fact that no armor can be pierced with bad projectiles. Cruisers annihilated some of the ironclads at the Yalu fight, and two of the most rapid of the latter succeeded in hiding until the Japanese settled the rest. This fact, however, is explained in an entirely different way. It is considered that the armor remained the victor in the fight:

this is not true, for we must not forget that a good gun causes victory, while the armor is capable only of postponing defeat.

Our opinion of types of ships remains the same. Ships should be of the same dimensions as formerly, and we consider, on a basis of data presented in our Elements of the Fighting Qualities of Men-of-war, that a fleet should consist of vessels of about 3,000 tons displacement, with armored decks. Guns should be placed upon upper decks exclusively.

Many think that a small ship will necessarily possess a very limited radius of action; but the radius of action is not to be sought in size but in auxiliary motors and in the absence of armor, which bears the vessel down. Remove the armor, introduce auxiliary motors, suppress electric lighting, and a ship of 3,000 tons will be able to proceed at a 5-knot speed from Kronstadt to Vladivostock without replenishing her supply of coal.

241. The necessity of agreement upon technical matters. In Elements of the Fighting Qualities of Men-of-war we stated that technical conditions to which ships should correspond would have to be established, and that every effort should be made to realize them in ship construction. We hold the same conclusions now, for our opinions have not changed since that time. Opinions upon details as expressed by us may be combated, for technical matters may be regarded in various ways, but we believe that no one will deny the necessity of deciding what technical qualities every fighting ship should possess. Without such a system shipbuilding becomes uncertain, and irregularity in types will exist as heretofore. Not only is uncertainty to be feared as regards types of vessels and systems of armor, concerning which we have already spoken, but in other matters, e.g., upon the question as to whether each ship should carry torpedo boats; whether she should have a net protection from torpedoes, etc. Some believed in torpedo boats, and now they either carry them or do not carry them.

While we are engaged in developing technique and conditions to which ships should correspond, everything remains uncertain as to what constitutes the relation of subordinate subjects to the whole.

242. *Unsinkability.* The absence of technical requirements in relation to war ships in general is especially felt in what relates to rational measures for preventing a ship from sinking. Parts of this subject are explained in our previous treatise. We will only refer to our chief proposition, which is that each ship after it is built should be fully tested as to its unsinkability. Each compartment, primary and secondary, should be filled with water to the top of the bulkheads. It is only after such a trial that a ship can be recognized as satisfactory in what concerns capability of not sinking.

Unsinkability is becoming more and more overlooked in all fleets, and even such catastrophes as the loss of the ironclad *Victoria* do not result in the establishment of the necessary precautions; they are still afraid to admit water in the necessary quantity and pump same out of ships. The people to blame in this regard are officers afloat, and they will be heavily punished in battle for their neglect if they do not take hold of this matter with both hands in peace time.

243. *Homogeneity in types of ships.* Similarity in types of ship's engines, etc., is required more now than ever before, since the desire to lighten machinery to the minimum of weight for the indicated horsepower has led to the construction of engines of metal of very high quality, and in case of any parts becoming broken they can be obtained only from special factories. In the year 1895, a cruiser remained more than half a year at Nagasaki because of a broken piston which could only be made at a special factory. How could vessels with such delicate mechanism repair injuries received in time of war in distant waters?

Unity in type of ships and engines would afford the possibility of making use of stores of supplies of these parts, and it might happen when the machinery in one engine was broken the parts could be replaced by those from another. On account of the difference in types of engines and of parts upon all ships, no such changes are possible, and each ship must repair independently, which requires a very long time and even the assistance of special factories, so that a war would end before even insignificant damages could be made good.

We repeat that the establishment of uniformity in types of ships and engines is highly important from a tactical standpoint.

244. The strengthening of the ram. It is necessary to strengthen the ram. In the form that it now possesses it would not withstand the shock of a moving vessel, and it is therefore in fact of no use in war. Whenever rams are broken, constructors make them a little stronger. But we can not blame them for not withstanding the shock of a moving vessel, for this requirement has not even been presented; should it be presented, it will be fulfilled.

In our opinion the ram would be much stronger if its vertical section had the form of a lozenge. In this shape its outer side would have the form of an edge that would tear away the plating of an antagonist upon contact, and therefore the fuller lines of this ram would not diminish the superiority of the sharp ram in the bows-on attack. The side ribs of the lozenge should be tooth-shaped, as shown in fig. 15.

245. Strengthening the boilers, etc., to resist the shock of ramming. All objects found on board of the ship are secured in place with sufficient strength not to move when the ship heels; they also say that constructors have borne in mind the conditions of a ramming encounter; but is this so? Actually, are boilers so secured in place that when an ironclad, moving at a speed of 18 knots, rams an antagonist the boilers would not move from their position? Such a technical problem has never been presented, and we believe it would be useful to offer it for consideration, for the displacement of boilers in time of war would produce a frightful catastrophe. In considering the matter, it must be remembered that a ramming ship stops, after moving a distance of a few feet, as soon as she strikes the ram against an enemy. Let us assume that this distance is 6 feet, and that the resistance offered by the side of the antagonist will be absorbed in traversing this distance. Have contractors so secured boilers that they will withstand the shock thus developed? If they are not torn away, they will nevertheless move forward a certain distance on account of the elasticity of the metal, and would not this result in the bursting of steam pipes?

The captain of the ship should know what ramming blow his vessel is calculated to stand, and this fact should be entered with other data relating to the ship, vouched for over the signature of responsible persons.

246. Means of saving the lives of the crew when the ship sinks in a battle. In the chapter "Preparations for war" we presented conclusions relating to ship's boats. In our opinion too many boats are installed on shipboard, and as they may be destroyed by shells it is useless to consider such boats as available for saving life. It would be more rational to supply cork or metal life buoys capable of floating one man, so he may throw the buoy overboard and support himself by it. Afterwards the buoys may be tied together so as to form floats for saving others. The above is presented as an idea, but if the details can be practically worked out such a contrivance would be wholly rational; we only desire to show that the excessive number of boats now carried is irrational. Merchant ships carry floating camp stools. Would it not be well to place upon warships floating bridges which in the moment of need could easily be thrown into the water by the simple movement of a lever?

In our Elements of the Fighting Qualities of Men-of-war we stated that it would be necessary to protect ourselves from ramming by beams of wood. A case in point occurred in the

British navy, where a torpedo boat that collided with a battleship made a hole in the side of the latter, which compelled the engineers of the fleet to cover the outside with wooden planks at the water line. Would it not be well to employ beams placed outside of the ship's side above the water line, so that they might serve for the main end of protecting the sides from damage in collision, while they may, by means of a simple appliance, be detached therefrom for saving the crew in case of the sinking of the ship in battle?

247. *Instructions to the engineering branch. Horizontal engines.*—We have called attention above to the fact that the war ship ought to be constructed for war, and we have considered matters from this standpoint. Engineers recognize, and justly, that vertical engines are superior to horizontal. This may be difficult to controvert, but from a fighting standpoint horizontal engines possess a strong advantage, as they are placed below the water line and out of reach of the enemy's shells. If they continued to endeavor to construct horizontal engines without succeeding in attaining good results, it would be useless to blame them; but as the construction of horizontal engines has almost entirely ceased, they are to blame in the matter. It is true also to state that seamen are to blame for not pressing their claims. One of the chief obstacles to the introduction of horizontal engines is the weight of the pistons, but now that the use of aluminum has been so greatly generalized it may become possible to save considerable weight in all horizontal bearing parts. We will not attempt to give directions how to do this, but it would be of the highest importance were a suitable modern type of horizontal engine suitable for war ships developed.

248. *Rapid formation of steam.* Engineers are now endeavoring to obtain each indicated horsepower with the least weight possible, but the rapidity with which each ship raises steam has been until very recently completely overlooked. In all fleets are to be found ships with cylindrical steam boilers

incapable of forming steam in less time than twelve hours. Under these conditions we are compelled to maintain steam continuously upon ships in time of war, and in so doing burn an enormous quantity of coal—a material of great importance in war, and in the absence of which the ship becomes helpless. The introduction of a quick method of forming steam is a matter of the highest importance.

249. *The subject of naval and military administration.* The art of military administration, as it is understood in Russia, is the science of investigating the laws of the formation and maintenance of armies. It deals with questions pertaining to—

First. Character of armies.
Second. Their organization.
Third. The organization of military administration.
Fourth. Performance of duty in military service.
Fifth. Military discipline and special methods for maintaining it.
Sixth. Military economics.
Naval administration investigates the same elements in relation to the naval fleet.

250. *Text-books.* We will not attempt to discuss in the present treatise the principles of administration governing ourselves. This has been the work of the late Commander Yenish, who prepared his text-book for the officers of artillery. We will only state that he was the first person to make this matter a special science.

In 1896 Colonel Dolgov prepared his admirable work, Outline of Naval Administration, which may serve each officer as an excellent handbook. Details on the technique of administration are not considered in tactics, but only those principles that may serve to indicate how to render a fleet fit for war.

251. *Promotion.* One of the most difficult matters of administration is how to establish a just system of promotion. In this regard tactics require that officers from whom good re-

sults may be expected in time of war should be advanced more rapidly than officers unfit for war. To this end we may promote some for excellence, and thus move them faster than others; or, while preserving lineal promotion, remove from the list those persons who are unfit for war conditions.

Justice is claimed in almost all fleets for the promotion of a few officers for excellence. It is a very difficult question to determine how to distinguish individuals who would prove capable for war from those who are less capable in this regard, and how to select these so as not to awaken dissatisfaction in all hearts. We have given examples of persons who have developed into talented commanders who did not seem to possess talents particularly adapted to the needs of the service in their youth, and who under these conditions would never have been advanced. The establishment of a criterion for the just estimation of officers is highly desirable. At present, persons in authority are often influenced by appearances, while it is desirable that some definite rules and procedure should exist. Manœuvers should be established as referred to in paragraph 98, which may enable us to recognize persons not possessing the qualities of seamen, from whom it is useless to expect the proper control of the ship, and thus to eliminate some and advance others in the service.

The establishment of a method of just removal for inefficiency and of promotion for excellence is of the highest importance, but it is so difficult to effect that we do not give any final opinion and will confine ourselves to general remarks.

Among all the duties of the commander in chief, the most unsystematized is that which relates to removing from the line of promotion persons unfitted to become good commanders. The chief who does this makes enemies, without doubt, of those persons whom he does not advance; but if he should do otherwise he would prove unfaithful to the fleet in which he serves. Colonel Orloff states in his Tactics that if in war a commander is found of little capability there are almost no ways of paralyzing his efforts. He presents an example (par. 59) of how, at the battle of Inkerman, they tried to have eliminated from the fight a corps commander whose abilities were in doubt, but without success.[1]

It would undoubtedly be better to retire an incapable captain, but this is not so easy to do, and if in time of peace little attention be paid to the choice of persons to whom is offered the possibility of advancement, and the places of commanding officers remain occupied by persons of little capacity, evil results will be felt in war time, when it will be too late to repair that which has been begun many years before. From a tactical point of view it would be well to establish such a system that in time of peace there would be indicated those upon whom choice would fall in time of war.

252. *Former conditions of service.* In former times, service duties aided to a certain degree the weeding out of incompetent people without producing general dissatisfaction. An officer in very early years of service was placed in such circumstances that he was forced to consider whether he was suitable for continuing his career or not. He was placed in charge of a watch, where he should develop the necessary skill—to know, for example, how to recover his place in the squadron as quickly as possible. If the watch officer did not possess the necessary ability, then, notwithstanding his other qualities, no commanding officer wished to take him on his ship, for to trust a watch to such an officer would be to place the ship in risk of a collision; this was a first-rate way of eliminating officers who did not possess seamanlike quality. It often happened that the officer who felt that he did not possess the necessary capacity, and recognized that he was unsuited for service, sought a place as hydrographer, instructor, or some position of activity on shore, and thus left the line. It

---

1. In this Crimean War battle, Russian troops, trying to cause an Anglo-French withdrawal, were badly led, repulsed, and defeated.

is true that he frequently continued on the list, but upon leaving active service he was no longer regarded as eligible to command at sea.

Advancement to the position of senior officer afforded still another powerful means of securing the advancement of the proper persons to the position of executive officer and furnished still another excellent way of preventing the promotion of officers who were unsuited for service. In former days captains chose their own executives, and, as it was highly important for each captain to have a good executive officer, poor ones were never chosen. In this way they were eliminated from the line of advancement. The desire to be chosen in his turn for the position of executive impelled all young officers to exert themselves that their seniors should consider them as well adapted for the service, and this in itself was productive of excellent results.

The above-described system of advancement must be regarded as fully satisfactory from the standpoint of tactical requirements. In this manner the officer in the old days was constantly undergoing a severe examination throughout his whole life—as to his qualities as a seaman. As an executive officer he was subjected to an examination more serious still—upon his general professional qualities.

Upon receiving further advancement in the service the officer continued to undergo no less severe tests of his capabilities, as he was placed in command of tenders, brigs, and finally of frigates. These ships performed the more unimportant duties of the squadron, and occasionally afforded their commanding officers opportunities of showing their qualities as such and of determining whether they were competent to command a ship of the line. Such an examination took place in the presence of the whole fleet, and no one could complain if there were no promotion in the service for him, as in such a case every one knew that the trouble was due to the lack of the proper officer-like qualities. In fact, officers themselves often acknowledged themselves incapable of receiving advancement, and willingly made way for others, returning to pursuits on shore, where they sometimes proved themselves very useful to the service.

The officer who finally successfully passed through all the above tests was given command of a ship, and after a few months afloat in this capacity had a chance to practice all that would be required of him in war, for squadron cruising in all weathers afforded an excellent opportunity for practice under circumstances closely allied to those actually obtaining in war.

253. *Conditions of service at the present time.* The conditions of naval service are now completely changed. The watch officer, even when afloat in the squadron, has very little chance to practice, as, with the usual sea formation in column, there is little or no occasion to employ the helm. The position of the ship, as far as the engines are concerned, is controlled by the range finder and engine-room signals. An officer who does not possess the necessary qualities of perception may be able to keep his place in line, for he has only to be attentive to the performance of his duty, and there is no call for the employment of higher qualities.

The officer who receives command of a torpedo boat has a chance to manœuver his ship; but, in the first place, not all officers are given the chance of practice in this school; in the second place, a torpedo boat may be regarded as a sloop in comparison to an ironclad; in the third place, if the command of a torpedo boat is to be considered the means of developing the qualities of an officer it must be looked upon somewhat differently from the manner in which it is now regarded.

Even after having been advanced to the command of an ironclad, the officer does not acquire practice in what he is called upon to do in battle, for the fear of collision, which now leads to such disasters, renders peace manœuvers, as conducted in all navies, quite dissimilar from those that would obtain in actual war. It would be superfluous to present here a full program as to how this matter should be adjusted. The problem of expedient promotion still awaits solution, and that fleet in which it shall have been most rationally solved will obtain therefrom a great military advantage.

254. Military ports. Questions concerning personnel are of great importance from an administration standpoint, but principles of administration should also be concentrated upon questions of military efficiency and the proper maintenance of matériel. Ships and ports must be kept in good order. Every port should be so constructed that the war ships assigned to it are maintained in full fighting order, so that they could put to sea upon short notice when war is declared.

Besides this, our ports should be supplied with all necessary materials and fighting appliances required for maintaining the fleet in time of war, and schemes should be devised for making up deficiencies and expenditures of such stores and supplies. Such a port should be capable of repairing, in a very short time, injuries that a ship might receive in battle. There is nothing new in these principles, and most of them have been taken legal cognizance of. The main point is that, while meeting peace requirements, consideration should be paid to demands of tactics based upon possible occurrence of war.

255. War ships. War ships should be built for war, and while cruising should be maintained in such a condition as to be ready to give battle upon short notice. To this end the matériel of every ship should be kept in good condition, and the personnel trained by exercises in manœuvers of all conditions that war or battle might present. Cruising life afloat should be passed with this end in view, and everything that does not touch directly or indirectly upon the matter should be eradicated as superfluous and injurious.

256. Conclusions. We shall conclude our work upon tactics with the remark that up to the present time all naval progress consists in the perfection of defects in various branches of naval technique. In some ways this work suggests the repair of an old building, where such attention is given to details that the chief object in view is completely lost sight of. From the standpoint of tactics we may justly ask: "Would it not be better to rebuild the entire edifice?"

We have considered the chief objects of tactics, and besides these the best methods of training people so that in time of war they may display the greatest development of the qualities of energy and understanding, as well as the utilization of those means of offense and defense with which ships are supplied. History affords us many incomparable examples as to how people should be trained and these may still serve us, for man remains just as he has ever been. As far as concerns matériel, the means we possess at the present time are in no way like those which were employed in the days of the old naval wars. If we exclude a few skirmishes, examples of modern naval war are wanting; therefore, in the conduct of war we should put more trust *in our common sense than in military precedents, which are completely insufficient.*

After the battle of Lissa everyone said that the best squadron formation was the echelon, that Admiral Persano made a great mistake in forming his fleet in line, and that he was beaten because he had not assumed the echelon formation. In the battle of the Yalu, the Japanese admiral, Ito, formed his fleet in column and the Chinese admiral disposed his vessels in line, which with its bent back wings resembled the echelon. The results of the battle, as far as relate to the formation, were exactly contrary to those in the previous case; that is, the column won, and the line or echelon lost.

We can only conclude that in both these actions the victory was lost in the one case and won in the other not on account of one formation or the other, but from other causes. We can not base tactical conclusions relating to formation upon the examples above cited, which only serve to confirm the truth that the side with the least daring will always lose.

INDEX

301

Hoste, Paul, 16–17
Hotham, Admiral, 58, 66

Inflexible, 24, 26
Initiative, 222
Inkerman, 296
Intelligence, 210–15
Isyères, 48
Ito, Yuko, 245

James, William, 68
Jena, 239
Jervis, Sir John (Earl St. Vincent), 49, 58, 62–63, 67
Jomini, Henri, 29, 36, 40, 94, 96, 100, 239
Jugan, Captain, 82

Karl, Erzherzog, 30
Kaznakov, Vice Admiral, 203
Khrushchev, Nikita, xxiv
Klado, N. L., 20, 46
Klausewitz, Carl von. *See* Clausewitz, Carl von
Kornilov, Vladimir, 231
Kronstadt, xvii, 228
Kronstadt Naval Club, 111
Krotkow, General, 116
Kutousow, 274

Lake Baikal, xxxi
Layman, Captain, 61
Lazarev, M. P., xv, 116
Leadership, 89–103, 296–98
Leer, G. A., 30, 38, 41, 46, 93–94, 240
Lestock, Vice Admiral, 48

Lissa, 245, 300
Lloyd, Henry, 237–38
Lonato, 84
Luce, Stephen B., 18, 90

Mahan, Alfred Thayer, ix, x, xi, xxv, xxvi, 28
Majestic, 25–26
Makarov, Stepan O., 110n, 240n, 267n
"Makarov's Little Cap," xxii, 141
Maneuver, 128–32, 151, 163, 182–83, 228–30, 244, 247, 250–53, 270, 279, 295
Marengo, 85–86
Marmont, Auguste de, 95
Masséna, André, 86, 239
Mathews, Admiral, 48–49
Merrimac, 245
Minotaur, 21–22
Montagu, Edward, 18
Montesquieu, Charles, 115
Morale, 38, 45–89, 153, 237
Moscow, xxi
Murat, Joachim, 93
Muraviev, Nikalai N., 165

Nagasaki, 290
Nakhimov, P. S., 50, 238–39
Napoleon, 31–32, 44–45, 50, 59, 61–63, 78–94, 116, 214, 237–42, 268
Naval science and art, 30–31, 35, 37–40, 52–55, 277
Navarino, 230
Navigation, 15, 285–87
Nelson, 21, 24

ABOUT THE EDITOR

Captain Robert B. Bathurst, USN (Ret.), an adjunct professor of national security affairs for the Naval Postgraduate School in California, is a leading expert on the Soviet Navy, past and present, and he has written extensively on Soviet and naval strategic questions. During his naval career he served as the Admiral Layton Chair of Intelligence at the Naval War College, the deputy chief for the Navy in London, and assistant naval and air attaché in Moscow.

Captain Bathurst first became fascinated by the "Russian Problem" at the age of sixteen, after reading Dostoevsky's *Brothers Karamazov*, a book he still considers essential reading for any informed adult. Fate also apparently intended him to be a Russian expert, for in his naval career he consistently drew assignments that deepened his experience in the field.

In preparation for introducing this volume, he read widely about Admiral Makarov in several languages and visited the Russian naval museum in Leningrad to view the Makarov exhibits. In writing his essay, he was able to draw not only on the theoretical knowledge gained from a broad range of research, but also on a lifetime of contact with Russians and their culture. His hope was to make it possible for the reader to understand the genius of the man and also to grasp the power of his spirit.

THE NAVAL INSTITUTE PRESS

CLASSICS OF SEA POWER

DISCUSSION OF QUESTIONS IN NAVAL TACTICS

Set in Sabon
by G & S Typesetters, Inc., Austin, Texas

Printed on 60-lb. Spring Grove Laid Text Ivory
and bound in Joanna Arrestox and Papan ESP
with Papan ESP endsheets
by The Maple-Vail Book Manufacturing Group,
Binghamton, New York